CULTURE AT WORK IN AVIATION AND MEDICINE

CULTURE AT WORK IN AVIATION AND MEDICINE
NATIONAL, ORGANIZATIONAL AND PROFESSIONAL INFLUENCES

ROBERT L. HELMREICH
ASHLEIGH C. MERRITT

Ashgate

Aldershot • Brookfield USA • Singapore • Sydney

Published by
Ashgate Publishing Limited
Gower House
Croft Road
Aldershot
Hants GU11 3HR
England

Ashgate Publishing Limited
Old Post Road
Brookfield
Vermont 05036
USA

British Library Cataloguing in Publication Data
Helmreich, Robert L.
    Culture at work in aviation and medicine : national,
    organizational and professional influences
    1. Social groups   2. Communication and culture
    3. Organizational behavior
    I. Title II. Merritt, Ashleigh C.
    302.3'5

Library of Congress Cataloging-in-Publication Data
Helmreich, Robert L.
    Culture at work in aviation and medicine : national,
    organizational, and professional influences / Robert L. Helmreich,
    Ashleigh C. Merritt.
        p.   cm.
    ISBN 0–291–39853–7 (hb)
    1. Air pilots—Professional relationships.   2. Operating room
    personnel—Professional relationships.   3. Teams in the workplace.
    I. Merritt, Ashleigh C.   II. Title
    TL553.H45   1998
    629.132'5216'023—dc21   98–2947
                                                             CIP

ISBN 0 291 39853 7

Printed and bound in Great Britain by
MPG Books Ltd, Bodmin, Cornwall

Dedication

To David Alexander, Carlos Canales and Teddy Gray, for their
support and encouragement

Contents

List of Boxes

List of Figures

List of Tables

Foreword

Stick: boomerang which, when thrown into the air, does not turn back.
(Australian popular wisdom)[p]

Beyond criticisms – and jokes – about ethnocentrism and parochialism rampant 'down under', this piece of Australian lore clearly articulates the fundamental role played by each of the shared sets of beliefs which define different cultures across the world in shaping perception of facts and, therefore, truth. The cultural underpinnings of this gem of Australian wisdom further open the door to a legitimate challenge to unsullied scientific knowledge as enshrined by people who only believe in demonstrable fact, 'hard data', or are simply captive to dogma. Not that such a challenge is anything new; after all, it was almost 400 years ago that Miguel de Cervantes Saavedra powerfully asserted – through his immortal Don Quixote de la Mancha – that reality as such does not exist. Truth, sanity and madness, Don Quixote proclaimed, whilst charging against perceived-to-be-villains/windmills, are merely a question of the perspective through which the observer calibrates the manifestation of events, which in turn define the mental construct we come to call reality. Philosophical meandering aside, contemporary cultural research would seem to support Don Quixote and suggest that, in the final analysis, nothing is clear-cut, black or white, true or false in life across the 'global village'.

Why should the aviation industry be interested in culture? What has culture to do with aviation's goals of safety and efficiency transporting people and goods? The answer is *much*; indeed, much more than an appraisal at face value might suggest. Of the many endeavors undertaken by humankind, modern aviation is *the* global undertaking by definition. Contrasting sets of beliefs about what is *perceived* to be safe and efficient generate subtle yet conspicuous differences in how the business of safe and efficient transportation of humans and merchandise is conducted in different contexts. These contextual differences are an integral part of aviation's fabric. Culture has been around aviation since Wilbur and Orville and *Kitty Hawk*, only they did not know then, and we did not know it – or pretended that we did not – for long thereafter. But the time to seriously think about cultural factors in aviation has come, as they have lately been brought to the forefront of attention by the always painful process of shifting through charred metal. Cultural factors are deeply embedded in the very nature of the aviation system, however, and it would be quite mistaken to consider them as yet another passing fad encouraged by media in the light of recent safety breakdowns.

My purpose in this foreword is to advance an early argument in favor of the influence of culture in the safety and efficiency of the aviation system, thus joining the many arguments so convincingly presented by Professor Robert Helmreich and Doctor Ashleigh Merritt in this book. Helmreich and Merritt direct their attention to applied research as well as to the search for practical tools to approach and deal with the relationship between culture, error and error management, and between culture and aviation human factors training for operational personnel. They devote particular attention to the link between culture and Crew Resource Management (CRM) training, a safety and prevention tool towards which few if any have contributed so much and so well as the authors of this book. They also extend their endeavors to medicine. I will limit my argument to aviation and to a conceptual discussion of the shaping influence of culture in aviation's safety process. But before I argue my case, I believe it appropriate to take advantage of the privileged position of industry safety observer that I have been extremely fortunate to hold for the last nine years. Being with the International Civil Aviation Organization, at the helm of its Flight Safety and Human Factors Programme over this period, has afforded me the opportunity to chart cultural endeavors across a broad spectrum. I will therefore start the take-off roll by attempting to draw a road map to the present-day situation, briefly reviewing the 'history behind the scenes' of cultural endeavors in aviation – as I perceive it – as well as a few accounts of human failures which strongly influenced this history.

On Squandering the Benefits of Foresight

Cultural factors drew the attention of aviation – and of the safety community in particular – through two avenues. The first avenue is the product of the insightful thinking of a meager handful of researchers, who in turn caught the attention of an even more meager handful of safety practitioners. It was the mid- to-late 1980s, and very early 1990s, a time when traditional, strongly-defended barriers and frontiers started crumbling worldwide. This was coupled with an equally resounding crumbling of social systems based on vanishing beliefs, thus laying the grounds for the dawning of the global village. It was

rather obvious to some observers within aviation that the consequences of such phenomenal change had to be properly addressed if
penalties in the system's performance were to be avoided. This concern was, however, a minority view, since the prevailing perception
within the industry was somewhat simpler: most provider and user
organizations felt that what was being faced was simply the case of a
growing market and new business opportunities.

On the other hand, aviation's historic love affair with and extreme
reliance on gadgets, training and adherence to rules as *the* method of
assuring safety – both inherent in the industry's professional culture
– undoubtedly fostered the impression that technology, training and
regulations were all that would be needed to cope with change.
Within such a context, aviation could continue conducting business
as usual, doing the same things, only on a larger scale and with new
tools. It is not far-fetched to suggest that, had someone argued in
those early days in favor of the importance of cultural factors, the
fate reserved for such a person would have been no different from
that suffered by Don Quixote, declared certifiably crazy by his con-
temporaries. Properly trained individuals using the latest available
technology and supported by regulations were the answer to the
challenges of change. Moreover, an airplane was an airplane, a cockpit was a cockpit, there was only one way of flying an airplane and
professionalism dictated that the cockpit was 'culture-free'. Or was
it?

The majority view thus led to a state of affairs in which, as on
myriad other occasions when safety issues are confronted, the opportunity to pursue a proactive avenue to deal with cultural factors
and their influence in aviation safety was squandered, in spite of the
fact that the theoretical framework to approach it was available.
Among the early advocates, Professor Michael Kaplan, then with the
US Army Research Institute, had been trying for quite some time to
gain acceptance (and obtain funding) to further applied research and
develop in practical terms his concept of *cultural ergonomics*. Professor Najmedin Meshkati, with the University of Southern California,
had extensively published alerts about the *cross-cultural issues involved in the transfer of technology* from industrialized to developing
nations. Professor Ron Westrum, of Eastern Michigan University,
had asserted the effects of *corporate culture in organizational behavior*,
in terms of both organizational safety and efficiency. France's René
Amalberti and Jean Paries had convincingly argued that *safety paradigms* varied across time and contexts, and that social beliefs and
culture were powerful determinants of contrasting safety paradigms
observed across time and contexts. But these and others were largely
conceptual endeavors, because of a Catch 22-type situation: the practical connection between culture and the aviation system's

performance was not obvious to most; therefore, funding for both basic and applied research was difficult to obtain; therefore, it was difficult to establish the practical connection between culture and the aviation system's performance.

An early breakthrough had been provided by the Flight Safety Foundation's 37th annual international air safety seminar held in Zurich, in October 1984. The program of this seminar featured a paper by S.G. Redding and J.G. Ogilvie, of the University of Hong Kong, on 'Cultural effects on cockpit communications in civilian aircraft'. Redding and Ogilvie argued that cultural levels of difference, although assumed not to effect the behavior of professional flight crews, might in fact operate unconsciously and in ways which were difficult to perceive. They supported their proposal with research data from an international study they had conducted. It is only fair to consider Redding and Ogilvie early trailblazers in the quest for the consideration of cultural factors in aviation, on at least three counts. First, their paper may well be considered the seminal 'applied' paper attempting to link the effects of culture in the aviation system's performance. Second, the notion that cultural factors might have practical implications on flight crew training and flight operations was exposed to a large operational audience for the first time. Lastly, and most importantly, Redding and Ogilvie had based their international cultural study on the framework provided by the work of Geert Hofstede, whose influence in later cultural endeavors in aviation would be pivotal. These were, however, early times, and it would be a fair assessment that Redding and Ogilvie attracted the attention of a scant few.

Nevertheless, all this early thinking did capture the attention of the International Civil Aviation Organization, a multicultural organization by nature and mission. ICAO had, in 1986, initiated its Flight Safety and Human Factors Programme, intended as a bridge between academic research and the aviation system's safety needs and realities. In fulfilling this bridging role, ICAO attempted by the early 1990s some initial skirmishes to catch the industry's attention. To this effect, it published early practitioner literature building upon the accounts described in the previous paragraphs, and it encouraged equally early attempts at applied cross-cultural research in aviation. Coincidentally – and fate is indeed the hunter – one of the authors of this book, Professor Robert Helmreich, became from 1990 a 'standard feature' of ICAO's newly started, globe-trotting program of regional Human Factors seminars. This was indeed a lucky break that afforded an insightful, sensible and sense-making researcher a first-hand appreciation of culture at work, as well as the potential contacts which would eventually allow him to pursue research into culture in action.

The turning point came in 1993, with the publication of the book, *Cockpit Resource Management*, edited by Earl Wiener, Barbara Kanki and Robert Helmreich. The problem the operational community was facing up to that point, in terms both of safety and of training practices, was that, in spite of the availability of theoretical knowledge and a growing recognition of the link between cultural factors and the system's performance, the lack of an applied model to deal with the practicalities of such a relationship hindered generalized understanding and, therefore, progress in the area. Add to this the fact that aviation was and remains a Western-dominated industry, that Americans 'own' a substanial part of this dominion, and that American ethnocentrism – a matter of anthropological fact – might turn a blind eye to the most compelling cross-cultural issues, and the reasons for the stalemate become obvious. Colonialism may take many forms, and aviation was facing a clear case of cultural colonialism: simply speaking, some people were deemed to have the 'right' culture, others the 'wrong' one; and the early solution to address the link between culture and system performance was obviously that the latter had to be indoctrinated into the former.

The answer to break the standoff came from the European side of the Atlantic. It took an Irishman known for his capacity to rebel against simplistic thinking and to come up with the most complicated answers to the simplest questions, but with an equal capacity to turn abstract thinking into tangible practice, to outsmart the status quo and free cultural factors in aviation from its prison of parochialism and ethnocentrism. Those familiar with his pioneering frame of mind were not surprised when Aer Lingus Captain Neil Johnston produced a seminal chapter on culture in aviation for the Wiener/Kanki/Helmreich book, taking over where Redding and Ogilvie had left off, and making Geert Hofstede an integral and extremely practical part of aviation Human Factors endeavors. The importance of this gem of applied cultural literature may never be recognized for what it meant at the time of its publication. Johnston introduced a practically compelling case about the relationship and influence of culture on CRM training in particular and on system performance in general. Moreover, he presented aviation with the means to deal with it: with Hofstede's model, aviation now had the foundations upon which to develop a practical tool to pursue cross-cultural research. In retrospect, Johnston's insight closed a loop by providing the badly needed missing leg to the three-legged stool upon which broad, systematic-oriented aviation safety and efficiency endeavors rest: the first leg constituted by Captain Frank Hawkins' (1988) SHELL model, to deal with human performance in practical terms; the second leg by Professor Jim Reason's (1990) accident causation model, to deal with system performance in practical terms; and the third leg by Hofstede's (1980) model, as a practical approach to cultural issues.

The point of no return had been reached, and Johnston's lucid account of culture's influence on aviation training and safety was the trigger to subsequent applied endeavors. The research group at the University of Texas at Austin under Helmreich quickly adopted the Hofstede model, and worked extensively to calibrate, validate, refine and extend it for application in the aviation environment. A last and exceedingly important event in the history of culture in aviation was the incorporation into Helmreich's research team of the very Australian co-author of this book, Dr Ashleigh Merritt (I have always thought of Australians as Latins – and more specifically, as Italians – who speak English). A powerhouse of applied research was set in motion, and the results of its endeavors fill – some scant four years later – this book.

On the Dubious Practice of the Benefit of Hindsight

The second avenue which brought the link between cultural factors and a system's performance to aviation's attention was the product of human failures. Aviation being an outcome-oriented industry, the early attempts narrated in the previous section were not enough to alert the community about the need to deal seriously with cultural issues in aviation. It was necessary to go through the reactive, expensive and painful approach of accident investigation privileged by aviation's prevailing professional culture when instances of human failures end up in proverbial trails of wreckage. Let us briefly review a few of these instances, all of which had determinant influences in the history being recounted.

In March 1989, an Air Ontario Fokker F28 crashed while attempting to take off in icing conditions with its wings contaminated with ice and snow at Dryden, in central Ontario. The report was one of the first investigations of a safety breakdown in which culture – corporate culture in this case – was discussed in considerable detail. The airline in question was the product of the merger of two quite different companies, and two incompatible corporate cultures therefore underpinned the newly created organization. The effects of such differences were enduring and difficult to change, were highlighted by the official investigation and were considered to have had a deleterious effect on crew coordination, thus becoming a contributing factor to the accident.

In January 1992, an Airbus A320 crashed into Mount St-Odile, near Strasbourg. Although the French Commission d'Enquête (quite wisely) never asserted *the* cause of the accident in its official report, it proposed that the crew might have erroneously mis-selected a switch in the autopilot mode selector control panel, ordering the aircraft to descend at 3300 feet per minute instead of at a stabilized angle of 3.3 degrees. The official accident report discusses in depth not only the influences of the corporate culture of the airline involved in shaping flight crew performance but also the influence of the social context within which the accident took place in shaping organizational performance. The St-Odile report is a turning point, not only in terms of the investigation of cultural factors in aviation safety, but also as a piece of accident investigation literature.

In June 1993, a Piper Navajo crashed while conducting a night circling approach to an uncontrolled airport in Young, New South Wales. The crew misjudged their position relative to the runway and the terrain, and flew the aircraft into the ground. The contemporary approach to the investigation pursued by the Bureau of Safety Investigation (BASI) of Australia includes a detailed discussion of the organizational, corporate and cultural factors – including both the operator and the civil aviation authority – considered to have had a bearing on this accident. Known as the 'Monarch report' after the name of the airline involved, and coupled with the two previous reports, this accident investigation completed a forward-looking trilogy which radically changed the approach to the safety investigation process.

In the meantime, between 1991 and 1994, the National Transportation Safety Board of the United States had published a number of accident reports in which the subject of corporate culture and its influence in shaping human and organizational performance received considerable attention. The thrust of the NTSB in that particular span of time is best summarized by a dissenting statement by then board member, Doctor John K. Lauber, in the aftermath of an in-flight structural break-up experienced by an Embraer 120RT, in September 1991. Organizational deficiencies had allowed the development of flawed maintenance practices and, under a combination of local triggering factors, an aircraft was released for revenue passenger flying with an unfinished maintenance job. This eventually led to a sudden in-flight loss of the left horizontal stabilizer leading edge and subsequent structural break-up of the airplane. Lauber's statement leaves no room for doubt: 'I believe the probable cause should read as follows … the probable causes of this accident were (1) the failure of [the operator] management to establish a corporate culture which encouraged and enforced adherence to approved maintenance and quality assurance procedures…'

All these accident reports defined a compelling case for the consideration of cultural factors in the aviation safety process. Change in aviation usually takes place within a window of opportunity defined by the emotional aftermath of tragedies, and these reports went on gradually building a momentum which set the foundations for the cultural window of opportunity. The momentum was furthered between 1994 and 1997, as a number of accidents involving Western-built technology took place in 'other cultures'. Contributing factors to the streak of accidents included misunderstandings in the use of the English language, contextually unfriendly human–technology interfaces and difficulties in Western – 'other cultures' human interactions. The evidence in favour of pursuing cultural factors in aviation became too compelling for even the greatest skeptics to ignore. By 1996, cultural factors in aviation were here to stay. The followers of Don Quixote had been spared his destiny.

What Aviation Sees is Not What Aviation Gets

It is sad that it had to take accidents before existing knowledge which might have been applied proactively to prevent unnecessary pain and destruction called aviation's attention to cultural factors. But then, I suppose this has always been, and will continue to be for the foreseeable future, the case in aviation. Our outcome-oriented professional culture demands that the system be broken before we start thinking about fixing it. Be that as it may, the important point is that, as a consequence of the investigation of facts and circumstances leading to human failures, the foundations were laid for fundamental changes in the prevailing perceptions about the way of doing business concerning aviation safety and efficiency. Equally paramount, the safety investigations following these accidents clearly illustrated that, beyond national culture, corporate culture and professional culture are significant determinants of the processes underlying the aviation system's performance.

At this point, the bridge between culture and aviation safety and efficiency became conspicuous and it began to be understood for what it really is because, indeed, safety is a social construct and, ultimately, a state of mind. Safety partly rests in formal structures and protocols, but fundamentally in attitudes. Safety intertwines with risk and human life. Perceptions of what constitutes risk and the value attached to human life are far from uniform across the global village. An unacceptable risk for one society might be quite tolerable for another. There are societies where, for example, body counting outweighs the social and cultural values deeply ingrained in other societies. There are also societies where legal liability becomes the basis for decisions about risk. In such societies, the bottom line is not risk and safety, but power. Indeed, there are many who believe that societies have the number of accidents (and loss of life) that they are ready and willing to accept before allocating resources to reduce risks. Far from suggesting amoral calculation, this rather implies that there is a strong cultural component associated with safety endeavors.

The existence of the link between attitudes about the value of human life and the allocation of resources to avoid injury or death is supported as a matter of indisputable fact by socioanthropological theory, although it does not sit very well with prevailing dogma. After all, decades of pontificating and smoke blowing about safety have led to the widely expressed contention that, in aviation, safety is first. This may certainly be true as a declaration of intent, but the imperative to remember when regarding safety as a social construct is to ask the question: what safety? Judging what constitutes an acceptable risk is a subjective, social activity which will be different in different cultures and societies and even in different organizations within a single culture or society. Following this line of reasoning, it is suggested that safety may be *judged* according to discrete standards but it can hardly be universally *measured*.

Therefore, before any safety endeavor is attempted, it is essential to put safety into perspective and decide where it fits within the cultural beliefs of a given social group. Such beliefs define the group's 'operational space', the outer boundaries of which are provided by national and professional culture and the inner by the corporate culture of the particular organization. In order to be effective, safety endeavors should be consistent with and not run counter to the shared beliefs of the receiving group. Safety and risk are not properties inherent in processes or artifacts, but they are constructed by common group history and experience. Rather than being the objective process that conventional knowledge would have the aviation industry believe, safety is a subjective process of quantifying and accepting risks. Risks – and safety – are simply in the eyes of the beholder.

Quo Vadis, Cultural Factors in Aviation?

I have recalled the history of cultural endeavors, and I have sketched my argument in favor of cultural factors in aviation. The remaining question before I rest my case and give way to Helmreich and Merritt is obvious: where to now? What does – or should – the future hold for cultural endeavors in aviation? While it is true that gigantic strides have been accomplished, it would be naive to think that the cultural question has been settled for good. The battle is not over. In fact, I believe that we are only in its beginnings. We may feel comforted by the ever-increasing state of awareness of the importance of cultural factors in aviation, but there is as yet no army behind those who truly believe in them. There are perhaps fewer 'colonialists' than before, but cultural colonialism is well and alive. During a recent meeting in which the subject under debate was the consideration of cultural issues in flight deck certification, somebody with the deep drawl peculiar to a corner of North America suggested that the solution to cultural issues in aviation was 'to bring those guys to think like us'. Likewise, a letter recently published in an industry magazine, submitted by a reader whose mother tongue happens to be English, suggests that the inability to master the English language is a handicap in human performance serious enough to render a person unfit to remain part of the aviation system. I hasten to add that, although to the best of my knowledge such glaring examples of ethnocentrism are not numerous, these two are not, unfortunately, isolated cases.

I fully agree with Bennett's advice (see Chapter 7) that any attempt to bring about cultural change must be approached with the greatest possible care, so as to avoid confusion, rejection and even bloodshed. I have been preaching the cultural gospel in conceptual terms for several years, but it was only in December 1997 that I went through my first 'applied experience', in South America. The event in question was held in sunny Cartagena, Colombia, and it was organized by Airbus Industrie. Probably because I am a native of the region, I was asked to discuss Latin American cultural dimensions and their shaping influence in CRM training, the human–technology interface and safety. I started with the usual caveats: that is, Latin American culture was the context and not the object of the exercise; serious cultural endeavors respect rather than challenge prevailing cultural beliefs, all cultures have strengths and weaknesses, cultural research aims at making the most of strengths while minimizing weaknesses, and so on and so forth. However, one-third of the way through the presentation, I was wishing I had brought a helmet and bullet-proof jacket in my luggage instead of suntan lotion. The stance adopted by most attendees was aggressively defensive and one of extreme denial. With very few exceptions (there are always instant converts), the consensus of opinion among participants was that training was the right and honorable mediator for those Latin American cultural beliefs and assumptions which might not be compatible with the cultural beliefs and assumptions of the contexts originating the training, technological and safety solutions, rather than cultural calibration of such solutions. Wording it somewhat differently, training can 'exorcise' cultural differences. On the face of it, one might think that professional culture prevailed: training and professional behaviors are *the* solution. It was a minor comfort that, towards the end of the presentation, grinding mental gears could be distinctly heard; but the message from Cartagena is, as far as I am concerned, loud and clear: there is a long and arduous road ahead.

In retrospect, the outcome of the event could not have been other than the one described. We are in the initial skirmishes of applied cultural endeavors. The data available from applied research essentially reflect attitudes expressed by the user population, but the feedback loop is still open: the users have told *us* how they perceive cultural issues, but we have not yet come back to the users, telling *them* what to do about it. People in aviation are exceedingly practical, and they are convinced by solutions. The solutions *vis-à-vis* cultural factors and system performance which have so far been sketched are to a large extent focused around CRM training, to a lesser one around error management, and to a considerable lesser one around safety practices. If we are going to break the armor of skepticism of the highly conservative flight crew and safety communities, we need to move further than this, and there are three areas which immediately come to mind as open grounds for cultural attack.

First, consideration of cultural issues should be an integral part of the design of technology. This will undoubtedly take time, and probably involve considerable expense. Therefore, in the intervening period, we should work at an interim solution in the interface between humans and technology: standard operating procedures. Cultural factors should be an integral consideration during design of SOPs; they should be discussed and agreed upon between the manufacturer and the operator before technology is delivered. In other words, SOPs should be culturally calibrated. Second, the safety investigation community must join the cultural endeavor, since it is illusory to view safety as a universal value. Cultural factors should routinely be considered during the safety investigation process, although this might be the toughest nut in the entire lot to crack, owing to the resilient conservatism of accident investigators. Finally, regulations are a social compromise reflecting a balance between the needs of the providers and of the users of services. International standards and regulations should therefore provide enough leeway to incorporate cultural factors which make such a compromise socially acceptable. An agenda for cultural research with applied solutions as the objective is a must.

In concluding, I would like to offer my perspective on a subject addressed by Helmreich and Merritt elsewhere: will the global village eliminate the differences and, therefore, the need for consideration of cultural factors? Like Helmreich and Merritt, I think not. I agree that there is a general tendency to move towards the Western/American way of doing business, but I view this as only a superficial manifestation of market-induced behaviors. In the global village, the Western way of doing business is essential for economic survival, and aviation is no exception to this rule. No matter what overt behaviors humans might have been indoctrinated into, no matter what overt behaviors humans might exhibit during routine situations, it is well known that in emergencies and life-threatening situations they revert to deeply-rooted behaviors. I am convinced that, under a cosmetic layer of declared acceptance, most of the user population still perceive cultural endeavors from an antagonistic perspective. Because of this, I further believe that native cultural beliefs and assumptions are alive and well under the facade of 'Westernization', ready to surface given the opportunity. The ethnocentrism (perhaps a product of professional 'groupthink'?) still prevailing in high places in aviation certainly does not help to improve this situation.

I would propose that the true challenge for those of us who believe that intelligent consideration and management of cultural factors will significantly improve the aviation system's performance is to foster an environment within which cultural differences become natural and compatible to the largest possible extent, so they can coexist without feelings of shame or blame. The international aviation community may well use the services of 'cultural architects', of individuals who can assume the role of mediators and, on a basis of trust and confidence, bring differences to the surface, so that they can be positively identified and cultural endeavors based upon data and not opinion can be pursued.

Cultural research, just like aviation human factors, is not an end in itself, a means of living for consultants, or an opportunity to generate research data and statistics. Just like aviation human factors, it is neither the last frontier of aviation safety nor a frontier of any kind. The incorporation and management of cultural factors into aviation operations and practices simply represent another tool to contribute to the aviation system's production goals. Encouraging progress has been made, but there is need for improvement. This book presents one possible way to move forward. At its foundation, it carries the belief – which I fervently share – that the proposal contained herein represents a solid contribution to the objective of anticipating human error rather than regretting its consequences. Please enjoy it.

CAPTAIN DANIEL E. MAURINO
Montreal, February 1998

Preface

Although our names appear as authors, this volume is the result of a collaborative effort that extends across five continents. We are indebted to many people and can only begin to identify those who have helped us in so many ways. Our deepest gratitude goes to our colleagues and students at the University of Texas Aerospace Crew Research Project, who have collected data, tortured them and provided invaluable, if not always flattering, feedback. John A. Wilhelm has been a colleague since the era of punchcard data entry. Without his analytic and critical skills, we would have been severely restricted. We want to express our gratitude to our students, graduate and undergraduate, past and present, for working so diligently with us. There has been so much help of so many kinds that we can only list them alphabetically: at the graduate level, Lieutenant Colonel Kathy Clothier, William E. Hines, Captain Dr Sharon Jones, James Klinect, Dr Randy Law, Dr Steven Predmore, Bryan Sexton, Dr Paul Sherman and Dr Mary Waller; we especially thank undergraduate research assistants including John Billimek, Kara Incalcaterra and Patrick Williams.

Our technical staff contributed their vast experience in aviation and aided in data collection and the development of training. We are deeply indebted to Captain John Bell, Captain Roy Butler, Peter Connelly, Leslie Partridge and William Taggart for their assistance and insights. Very special thanks go to our executive assistant, Lou Montgomery, who gave us, not only technical support of the highest caliber, but emotional support when we most needed it.

Captain Daniel Maurino has been the spiritual Godfather of our work. He first gave us entrée into the wonderful universe of global aviation and has been a constant support as well as a delightful travelling companion across five continents. We also are extremely grateful to those colleagues who shared their experiences in personal essays which appear in the text. Their biographies are found on pages xxvii–xxix. We thank all the pilots, flight attendants, maintenance personnel, trainers, check airmen and airline management who participated in the project over the past five years – your contributions have allowed us to make important discoveries about global aviation. We thank all 17 000 plus of you!

In the medical area, our deepest gratitude is to the late Dr Hans-Gerhard Schaefer, who opened this exciting world to us. Our colleagues at the University of Basel Kantonsspital have been enormously supportive. They include Drs Dieter Betzendoerfer, Felix Harder, Stephan Kocher, Daniel Scheidegger and Sven Staender. The ability to collaborate on medical behavior and the nature of error with Dr Jan Davies of the University of Calgary Foothills Hospital has been an unending source of intellectual and social stimulation.

The Honorable Dr John K. Lauber provided the initial opportunity to explore the fascinating world of aviation and crew behavior while he was at NASA-Ames Research Center. He continued to provide encouragement and sage counsel during his tenure as a member of the National Transportation Safety Board. We are also indebted to Captain Neil Johnston of Aer Lingus, whose seminal work in relating the aviation system to a theoretical model of national culture provided us with a critical roadmap.

We would also like to acknowledge the academic support of Professors Michael Harris Bond of the Chinese University of Hong Kong and Geert Hofstede of the IRIC in the Netherlands. Naively, we stumbled into the world of cross-cultural psychology, yet these gentlemen were kind enough to guide us toward cultural discovery. We are indebted to them for their time and sage counsel.

We also want to thank our publisher, John Hindley, for continuing understanding and encouragement, and our editor at Ashgate, Sonia Hubbard, for her guidance.

Notes on the Contributors

Graham Braithwaite, Ph.D., is a researcher at the Department of Aviation at the University of New South Wales, Sydney, Australia. Born in the UK and educated at Loughborough University, he has spent a number of years looking at Australian aviation safety. This work included looking at the influence of culture at its many levels from work group and organizational to industry and national culture.

Captain Robert R. Bumgarner received his US Navy wings in April 1961. After two tours of carrier duty, he left the Navy for airline flying and has now accumulated 34 years of worldwide service as a pilot, flight instructor and check airman. Captain Bumgarner has produced and taught CRM and LOFT training courses for multinational airlines and has extensive experience in the design of pilot recruitment, selection and motivation systems. He currently flies as a B-747-400 captain and instructor pilot for a Taiwanese airline.

Dr Jan M. Davies is a professor of anesthesia in the Faculty of Medicine at the University of Calgary. Born in Australia and educated in Canada, she has spent more than a decade reviewing and researching key issues in anesthetic safety, including patient-specific factors, the personality of anesthetists, and noise in the operating room. She has borrowed heavily from aviation, believing that the analogy between aviation and anesthetics provides a ready source of information about safety-related issues. In addition, she has acted as a consultant to the Bureau of Air Safety Investigation in Australia and the human factors and simulation project at the University of Basel/Kantonsspital. She continues to see patients in consultation at the Foothills Medical Centre and other hospitals in the Calgary Regional Health Authority.

Juergen Hoermann has been working as an aviation psychologist in the German Aerospace Center (DRL) in Hamburg since 1986. He serves as consultant for airlines in Europe and Asia for the development and evaluation of pilot recruitment and selection strategies. Individual and cross-cultural differences of risk perception and decision making as well as their malleability through training or system design are his primary research interests.

Captain Dr Sharon Jones started college at the University of Texas at Austin and completed her BS in Aeronautical Science at Embry Riddle Aeronautical University in Prescott, Arizona. She flew for several regional airlines before simultaneously becoming a pilot for Southwest Airlines and a doctoral candidate in psychology at the University of Texas at Austin. She received her PhD in social psychology in 1996, with dissertation research on error in the air traffic system. She is currently a captain for Southwest while continuing her research efforts with the University of Texas Aerospace Crew Research Project.
Captain Azmi Radzi trained as a cadet pilot with QANTAS in 1972, and graduated with the Australian Airline Transport Pilots' Licence. He flew as a co-pilot with Malaysia Airlines on the Fokker 27 and Boeing 737, and became a commander on the F-27 in early 1979. He has been a captain and check pilot on various fleets, including the B737, Airbus A-300, B747-200 and -300 and is now a captain on the Boeing 747-400. Keeping busy, Azmi graduated from the University of Hull/Malaysian Institute of Management with a Master's degree in Business Administration in 1995, majoring in Human Resource Development.
Captain Surendra Ratwatte is a Boeing 777 captain with Emirates Airlines in Dubai. Born in Sri Lanka, Surendra completed his undergraduate work at Embry Riddle Aeronautical University in Prescott, Arizona. He flew the B737 and L-1011 with Airlanka before moving to the Persian Gulf in 1989, where he initially flew the Airbus A-300-600 and A-310. He is currently pursuing a Master's degree in Aviation Safety through Embry Riddle's distance learning program.
Antonio Schuck   Before arriving in the USA in 1987, Antonio was a flight attendant for VARIG Airlines, based in São Paulo, Brazil. He began his flight training in 1989 at the University of New Haven in Connecticut. In 1991, he transferred to Purdue University, where he graduated in 1993 with a BS in Aviation Technology. Right after graduation he was employed by NATCO (Northwest Airlines Training Corp) to translate CRM material into Portuguese and to teach Brazilian CRM facilitators at TransBrasil Airlines. In October of 1997, he wrote a CRM curriculum for TAM Airlines, also based in Brazil. This airline now runs a full-fledged CRM program and it reports that the course is a great success. Currently, he is in negotiations to write a CRM program for two other South American airlines and a CRM curriculum for a university in southern Brazil. He is a line pilot for Atlantic Southeast Airlines (ASA), based in Dallas, where he lives with his wife.
Bill Taggart is a training specialist with broad experience in human factors training systems. Bill received his undergraduate education at Muskingum College in Ohio, and his graduate-level studies at Carnegie-Mellon University. He helped United Airlines with the

development of their landmark Crew Resource Management program in 1980, and later worked with US and international airlines, ranging from Southwest Airlines to QANTAS. Bill joined the University of Texas Aerospace Crew Research Project under Bob Helmreich in 1990, and has participated in several FAA and NASA-sponsored research projects. He has also applied the lessons learned from aviation to medical settings and other complex, high-risk organizational settings. He and his wife Debbie reside in Austin, Texas.

1 Groups and Cultures in Aviation and Medicine

The great tragedy of Science – the slaying of a beautiful hypothesis by an ugly fact. (Thomas Huxley, *Biogenesis and Abiogenesis*, 1870)

Culture fashions a complex framework of national, organizational and professional attitudes and values within which groups and individuals function. The power of culture often goes unrecognized since it represents 'the way we do things *here*' – the natural and unquestioned mode of viewing the world. However, the reality and strength of culture become salient when we work with a new group (whether in a new country, a new organization or a new profession) and interact with people who have well-established norms and values.

We report here the results of our ongoing exploration of the influences of culture in two professions, aviation and medicine. Our focus is on commercial airline pilots and operating room teams. In both of these domains, work requires high levels of interpersonal collaboration, communication and coordination. The fact that teamwork is an essential element of these domains is both an advantage and a disadvantage for the investigator. Research is facilitated by the fact that group interaction and communication can be observed and measured. However, the dynamics of multi-person interactions are highly complex and are difficult to decompose and understand. As a result, the study of group behavior has lagged behind other areas of psychology.

The study of culture poses its own set of challenges. Culture is an abstract construct that must be inferred from behavior, self-report and artifact. In our case, we are interested in three types of cultures – those associated with national heritage, with organizational membership and with professional allegiance. In this chapter we discuss methodological issues surrounding the study of groups and their behavior and provide the reader with an overview of the work environments we have studied in aviation and medicine.

The Methodological Morass of Group Research

The investigator interested in group behavior must answer two important questions: should I conduct my research with natural groups in a field setting or in the laboratory, and should my investigation be correlational or experimental in nature? The problems facing the field investigator are daunting ones. Natural groups function in real settings where behavior is determined by multiple factors outside the control of the investigator. Studies in the natural world are more likely to deal with correlations among variables that are embedded in a highly complex environment. In correlational group research the inability to specify causal relationships is a major barrier to understanding. However, the experiment poses its own set of methodological problems.

The prototypical social psychological experiment on work groups examines the behavior of 'pseudo-groups' of undergraduates formed in the laboratory to work briefly on a relatively meaningless task (Helmreich, 1975; 1983).[1] Unlike correlational research where causality is necessarily indeterminate, the laboratory experiment, where the researcher can control and manipulate conditions, allows clear specification of causality. However, ethical constraints preclude using powerful or long-lasting manipulations with experimental subjects. In contrast, 'real' work groups typically have a considerable lifespan and the efforts of participants are highly consequential. Performance of the group's tasks often determines success in terms of pay and promotion and, in military and other hazardous environments, may determine life or death. Given the limitations of the laboratory, it seems unreasonable to assume that most findings from laboratory groups can be generalized in meaningful ways to the workplace.

After considering the trade-offs, we concluded that meaningful data in our areas of investigation could only be acquired in real work settings. Despite the real limitations of field research, it is our belief that lack of control can be largely offset by replication in diverse settings and through the use of multiple measures of constructs and behaviors. Thus our commitment is to the study of groups in natural settings.[2]

The decision to study natural groups *in vivo* was further reinforced by consideration of what was known as the 'crisis in social psychol-

1   By 'pseudo-group' we mean that research subjects are formed into groups for the sole purpose of participating in the experiment. The groups have no life following the experimental procedure.
2   Since cultures are acquired through experience and across time, the artificial creation of group cultures in the laboratory strikes us as a very questionable research strategy.

ogy' during the late 1960s (McGuire, 1967; Ring, 1967). Kenneth Ring, one of the harshest critics of academic social psychology, argued that theoretical social psychologists avoid the study of fundamental social issues while pursuing theoretical problems of little or no import. The acrimonious exchanges that dominated professional meetings during this era degenerated into a schism between those doing applied research and those committed to theoretical inquiry in social psychology. Members of each faction openly questioned the values and contributions of the other. Such polarization seems ironic since Kurt Lewin (1946), who is acclaimed as the intellectual father of modern social psychology, followed a strategy that he called 'Action Research'. Action research pursues theory development and application as complementary goals. Investigation of important social issues is not inconsistent with the development of basic theories of social behavior. It is our conviction that the study of natural groups engaged in meaningful work provides the opportunity for both pursuits.

At the same time that we committed the project to naturalistic, action research, we initiated a research philosophy that endures today. In exchange for access to their operations for research, we provide participating organizations with detailed feedback on findings about their operations and make recommendations for action. Organizations, in turn, agree that data collected can be published in de-identified form and share in funding the research.

Box 1.1   From the bridge to the classroom to the cockpit

I was commissioned as a line officer in the US Navy after graduating from Yale University with a major in Culture and Behavior, which included Anthropology, Biology, Psychology and Sociology. My honors thesis had been on the physiological effects of stress, reflecting an early interest in reactions to extreme environments. I served on destroyers in operations and as officer of the deck for combat and refueling. The period of the 1960s when I was on active duty was one of heightened international tensions. It included the Cuban Missile Crisis, the building of the Berlin Wall and the onset of conflict in Southeast Asia. Serving on destroyers on deployments of six or more months served to focus my interests on the behavior and performance of groups living and working under stressful conditions. Observing and experiencing the diverse responses of shipmates, including peers, subordinates and superiors, convinced me that research into group behavior should be at the heart of my graduate studies.

After completing my active duty service, I returned to Yale and enrolled in the PhD program in personality and social psychology.

My early graduate research involved the study of undergraduates exposed to modest levels of stress in the laboratory. It became apparent to me that the reactions of students to the stressors imposed in brief experimental sessions were probably not representative of those of groups exposed for long periods to life-threatening events such as combat.

Fortunately, because of my military and diving background, I was able to conduct my dissertation research as a field study of the reactions of aquanauts living and working on the ocean floor under extremely hazardous conditions as part of the Navy's Project Sealab (Radloff & Helmreich, 1968). This experience convinced me that some aspects of human behavior, including reactions to prolonged and high stress, must be studied in natural settings.

After completing my dissertation, I joined the faculty at The University of Texas at Austin. My research in performance and adjustment under stress was supported by the Office of Naval Research and NASA. NASA's goal in sponsoring this research was to generate data relevant to selection, training and management of long-duration spaceflight. This included further investigations of the performance of aquanauts living and working in habitats on the ocean floors (Bakeman & Helmreich, 1975).

A serendipitous event changed the research setting dramatically. NASA, of course, is the National *Aeronautics* and Space Administration. As part of its efforts in aviation in the 1970s, scientists at NASA's Ames Research Center investigated the causes of jet transport accidents and came to the then startling conclusion that human error was a root cause of the majority. In 1978, NASA hosted a workshop for the aviation industry to share these findings and I was invited to give the keynote address on social psychological factors in the cockpit (Cooper, White, & Lauber, 1979; Helmreich, 1980). Representatives of several of the airlines present felt that the research approach described was as relevant to aviation as to space and invited our group to study pilot behavior and performance in their organizations. From this almost casual beginning, a project that is now in its nineteenth year was born.

An equally serendipitous event led to the current research with medical teams. A Swiss anesthesiologist, Hans-Gerhard Schaefer, saw the links between medicine and aviation and introduced me to a remarkable environment with daily life and death encounters.

A major theme underlying my career is the commitment to research that addresses social issues as well as theoretical concerns. Both aviation and medicine provide settings where research has the potential to increase safety and save lives. (Robert Helmreich)

Box 1.2   From Oz[3] to Austin: an Australian discovers culture

I was born and raised in Australia, and completed my undergraduate and honours studies in organisational psychology at the
University of Queensland. I lived in London for two years some
years ago, and came to understand some of the English influence
upon Australia. When it was time to do my doctoral work, I decided to go to the USA so that I could study Americans 'up close'.
Along with England, the USA exerts a strong cultural influence on
Australia, and I wanted to understand how a country that was
populated by Anglos at about the same time as Australia, could
have developed so differently from Australia. For example,
Australians are blessed and handicapped with the 'tall poppy syndrome', a tendency to cut anyone back down to size who tries to
stand out too far from the other flowers in the field. Based on my
observations of the last eight years in the USA, I believe Americans
embrace the opposite syndrome, which I call 'I'm special'. This
national belief system seems to blend self-esteem with entitlement,
allowing individuals to believe that they are worthy of special consideration – a whole nation of tall poppies if you will. (To avoid
a clamor of complaints, let me state that, yes I honestly believe that
each value system has its advantages and disadvantages.)

It was chance and good fortune that brought me to Bob
Helmreich's door –we bonded on our mutual distrust of psychology studies conducted in laboratories with psychology
undergraduate students. With Bob's help and guidance, I navigated my way through a study of national culture and pilots'
attitudes, and much of the material in Chapter 3 is based on my
doctoral dissertation. The more we delved into national culture,
however, the more we realized the story was not that simple, and
we began to look more closely into organisational culture, and
later, professional culture. Understanding the complex interactions
of these cultures has proved to be a fascinating research arena.
(Ashleigh Merritt)

The Research Environment

In this section we describe relevant characteristics of the cockpit and
operating room (OR) environments. We then consider the similarities

---

3   'Oz', the mythical land from Hollywood movies, is also a favorite short-hand
term for my home country. If you pronounce the first syllable of 'Australia' with
a very broad 'Crocodile Dundee' accent, you'll get to 'Oz'.

and dissimilarities of these domains and, finally, evaluate them as research venues.

The Cockpit

Commercial jet transports are operated by a crew of two or three pilots, depending on the design and level of automation present.[4] Pilots are qualified and licensed professionals who perform the same duties in every nation and organization. During flights, crews operate as semi-autonomous work groups, responsible for the conduct of the mission. They also have responsibility for coordinating and directing the activities of the cabin crew.

Although separated from their company and its management, crews do not operate in a vacuum. They are members of an airline that has formal rules governing the conduct of their jobs. Their flights are conducted as part of a complex and regulated aviation system that has formal rules for the operation of aircraft. The specific direction of flight is coordinated by air traffic controllers who issue commands by radio regarding navigation, speed and destination, based on formal flight plans filed by each company. During flight, crews must also coordinate their activities by radio with their company's flight operations department.

Helmreich & Foushee (1993) proposed an *input–process–output* model of flight crew performance that is shown in Figure 1.1. The model illustrates how the behavior of pilots in the cockpit is influenced by a variety of *input factors*, including individual attitudes, values and capabilities, and organizational and environmental conditions. Influenced by the multiple input factors, the crew conducts a flight through *processes* that include both technical tasks, such as controlling the aircraft, and team responsibilities, including communications, decision making, task allocation and planning. The desired *outcomes* of a flight are safety and efficiency (along with the comfort of passengers), but the dynamics of interactions also shape and interact with the attitudes and morale of the crew members. These, in turn, become inputs to processes in subsequent flights. Thus the model is both dynamic and recursive.

The aviation system is very safe and the overwhelming majority of flights are routine and without incident. However, even on a routine flight the crew's workload varies greatly. Both departures and landings involve the accomplishment of numerous tasks simultaneously. These include monitoring aircraft systems, completing checklists, re-

4 Most advanced technology aircraft have a flight management computer which controls many of the functions formerly filled by the third crew member or flight engineer. On very long flights, even in highly automated aircraft, additional crew members are rostered to allow crew members to rest.

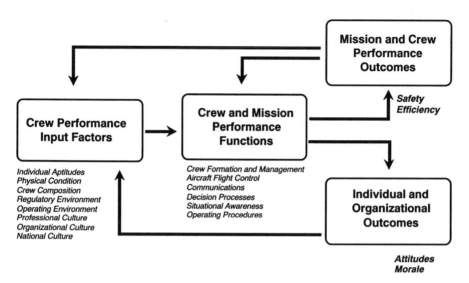

Source: Adapted from Helmreich & Foushee (1993).

Figure 1.1   A model of crew performance

viewing approach and departure charts, listening for and answering radio communications, looking for other, conflicting traffic, and co-ordinating cabin crew activities. Multi-tasking is a demanding and important aspect of team performance in the aviation environment (Waller, 1997; Waller, in press).

The cockpit is also distinguished by clear lines of authority, with the captain having ultimate responsibility for decisions and the conduct of flight. Pilots' tasks are directed by Standard Operating Procedures (SOPs) and a variety of checklists and manuals dictating actions in normal and emergency situations. Despite this formalization of procedures, there are vast opportunities for variation and the combined influences of weather, air traffic and mechanical problems frequently require decision making and prioritization among a variety of alternatives. Many abnormal situations involve *combinations* of conditions (for example, weather and mechanical failure) that are not covered by SOPs.

The introduction of increasing levels of automation has changed the work of pilots in a variety of ways, some positive and some not. Transferring functions from the human to the computer may increase efficiency and reduce some kinds of errors. On the other hand, it can reduce the sense of autonomy and self-worth of pilots and may, at times, increase pilot workload (for example, when unforeseen changes in flight plans require extensive reprogramming of the flight management computer). Helmreich (1987) has referred to the onboard computer as an 'electronic crewmember' with whom the crew must work. Also, as anyone who has used a personal computer will readily acknowledge, entering data into computers offers many opportunities for error and these can have tragic consequences in aviation.

Box 1.3   Teamwork in the cockpit: a flight vignette

The crew for this flight consisted of two pilots flying an advanced technology aircraft that has a flight management computer capable of navigating the aircraft horizontally (point to point) and vertically (maintaining and changing altitude) at programmed speeds.

Meeting in the operations room at the airport, the crew introduced themselves and reviewed the dispatch release (a document containing the route of flight, fuel required and so on) for the 1500 km trip, the weather forecast, and Notices to Airmen containing information about any special conditions that might be encountered on the route of flight. Both pilots noted that weather conditions at the destination were deteriorating and discussed conditions at an alternative airport. After discussing the possibility of en route delays and the performance capabilities of the aircraft with its load, they agreed that it would be prudent to add 2000 pounds of fuel and ordered that it be loaded.

At this point the first officer began a visual inspection of the outside of the Boeing 737-500, which was parked at the gate, while the captain boarded the airplane. On completing the inspection, the first officer boarded and the captain gathered the flight attendants and the first officer in the First Class cabin for a briefing. The briefing contained two major elements: the first consisted of forming an effective team by stressing shared responsibilities and the need for open communications, including the obligation to express any concerns or questions regarding the flight; the second discussed technical aspects of the flight (anticipated weather, delays, and so on).

In the cockpit, the captain and first officer reviewed the logbook for the aircraft, noting its history of recent maintenance. They then discussed how the flight management computer would be used (for example, when to disengage and when to reprogram if the flight plan changed) and confirmed that all changes entered into the computer would be announced and verified. They also affirmed the division of duties between the pilot physically flying the aircraft and the other crew member. The non-flying pilot would be responsible for support activities, including monitoring flight path and aircraft systems, communicating on the radios and coordinating cabin activities. The captain remarked that he would prefer to be the flying pilot on this segment and this became the plan. The first officer then programmed the flight plan, including navigational fixes, altitudes, projected landing runway and alternative destination, into the computer.

After the captain taxied to the runway and the first officer received the clearance to take off from air traffic control, the plane lifted off and the first officer was directed by Air Traffic Control (ATC) to shift to another radio frequency. The plane was cleared to climb in accordance with the flight plan and the captain engaged the flight management computer to control navigation, altitude and speed.

As the aircraft leveled off at its assigned cruising altitude of 35 000 feet, the first officer spoke to the passengers over the public address system. While at cruising altitude, the crew received frequent calls from air traffic controllers, who shifted them from one radio frequency and facility to another as they proceeded toward their destination. During this period, the workload was low and the crew engaged in casual conversation while monitoring navigation, radios and the status of all onboard systems, including the flight management computer. Because of concerns about the weather, they regularly listened to reports of conditions at the destination airport. Prior to the scheduled initiation of the descent for landing, both pilots reviewed the plan for approach and landing and discussed what they might do if the weather continued to deteriorate. They also examined navigational charts and the captain briefed the details of the approach to the scheduled runway.

Shortly after beginning to descend, a warning bell rang, indicating a possible fire in the number two (right side) engine. At the same time, the flight attendant knocked urgently on the door and entered the cockpit to report smoke coming from that engine. The first officer used a handle in the cockpit to discharge a fire extinguisher into the engine and began consulting the emergency checklist for an engine fire. The fire indication did not cease, so a second extinguisher bottle was discharged, with no noticeable effect.

At the captain's direction, the first officer declared an emergency to air traffic control and requested a clearance to the nearest available airport. ATC informed them that an airport with suitable emergency equipment was about 50 miles away. The crew accepted this destination, disengaged the automation and turned toward the new destination while continuing to descend. During the next 10 minutes the crew had to accomplish the following tasks:

1   navigate the aircraft to the new airport;
2   complete the emergency checklist for engine fire, including shutting down the burning engine;
3   monitor the status of the fire and conduct damage assessments and projections based on instrument readings and pilot and flight attendant observations;
4   monitor and comply with route instructions from air traffic control;
5   advise company dispatchers (either directly or by having air traffic control relay messages) of their status and intentions;
6   verify with air traffic control that emergency equipment was ready;
7   brief the lead flight attendant on the situation and instruct her to prepare the passengers for an emergency landing and evacuation;
8   review charts needed for landing at the chosen airport;
9   complete checklists for landing with an engine inoperative and on fire;
10   configure the aircraft for landing;
11   land;
12   evacuate the passengers.

The lead flight attendant briefed the other cabin crew about the situation and they consulted their manuals to ensure that all preparations of the cabin and passengers were completed (this included stowing loose material and instructing the passengers on how to assume a brace position for a possible crash landing). They also had to comfort passengers who were aware of the visible engine fire and becoming increasingly anxious. The first officer interrupted his tasks to make a brief, reassuring announcement to the passengers over the PA.

As the airplane descended through 3000 feet (approximately three minutes from touchdown), the captain instructed the first officer to lower the landing gear. The green light indicating that the right landing gear was down and locked did not illuminate. The crew discussed the possibility that the fire had made the gear inoperable, and the first officer reached for another abnormal checklist. The crew was then faced with a critical decision: whether to abort the approach and attempt to solve the problem or to continue the approach with the possibility of one gear not being lowered.

After a brief discussion, the captain decided to make an immediate landing because of the risk that the fire could cause structural damage if the plane remained in the air. The flight attendant was called to verify that the passengers were prepared for an emergency landing and subsequent evacuation. The captain then landed the airplane and it skidded off the runway into the grass. The crew shut down the left engine and signaled the flight attendants to begin emergency evacuation on the left side (away from the fire). They then secured the aircraft's systems and left the cockpit to assist the flight attendants in evacuation of the passengers.

Overall, the cockpit is an environment that requires high levels of both technical and interpersonal skill. Crews must be able to maintain appropriate vigilance during extended periods of low workload and to make an abrupt transition to demanding, overload conditions (National Research Council, 1993). As noted, they must often form a team from a group of strangers and immediately begin to perform demanding work.

Research into the causes of air disasters during the late 1970s led investigators to the disturbing conclusion that more than 70 per cent of air crashes involve human error rather than failures of equipment or weather. The majority of crew errors consist of failures in leadership, team coordination and decision making (Cooper *et al.*, 1979). The response of the aviation community was to develop new kinds of psychological training for flight crews that focus on group dynamics, leadership, interpersonal communications and decision making (Helmreich & Foushee, 1993; Wiener *et al.*, 1993). These programs were known initially as Cockpit Resource Management (CRM). CRM training represented a massive shift from traditional pilot instruction and evaluation, which had focused almost entirely on the technical (stick and rudder) aspects of flying. More recently, the scope of training has expanded to include other personnel such as flight attendants and air traffic controllers and the name has changed to *Crew* Resource Management, although the acronym remains the same. An essential feature of CRM training is the use of high-fidelity flight simulators to allow crews to practice interpersonal skills in the context of technical flying.

Influenced in part by concerns of the flying public, intensive investigations are held into air crashes and the findings are used to guide regulations and training. In the USA, the National Transportation Safety Board, an independent government agency, is charged with accident investigation and with making recommendations to enhance the safety of the aviation system. There is also increasing reliance on incident-reporting systems in aviation. These systems, which range from an independent, government-sponsored entity, the Aviation Safety Reporting System, to partnerships between organizations and government, allow pilots to report errors and safety-related events without fear of punishment. The data, in turn, aid in training and organizational actions to prevent recurrence.

A flight crew typically begins a trip in the airline's operations room at the airport. Because crew members bid for flight sequences as a function of seniority in their position (captain, first officer, flight engineer), this is frequently the first time the group has met. When the crew is composed of strangers, the initial task is to form and maintain a team that can deal with both normal and abnormal situations effectively.[5]

Overall, flight crews operate in a controlled and highly regulated environment, but one that can provide many complexities and rapid changes. The element of danger, to self and passengers, is an underlying theme in all operations.

The Operating Room

The operating room (OR) is a milieu where a number of professionals must come together to perform multiple and complex tasks in a noisy and cluttered environment.[6] The staff of the OR come from multiple professional specialties. A number of subgroups – surgeons, anesthesiologists, nurses, technicians (for example, perfusionists for procedures such as coronary bypass operations) and orderlies – must coordinate their activities to complete the operation successfully. Other than the well-being of the patient, individuals and subgroups may have different and competing agendas and requirements. Adding to the complexity of the environment, the condition of patients is highly variable and frequently unpredictable (Helmreich & Schaefer, 1994).

Status inequalities in the OR are pervasive and readily observable. All physician groups have higher status than surgical and anesthesia nurses and do not hesitate to invoke their authority.[7] However, the authority structure in the OR is not clearly defined. Surgeons are, of course, responsible for whatever surgical procedure is being con-

---

5   Research into accidents involving human error by the US National Transportation Safety Board has shown that a disproportionate percentage of accidents happen to crews who are flying together for the first time. This suggests that the team formation process is frequently imperfect. Conversely, crews who fly together for extended periods of time may fall victim to complacency and tendencies to shortcut standard operating procedures.

6   In contrast to the flightdeck, which is engineered in an integrated fashion by a single manufacturer, the operating room is a noisy setting (hygiene precludes sound insulation that could trap germs) where a variety of different equipment (such as monitors and sensors, intravenous preparations, electro-cautery devices and so on) made by different manufacturers are linked together by cables and tubing. It is not uncommon for a staff member to trip over a cable or accidentally disconnect an intravenous (IV) line.

7   In many cases, the nurses are much more experienced than residents. This also can lead to difficult interactions. A similar situation is often found in the military, where senior sergeants have much more knowledge than junior officers and control situations by indirection.

ducted. However, the anesthesiologists are responsible for the induction, maintenance and resuscitation of the patient. On many occasions there may be disagreements about how to deal with unexpected contingencies during an operation.[8]

Box 1.4 Teamwork in the operating room: a medical vignette

The events during this hypothetical operation give a sense of the sequence of activities and the nature of team interaction in the OR. Although there are many differences in procedures and practices between hospitals in one country and between those around the world, overall activities are similar, wherever the venue. This episode has a scenario that has been used in one hospital as a model for training OR teams in more effective teamwork. It depicts an operation to remove a possibly malignant tumor from the abdomen of an obese, 75-year-old patient with moderately severe emphysema and chronic bronchitis.[9] He had smoked a pack of cigarettes each day for the past 50 years. He was unable to climb one fight of stairs without shortness of breath, nor could he speak a complete sentence without stopping to take a breath. He was admitted to hospital two days before the operation to facilitate an increase in his medications and to provide chest physiotherapy (in the form of special breathing exercises).

On the night before the operation, the patient was visited separately by the attending surgeon and anesthesiologist. These visits served both to reassure and to assess the patient. Because of the patient's age, weight and breathing problems, his level of risk was classified as above average.

On the morning of the operation, the surgeon and anesthesiologist arrived in the changing rooms adjacent to the OR. While changing into special OR clothes, they discussed the patient's condition, the proposed operation, and plans for the anesthetic.[10] The surgeon reminded the anesthesiologist that he wanted to send a specimen of the tumor to the Pathology Laboratory to obtain a diagnosis while

---

8   When one of us (RLH) was giving a talk on interpersonal issues in the OR to a group of surgeons and anesthesiologists, the question was posed, 'Who is in charge in the OR?' This resulted in heated exchanges between the two groups.

9   We are indebted to Dr Jan Davies of the University of Calgary/Foothills Hospital for her wise counsel. The vignette is designed to represent a typical layout and procedure. In some hospitals and countries, different physical layouts and procedures are found. For example, in the Swiss hospital where we have conducted research, the patient is anesthetized in an adjacent room and not taken into the OR until induction is complete.

10 In our hypothetical operation, both the surgeon and anesthesiologist are male, as this is representative of the gender distribution. If they were of different sexes, the informal, but critical, briefing during robing would not be possible.

the operation was still proceeding. (This would be accomplished by the pathologist taking a section of the tumor, freezing it and examining it under the microscope, while the patient was still anesthetized.) The anesthesiologist then remarked that he would be inserting extra monitoring devices, to provide more thorough assessment of the patient's condition. The insertion of these devices would take additional time during the anesthetic induction.

While the surgeon and anesthesiologist were discussing their patient, he was being transported to the OR, to wait in a central holding area with several other patients.

The anesthesiologist left the changing room and went into the assigned operating room while the surgeon went off to make rounds of several other patients. In the OR, the anesthesiologist then carried out a pre-anesthetic check of all equipment (including the anesthesia machine, ventilator and monitors) using a checklist. He then drew the necessary drugs into syringes (including the normally used anesthetic agents and two drugs which might be needed in the case of marked changes in blood pressure or heart rate). While doing this, he discussed the day's operating list with the nurses who were carrying out their own preparations for the procedure. He briefly described the first patient's problems and answered questions posed by the nurses.

Once ready, the anesthesiologist and one of the nurses went to the holding area where they introduced themselves again to the patient and accompanied him to the operating room. When the patient was positioned on the operating table, the anesthesiologist, with the help of a nurse, inserted an intravenous (IV) line and attached sensors for blood pressure, heart rate and blood oxygen. After injecting a local anesthetic, the anesthesiologist inserted a small plastic catheter into the artery of the left wrist and connected this via a tube to a blood pressure sensor. He then injected a number of drugs through the IV, including one to induce loss of consciousness, a narcotic used with other agents to abolish pain from the surgical procedure and a muscle relaxant to paralyze the patient's muscles. An oxygen mask was placed over the patient's face and oxygen was administered, first with the patient breathing on his own and then with the anesthesiologist assisting the patient's efforts which were observed to grow progressively weaker as the anesthetic agents took effect. Once the patient was evaluated as being unconscious, with muscles completely relaxed, a tube was inserted through his mouth into the trachea. Tubing from the tracheal tube was then connected to an anesthesia ventilator, which assumed the breathing function, pushing a mixture of gases from the anesthesia machine into the patient's lungs. As well as oxygen, the gases consisted of nitrous oxide and an inhalational anesthetic agent which maintained the patient in a state of unconsciousness, since the effect of the intravenous sedative was starting to abate. The anesthesia machine, ventilator and sensors were connected to a video monitor which continuously displayed the patient's heart rate, blood pressure, electrocardiogram (EKG), blood oxygen saturation, amount of carbon dioxide exhaled with each breath and several other critical measurements. In addition to visual displays, the monitors were capable of providing audible alarms if the patient's status changed from acceptable limits. After being assured that all vital signs were stable, the anesthesiologist then lowered the head of the operating table slightly to facilitate the insertion of a large intravenous line into the patient's right jugular vein. This line would permit the anesthesiologist to administer large amounts of intravenous fluids rapidly and also to measure the pressure in the venous part of the patient's circulation, by connecting the IV to a special pressure sensor.

During this time, the surgical (scrub) nurse was preparing the instruments, assisted by another (circulating) nurse who would obtain necessary supplies from cupboards and shelves. Outside the OR, the surgical team, consisting of the attending surgeon and a surgical resident, was scrubbing in preparation for the operation.

After induction of anesthesia was complete, and the anesthesiologist was satisfied with the condition of the patient, notations were made on the patient's anesthetic record as to drugs administered and the values of the various monitor readings. And after receiving instruction from the anesthesiologist, the scrub nurse uncovered the patient's abdomen and cleaned the skin with an antiseptic solution.

As the surgeon was drying his hands and arms with a sterile towel, he asked the anesthesiologist how the patient was doing. The anesthesiologist responded that the monitors showed that the patient was stable and that his blood oxygen saturation had increased. After receiving this update, the surgeon helped the scrub nurse drape the patient's abdomen and chest with sterile sheets. One sheet was attached to the two poles supporting the IV at the head of the table, forming a screen between the anesthesiologist and the surgical field. The anesthesiologist adjusted the height of the poles so that he was able to view the surgical field.

Once all preparations were complete, the surgeon asked if the patient was ready for the incision and, receiving an affirmative response, began the scheduled two-hour procedure.

As the surgeon proceeded to isolate the tumor, the anesthesiologist monitored the patient's condition. During this period the sensors emitted occasional spurious audible alarms, suggesting low blood oxygen saturation or blood pressure. These were noted and verified as false, and probably originating from electrical interference from the electrocautery unit used by the surgeon to heat-seal blood vessels.

An hour into the operation, the surgeon inadvertently perforated an artery, which resulted in massive loss of blood. Simultaneously, the anesthesiologist noted decreasing blood pressure and, with the nurse, initiated efforts to restore the volume of blood in circulation and blood pressure.

After several minutes, the surgeon managed to staunch the bleeding and prepared to resume the operation. However, the anesthesiologist suddenly cautioned that blood oxygen saturation was now dangerously low and suggested not proceeding until the patient could be stabilized. He also argued that, if stable vital signs could not be rapidly restored, the operation should be terminated and the patient sent to the Intensive Care Unit. After some debate, the procedure was halted and the anesthesiologist and nurse worked to achieve a normal EKG and blood oxygen saturation. Using a stethoscope, he listened to the lungs and heard decreased breath sounds from the right lung. He asked the surgeon to stop operating and then inserted a large needle into the patient's chest. An audible hiss of escaping gas was heard by all in the operating room, confirming the anesthesiologist's diagnosis of a pneumothorax (an abnormal accumulation of gas between the lung and the chest wall) due to a ruptured bleb or blister on the surface of the lung. The anesthesiologist turned off the nitrous oxide and administered one hundred per cent oxygen. He then asked the surgeon to insert a large tube into the chest, to aid in evacuation of the gas. He also suggested not proceeding until the patient could be stabilized. He again said, if stable vital signs could not be rapidly restored, the operation should be terminated as quickly as possible and the patient sent to the Intensive Care Unit. After 15 minutes, the patient was stabilized, the operation was resumed, and the tumor was excised. It was dispatched to the laboratory for immediate examination by a pathologist to determine if it was malignant. While waiting for the results, the surgeon and anesthesiologist reviewed the dynamics of the operation, the management of the hemorrhage and efforts to stabilize the patient.

When the pathologist reported that the tumor was actually malignant, the surgeon proceeded to remove additional tissue in the surrounding area. Finally, after four and a half hours, the surgeon delegated the task of closing the incision to the assisting resident. Following this, the anesthesiologist and nurse began the process of preparing the patient for transfer to the Recovery Room and then to the Intensive Care Unit.

> *This hypothetical operation is not unique in showing how a team re-sponds to a medical crisis such as massive bleeding or experiences conflict over whether or not to continue or terminate a surgical procedure. It may, however, be atypical in depicting a high level of open communica-tion between the professional specialties in the OR. Observational data suggest that briefings and debriefings are infrequent and that there are often misunderstandings and miscommunications in this environment (Helmreich & Schaefer, 1994; Sexton et al., 1997a).*

Medical catastrophes also come under investigation, but not as publicly or intensively as air disasters. The figures for anesthetic mishaps are strikingly similar to those found in commercial aviation. Investigations of incidents in anesthesia suggest that between 75 per cent (Chopra *et al.*, 1992) and 80 per cent (Kumar *et al.*, 1988) include human error. Helmreich & Schaefer (1994) report that many of the errors involve failures in communication, decision making, interper-sonal conflict and teamwork. Errors are of both commission and omission (Davies, 1995; Runciman *et al.*, 1993). More striking are the results of a survey of anesthesiologists in which 24 per cent admitted committing an error with lethal consequences (McDonald & Peterson, 1985). Systematic data on the frequency and severity of surgical error are not available, but there is no reason to assume that the incidence rate is lower than in anesthesia. Leape and his colleagues (Leape, 1994; Leape *et al.*, (1991) studied errors associated with hospitaliz-ation and concluded from a sample of 25 000 hospital records that more than 3 per cent of patients hospitalized are the victims of errors by medical personnel which result in permanent damage.

The medical community has begun to respond to findings of hu-man error and failures by initiating psychological training that deals with team issues and crisis management (Davies & Helmreich, 1996; Helmreich & Davies, 1996; Howard *et al.*, 1992). These efforts have drawn heavily on experiences in aviation. The major impetus for human factors training has come from anesthesiologists (Howard *et al.*, 1992; Helmreich & Schaefer, 1997), but surgeons are becoming increasingly involved. The use of simulators is also growing for team training of surgeons, anesthesiologists and nurses (Helmreich & Schaefer, 1997; Davies & Helmreich, 1996).

Medicine is also beginning to initiate confidential incident-report-ing systems that allow personnel to report instances of human error without fear of retribution (Runciman *et al.*, 1993; Staender, 1996).

Similarities and Differences between the Cockpit and the Operating Room

The late Hans-Gerhard Schaefer, an anesthesiologist from the University of Basel Kantonsspital in Switzerland, provided the original impetus for our research in this setting. Through immersion in both environments, he concluded that the group dynamics of the OR have much in common with those of the flightdeck (Helmreich & Schaefer, 1994). Schaefer worked on the development of a conceptual model of team performance in the OR. The model which is shown in Figure 1.2 is highly similar to that defined for the flightdeck. The input, process and outcome factors are conceptually the same, although the specifics differ widely.

The operating room is a much more complex environment psychologically than the cockpit. In the cockpit, a small team, working for the same organization, conducts a flight in accordance with clear rules and regulations. Although the flight crew must interact with other groups in the system, their primary workplace is clearly defined and isolated. In contrast, the operating room, with its many subgroups, is a much more fluid and dynamic setting, without the same formalized control mechanisms. Although there are clear lines of authority within subgroups, for example, between attendings and residents and physicians and nurses, the ultimate authority in the OR is not clearly defined. The absence of a clear authority structure is an invitation to conflict. The *Oxford English Dictionary* defines a

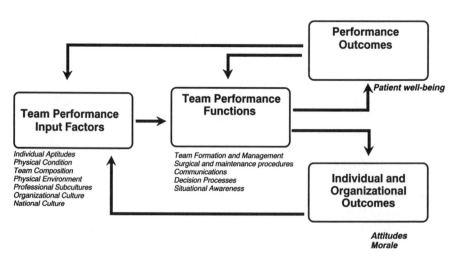

Source: Adapted from Helmreich & Schaefer (1994).

Figure 1.2   A model of operating room team performance

Doctors Fined for Fight in Operating Room

Worcester, Mass. Nov. 27 (AP) — A state medical board has fined a surgeon and an anesthesiologist $10,000 each for brawling in an operating room while their patient slept under general anesthesia.

After their fight, the anesthesiologist, Dr. Kwok Wei Chan, and the surgeon, Dr. Mohan Korgaonkar, successfully operated on the elderly female patient.

In addition to imposing the fines, the state board of Registration in Medicine last week ordered the doctors to undergo joint psychotherapy. It also directed officials at the Medical Center of Central Massachusetts, who had already put the doctors on five years' probation, monitor Drs. Chan and Korgaonkar for five years.

The medical board said that on Oct. 24, 1991, Dr. Korgaonkar was about to begin surgery when he and Dr. Chan began to argue. Hospital officials would not provide the nature of their disagreement.

Dr. Chan swore at Dr. Korgaonkar, who threw a cotton-tipped prep stick at Dr. Chan, the board said. The two then raised their fists and scuffled briefly, at one point wrestling on the floor. A nurse monitored the anesthetized patient as the doctors fought.

Figure 1.3   Conflict in the operating room

cockpit as 'an enclosed space for fighting'. From systematic observations of interactions in the OR, it was noted that the setting on occasion comes close to the Oxford definition of a cockpit (Sexton *et al.*, 1997a). While conflict does occur among flight crews, the cockpit is more often the venue where teams interact harmoniously with technology. Figure 1.3 is a vivid example of conflict and conflict resolution in the operating room.

Box 1.5   At the cutting edge: from the operating room to the cockpit

Hans-Gerhard Schaefer was responsible for the extension of our research into medicine. Although he died tragically in 1995, his initiative and wisdom have launched a new line of research and training. This is to recognize his outstanding contributions to the human factors of medical teams.

As an attending anesthesiologist at the University of Basel Kantonsspital in Basel, Switzerland, in the early 1990s, Schaefer became concerned by the extent of human error and by breakdowns in communication in the operating room. While investigating the literature on human error, he came across research into flight crew performance and the development of Crew Resource Management training for pilots. He hypothesized that the problems were similar and that similar solutions might increase safety and team effectiveness in the operating room.

Schaefer spent a sabbatical leave with our research group at the University of Texas at Austin where he immersed himself in both aviation research and approaches to team training. Following his stay in Texas, three of the research group (Helmreich, William Hines and Bryan Sexton) went to Basel to study human factors issues in the operating room. Observing team interactions and the nature of errors confirmed that the team dynamics were highly similar.

On the basis of his experience, Schaefer concluded that team simulation training similar to that employed in aviation would be the most effective way to change behavior and promote safety. With the strong support of the departments of Anesthesia and Surgery, a complete operating room simulator was designed and constructed at the Kantonsspital in Basel. The facility includes a fully instrumented mannequin (named Wilhelm Tell). Both anesthetic and surgical procedures can be conducted.

The program at Basel represents the most faithful translation of aviation training approaches to human error. A multidisciplinary team manages the program and has conducted simulator training for faculty, anesthesia and surgical residents, nurses and orderlies since 1995.

Hans-Gerhard Schaefer was born in Germany in 1951. He completed his medical studies and residency at Oxford University in England. He served as an attending anesthesiologist at the University of Basel Kantonsspital from 1987 until his death in 1995. His dedication to improving the human factors of the operating room led to the development of the first full operating room simulator and continues to inspire his colleagues.

The types of errors involving communication, decision making, conflict resolution and so on are highly similar in the two environments and the percentage of adverse events that involve human error appears to be nearly identical.[11] However, there is a critical difference in reactions to error in medicine and aviation. When a

---

11 While the base rate of accidents is well established in aviation (for example, one fatal crash in just under a million flights), comparable data are not available in medicine. If the data from the study of errors in general hospitalization can be generalized, the rate of catastrophe is much higher in medicine than in aviation.

patient dies in the operating room, it is an unfortunate, but singular, event. When an aircraft crashes because of team error, it is a highly visible event that receives wide media publicity and results in demands for investigation and remediation and/or punishment of the 'guilty'. It is a cynical truism that, while pilots are the first at the scene of an accident and more often than not perish as a result of their errors, doctors can commit an error with a lethal outcome in the morning and can play golf that afternoon. Exacerbated in the USA by the specter of malpractice litigation and enormous financial damages, many errors are covered up or not investigated rigorously. Recently, however, more light has been cast on medical mishaps ranging from errors in drug doses to operating on the wrong side of the brain or amputating the wrong leg (Belkin, 1997; Bogner, 1994).

The Cockpit and Operating Room as Research Settings

The cockpit of a jet transport is a splendid place to study individual, group, organizational and national factors involving human interaction and the interface between teams and technology. The vast majority of the world's transport aircraft are built by a small number of manufacturers in the USA and Western Europe. Thus the same work environment can be found in Asia and Africa. There are also large numbers of crews conducting the same meaningful (and sometimes dangerous) work, thus providing an enormous potential research population (Foushee, 1984). The behavior of flight crews is observable and measurable, making systematic investigations possible. In addition, the widespread use in training of advanced simulators that recreate all aspects of flight (controls, outside view, motion, communication between cockpit and cabin, communication with air traffic control, mechanical problems, adverse weather, and so on) allows for quasi-experimental research under well controlled conditions. For example, NASA researchers assembled 24 crews of experienced airline pilots who were assigned to one of three groups on the basis of the captain's personality characteristics (Chidester *et al.*, 1990). Each crew then conducted five complete flights over a two-day period, with the major dependent variables being expert ratings of performance and number of errors committed by the crews. The results showed significant differences in overall team performance as a function of the leader's personality.

The operating room is also a rich research environment. It provides a setting where various subgroups must cooperate in the service of common goals – completing the necessary procedure with the best outcome for the patient, minimizing the probability of human error and mitigating the consequences of errors that do occur. It is also an excellent venue for investigation of the way in which professional and organizational cultures influence actions. Given the greater safety of aviation, research that enhances the effectiveness of medical teams and reduces the incidence of adverse events may have a greater potential for social benefit than similar research in aviation.

Aviation and medicine differ greatly in their acceptance of the type of research into group behavior that concerns us. Because everyone in aviation shares a concern with safety, organizations are open to research that has the potential to decrease the likelihood of accidents. Although fierce competitors in the market-place, airlines willingly share data on issues that involve safety. Research in aviation is facilitated by archival data available from accident investigations and from incident reports. In addition, regular recurrent training and performance evaluation of flight crews in both simulator and aircraft is required, providing another opportunity for data collection. In contrast, medical practice is driven to a considerable extent by fear of litigation should evidence of error or substandard performance emerge. Thus there is neither a tradition of research into group processes and error nor a general willingness to share what data are available on human performance. There is also lacking a tradition of formal job performance appraisal after completion of medical school. The type of psychological training in individual and team performance issues that so greatly facilitated our research with pilots is in its infancy in medicine. However, we see indications that acceptance of the need to investigate and ameliorate the interpersonal team aspects of medical practice is growing.

Our research strategy is based on the use of multiple methodologies and measures in many organizations (Helmreich & Foushee, 1993). One of our primary methods is the use of surveys to assess attitudes regarding teamwork, leadership, vulnerability to stress, organizational factors, and so on. A second approach consists of systematic observation of crew performance in normal and simulated flights or in the OR, using a detailed and reliable coding scheme. A third method utilizes records of accidents and incidents as sources of data and hypotheses.[12]

Context Factors

As the two models of team performance indicate, cockpit and OR teams function in the context of the physical environment and the psychological environment provided by their attributes and experience. Experimental research in social psychology that is conducted in

---

12   For example, Helmreich conducted detailed analyses of system, organizational and individual factors in several air crashes in Canada and the USA (Helmreich, 1992; 1994).

laboratory settings either controls or ignores context effects, in our view seriously limiting the generality of findings.

When we began our research in US airlines, we were unaware of the nature and power of many of the context effects that are the inputs to group processes in the cockpit. We were beneficiaries of the growth of CRM training throughout the aviation community. Organizations realized that empirical data were needed to provide information on the behavioral and attitudinal impact of training, and guidance in curriculum development and refinement. As a result, our project grew rapidly as more and more airlines asked to participate. As we began to collect both survey and behavioral data, we were not surprised to find substantial variability in attitudes about the management of flight and highly significant differences between airlines in attitudes about the interpersonal aspects of flying. These differences seemed to correspond to recognizable aspects of the organizational cultures of the airlines involved. More important, the attitudinal measures proved to be valid predictors of the behavior of crews in flight operations (Helmreich *et al.*, 1986).

At the same time, airlines in other countries also sought to increase crew effectiveness and reduce human error. Many imported existing CRM training from the USA. Some of these programs proved to be less than successful when applied in other cultures, but the reasons for their failure were not readily recognized. Several foreign airlines that were struggling to implement CRM training asked to participate in our research and we began to collect data in Asia and Europe.

We began our research accepting the widespread assumption that the task of flying an aircraft from one point to another is universal and culture-free. After all, the task and airplanes are the same. We were surprised to find that national differences on the attitudes measured on our survey were much larger than the differences between organizations that we had found in the USA. Several items assessing attitudes about the use of cockpit automation had also been included in the survey and these also showed large national differences.

Our initial cross-cultural findings made it clear that we needed to include national culture as one of the input factors to be investigated. The factors that make the cockpit an excellent research environment for studies within a culture also recommended it for cross-cultural investigation. A major convenience for the researcher is the fact that English is the global language of aviation.[13]

13 Indeed, many international airlines not only require proficiency in English as a prerequisite for being a pilot, but also require crews to use English as the language for intra-cockpit communication. However, we rapidly discovered that the assumption that crews will be fluent in English is not universally correct. As a result, some of the data collection was accomplished with versions of our instruments translated into the native language of the respondent.

We now know that the contextual inputs to group behavior in aviation and medicine include professional, organizational and national cultures. The influences of these multiple cultures on human interaction are the focus of the book.

The Structure of the Book

Our goal is to use the two environments, aviation and medicine, to illustrate the nature and consequences of professional, national and organizational cultures for individual attitudes and values and team interaction. The majority of the data come from aviation, as that has been our primary research area, but we feel that contrasting two professions that make strong interpersonal as well as technical demands on their members can illustrate the breadth and importance of cultural issues in the workplace.

Chapter 2 explores professional cultures in aviation and medicine in greater depth. Formal definitions of professional culture are discussed and data from aviation and medicine in several countries are presented. Positive and negative aspects of professional culture are considered. Finally, the extent to which individuals with particular personality attributes self-select into different professions is explored.

Chapter 3 begins with a review of the relevant research on national culture and methodological issues and challenges that confront researchers. Data from pilots in 22 countries are presented and the results of this investigation are placed in the context of earlier research into the dimensions of national culture. We use reactions to automation as an example of the way technology is strongly influenced by values associated with national culture.

Chapter 4 addresses the cultures of organizations. The organization is seen as the modulator of the influence of national and professional cultures. We focus on those organizational issues that affect the safety of organizational function and the relationship between safety and organizational cultures. Comparative data from airlines and a more limited number of medical organizations are presented.

Chapter 5 describes a model of human error and its management. We suggest that error management can provide a universal model for training in safety-sensitive, high-risk organizations. The error model is based on cultural universals (human limitations and the value of safety) and is a strategy for developing organizational practices to enhance safety. The chapter concludes with a description of methods to diagnose the status and needs of organizations. Chapter 6 focuses on the implementation of error management in organizations, with particular emphasis on fitting the strategy to the organizational and national culture. Case studies illustrate the special circumstances that may influence outcomes in particular organizations and cultures.

Chapter 7 considers the special case of multicultural organizations. It examines not only organizations staffed by individuals from different national cultures but also the strains that arise when organizations merge within cultures. Finally, Chapter 8 is a discussion of the ways culture may be addressed more effectively by organizations and how the next generation of researchers may be trained.

Our hope is that this book will be accessible both to practitioners and managers and to members of the research community with an interest in each of the types of culture. To accomplish this we relegate highly technical methodological discussions and detailed statistical analyses to appendices. A methodological appendix describes particular techniques we have employed to enable appropriate analyses. A statistical appendix presents results of complex analyses. Finally, the various research instruments we have utilized in our research in both domains are provided.

2 Professional Culture

Our data suggest that aviation and medicine have strong and distinctive professional cultures. We feel that defining and isolating the positive and negative attributes of these cultures can give us greater insight into the context that surrounds and influences the work of pilots and OR teams.

Vocation or Profession

One of the defining attributes of a profession is that its members have special expertise: they can perform actions or deliver services that the lay person cannot (Hughes, 1958). Selectivity and competition are also defining characteristics of professions; far more apply than are accepted. The process of acquiring such expertise usually requires the novice to undergo lengthy, demanding training. Military and airline pilots undergo rigorous training, often with substantial attrition. Similarly, doctors face a lengthy training process that begins with medical school and internship and, in the case of specialties such as surgery and anesthesia, also includes a lengthy and demanding residency.

Justifying the sacrifices associated with attaining professional status, many professions provide their members not only with prestige but also with high monetary rewards.[1] In general, the public trusts professionals and relies on them.[2] Reflecting the reward structure and also the sacrifices they have made along the way, few leave professions once they have achieved full membership.

1   Academics at the college and university level are recognized as professionals, not only as educators but also as members of their disciplinary specialties. While these professional affiliations have historically been prestigious, they have not been highly rewarding financially. Perhaps the organizational assumption is that prestige alone is sufficient to provide fulfillment.
2   There are exceptions to this generalization. Many deride the ethics and behavior of members of the legal profession (a tradition that may be traced back to Shakespearean England).

Professions typically employ symbols that differentiate their members from laypersons (Greenwood, 1957). The symbols are so ubiquitous that people can readily recognize members. Pilots and doctors possess these badges to an extraordinary degree. The symbols of medicine are universal and have been reinforced by countless television series beamed around the world. The stereotypical doctor is a caring (often graying, but sometimes young and intense) individual in a white smock with stethoscope loosely carried around the neck. Doctors and pilots have historically been male, but this is slowly changing and the process is creating new tensions as traditional male bastions are breached and cultural stereotypes are threatened. We will explore gender issues further in our discussion of professional subcultures.

Aviation is less than 100 years old, but it rapidly acquired symbols that have endured to the present. World War I gave us the image of the lone warrior battling a heroic opponent while following the code of chivalry. Von Richthofen from Germany and Rickenbacker from the USA became household names and role models for the youth of their countries. After the war, the initiation of mail service further established the image of the intrepid aviator braving the elements, aloft and alone, with white scarf trailing in the wind. The aircraft of the time were flimsy and unreliable and navigation aids and accurate weather information were only dreams. Although the fatality rate was appalling, the romance of flight continued to attract risk takers. Antoine de Saint Exupéry (1942) and Ernest K. Gann (1961) have poetically chronicled the life (and death) of the early mail pilots. The current symbol of the airline pilot is a sharply tailored uniform with multiple golden stripes and wings. The prototypical aviator also conveys an air of knowing, imperturbable competence communicated in a laconic speech style captured wonderfully by Tom Wolfe in *The Right Stuff* (1979).

Box 2.1   Excerpt from *The Right Stuff*

Along with his description of the culture of the first astronauts, Tom Wolfe paints a vivid picture of Chuck Yeager, the test pilot who first broke the sound barrier, as the ultimate role model for today's airline pilot.

'Now folks, uh … this is the captain … ummmm … We've got a little ol' red light up here on the control panel that's tryin' to tell us that the landin' gears're not … uh … *lockin'* into position when we lower 'em … Now … I don't believe that little ol' red light knows what it's talkin' about – I believe it's that little ol' red light that iddn' workin' right'… faint chuckle, long pause, as if to say I'm not even sure all this is really worth going into – *still, it may amuse you...*'But ... I guess to play it by the rules, we oughta humor that little ol' light ... so we're gonna take her down to about, oh, two or three hundred feet over the runway at Kennedy, and the folks down there on the ground are gonna see if they caint give us a *visual* inspection of those ol' landin' gears' – with which he is obviously on intimate ol'-buddy terms, as with every other working part of this mighty ship – 'and if I'm right ... they're gonna tell us everything is *copacetic* all the way aroun' an' we'll jes take her on in'... and, after a couple of low passes over the field, the voice returns: 'Well, folks, those folks down there on the ground – it must be too early for 'em or somethin' – I 'spect they still got the sleepers in their eyes ... 'cause they say they caint tell if those ol' landin' gears are all the way down or not ... But, you know, up here in the cockpit we're convinced they're all the way down, so we're jes gonna take her on in ... And oh'... (*I almost forgot*) ...'while we take a little swing out over the ocean an' empty some of that surplus fuel we're not gonna be needin' anymore – that's what you might be seein' comin' out of the wings – our lovely little ladies ... if they'll be so kind ... they're gonna go up and down the aisles and show you how we do what we call "assumin" the position' ... another faint chuckle (*We do this so often, and it's so much fun, we even have a funny little name for it*) ... and the stewardesses, a bit grimmer, by the looks of them, than that voice, start telling the passengers to take their glasses off and take the ballpoint pens and other sharp objects out of their pockets, and they show them *the position*, with the head lowered ... while down on the field at Kennedy the little yellow emergency trucks start roaring across the field – and even though in your pounding heart and your sweating palms and your boiling brainpan you know this is a critical moment in your life, you still can't quite bring yourself to believe it, because if it were – how could *the captain*, the man who knows the actual situation most intimately ... how could he keep on drawlin' and chucklin' and driftin' and lollygaggin' in that particular voice of his –

Well! – who doesn't know that voice? And who can forget it? – even after he is proved right and the emergency is over.

That particular voice may sound vaguely Southern or Southwestern, but it is specifically Appalachian in origin. It originated in the mountains of West Virginia, in the coal country, in Lincoln County, so far up in the hollows that, as the saying went, 'they had to pipe in daylight'. In the late 1940s and early 1950s this uphollow voice drifted down from on high, from over the high desert of California, down, down, down, from the upper reaches of the Brotherhood into all phases of American aviation. It was amazing.

It was *Pygmalion* in reverse. Military pilots and then, soon, airline pilots, pilots from Maine and Massachusetts and the Dakotas and Oregon and everywhere else, began to talk in that poker-hollow West Virginia drawl, or as close to it as they could bend their native accents. It was the drawl of the most righteous of all the possessors of the right stuff.
(*The Right Stuff*, pp.44–6)

Characteristics of Professional Cultures

The culture of a profession is manifested in its members by a sense of community and by the bonds of a common identity (Goode, 1957). The norms and values of the profession are exemplified by its senior members and passed on to recruits. Because the knowledge required of the professional is esoteric, the policing of the profession is typically by its own members – as illustrated by the control that medical societies exert over their members. By monitoring its own, a profession accords its members protection from the lay community. However, in exchange, the professional must accept the social control of his or her peers. This type of control serves to maintain and strengthen the professional culture of medicine. In contrast, because commercial aviation consists of a complex system and carries the risk of large-scale catastrophe, it is strongly regulated at the national level in most countries. This level of regulation makes it more difficult for an 'old boys' network' to protect members of the profession who err.

The strong stereotypes associated with medicine and aviation greatly facilitate the socialization of new members, making the process direct and successful. Having been indoctrinated into the professional culture, doctors and aviators from all parts of the world feel a common bond. Indeed, professional membership can provide a much stronger bond than company loyalty or national identity.

Professional Commitment

Members of a strong professional culture typically place great value on their work. Our data in aviation and medicine show this high regard for the work. Members of both professions, with few exceptions, report that they like their jobs a great deal. Figure 2.1 shows the responses of more than 12 500 pilots from 19 countries to the survey item 'I like my job'. Answers were on a five-point Likert scale where 1 indicates 'disagree strongly', and 5 'agree strongly'. The overall average score for liking the job was an extraordinary 4.7 out

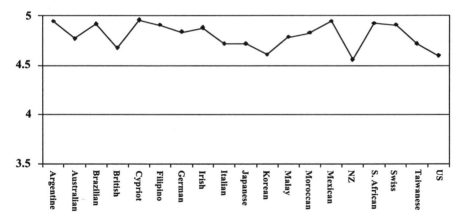

Scale 1 = disagree strongly 3 = neutral 5 = agree strongly

Figure 2.1   Pilot responses in 19 countries: 'I like my job'

of a possible 5. Put another way, more than 75 per cent of all re-spondents *agreed strongly* and another 17 per cent *agreed* with the statement; only 4.5 per cent disagreed. In contrast, a Gallup survey of a random, national US sample of working adults found that only 36 per cent were extremely satisfied with their jobs (Seglin, 1996).[3] Per-haps representing a sample closer to the professionals in our data, a Cornell survey of more than 3800 managers and executives, all col-lege graduates and 55 per cent with Masters or higher degrees, conducted in 1995, found that these senior personnel reported being satisfied with their jobs 54 per cent of the time, dissatisfied 27 per cent of the time, and neutral 19 per cent of the time.

While liking for the job is a professional pilot universal, there is variability in overall job satisfaction. Liking for the job does not imply that pilots are happy with their organizations or working conditions. Organizational context is a significant determinant of job satisfaction. In the USA, where data from nine airlines are available, the percentage of pilots who agreed that they liked their jobs ranged from 77 per cent to 98 per cent. However, even in the airline where pilots liked their jobs least, only 11 per cent disagreed at all with the statement.

The medical personnel we have surveyed also like their work. Overall liking for the job is somewhat less in medicine than among

3   In the best of all worlds, survey items would be identical and comparisons could be readily made. We assume that 'liking for job' and 'being satisfied with one's job' are roughly comparable.

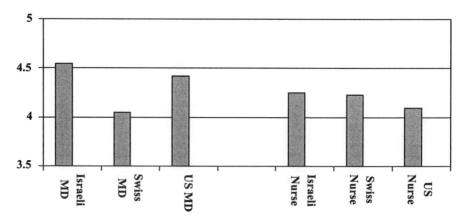

Figure 2.2   Doctor and nurse responses in three countries: 'I like my job'

pilots, as shown in Figure 2.2.[4] As the figure shows, the least satisfied pilot group (New Zealanders) was equal to the highest medical group. We can only speculate about what might lead to differences in job satisfaction between the professions. One possible explanation is that pilots, without exception, love to fly and enter the profession with a strong commitment. In contrast, those who enter medicine may be impelled by a variety of reasons, including parental pressure and the lure of high earnings as well as the appeal of science and service to humankind. The inevitable deaths of some patients may also serve to reduce satisfaction. We cannot discount changes in medical practice as determinants of job satisfaction. Programs such as managed health care in the USA, reduce doctors' freedom of choice in patient treatment and, in some cases, their income.

Despite variability, we can still conclude that the majority of both groups have a high regard for their jobs. It is certainly true that there is an aura of romance associated with being a pilot or a doctor. While children may dream of being pilots or doctors, few fantasize about being government bureaucrats (or academic researchers).

It is also possible that cognitive dissonance phenomena may account in part for commitment to the professions. Festinger's theory of cognitive dissonance (Festinger, 1957) posits that individuals strive for cognitive consistency and that inconsistencies create a negative psychological state (dissonance) that motivates the individual to take

4   Our research in medicine is much less developed than that in aviation. The data discussed here come from just over 500 personnel in five hospitals in three countries.

steps for its reduction. In a laboratory study, Nel *et al.* (1969) argued that dissonance is caused by discrepancies between one's actions and self-esteem, the sense of personal worth as an individual who makes rational and worthwhile decisions. Aronson and Mills (1959) demonstrated that individuals who undergo a severe initiation to become members of a group or organization will reduce the dissonance created by finding out that the group is of little value by (unrealistically) perceiving it as worthwhile. The dissonance rationale has been applied to the training regimens of organizations such as the Marine Corps that subject their candidates to severe training in the expectation that those who succeed will not only be well prepared but will also have a high regard for the organization and their personal capabilities as a result of having survived the initiation ordeal. In the case of our professions, the same logic can be invoked: 'I would not have put up with the stress and duration of training and initiation if the outcome was not wonderful.' In the same vein, pilots may use love of the job as a justification for the inevitable risks that are associated with flying. The premise of dissonance theory is that humans are rationalizing rather than rational creatures.

Professional Culture and the Self-concept

The term 'self-concept' is applied to the self-evaluations that people apply to their capabilities contrasted with reference groups such as professional peers. Each of us has a global sense of personal worth, often called 'self-esteem', as well as concepts of competence in more specialized domains such as athletics or scholarship (Helmreich & Stapp, 1974; Swann & Read, 1981a). Maintaining self-concepts is a major element of being human. Since work is a central (for some, *the* central) aspect of being for many, the internalized values of professional culture are likely to be important components of the self-concept. The positive aspects of professional culture, including prestige, contribute to a positive self-concept in the work domain and to self-esteem. Unfortunately, the negative aspects of the culture, including the sense of invulnerability, also become integral parts of the self-concept. One of the more provocative findings regarding the self-concept is that individuals seek to maintain their established self-concepts, even when they are recognized as negative (Josephs *et al.*, 1992; Swann, 1996; Swann & Read, 1981b). The resistance of self-concepts to disconfirming evidence can explain why attitudes about personal limitations seem to fall on deaf ears and why change proceeds at a slow pace.

Strengths and Weaknesses of Professional Culture

Strengths of Professional Cultures

The achievements of members of strong professional cultures provide concrete evidence of the positive aspects of these professions. The heroic actions of pilots under conditions of extraordinary stress add to the luster of the profession. Dedication to job and maintenance of composure under extreme circumstances have saved many lives. Unfortunately, because of the nature of the aviation system, the avoidance of accidents and the mitigating action of pilots is seldom documented. One shining example of effective behavior was the performance of a United Airlines crew when their DC-10 lost all flight controls after the catastrophic failure of an engine (NTSB, 1990; Predmore, 1991). The actions of the crew in maintaining open communication and coming up with a creative means of controlling the aircraft, by manipulating thrust on the two remaining engines, enabled them to make a crash landing. Their performance was singled out as minimizing the loss of life in a near-impossible situation. Similarly, the dedicated doctor has been a revered figure in society for the skill and effort brought to bear on illness and trauma. The esteem in which professionals are held is justified by real accomplishments.

The Dark Sides of Professional Cultures

The elements of self-perception that give professionals the confidence to persevere in the face of great challenges also have negative sequelae. Pride in doing one's job well can lead to flying when fatigued or suffering from a serious head cold. This can result in a crew not fully capable of coping with emergencies. The same pride may make pilots reluctant to admit error, which in turn can keep valuable information about human limitations from the organization (a point we will address in Chapter 5). Confidence can turn into arrogance, and machismo can lead to a disregard of others' opinions and a failure to consider alternative courses of action. The negative consequences of perceived invulnerability are readily found. An unrealistic view of normal human limitations may lead pilots to disregard standard operating procedures, to proceed into dangerous situations to complete a flight and/or to fail to utilize other crew members as safeguards against mishap. The 1979 crash of an Air New England flight into Hyannis, Massachusetts, is illustrative (NTSB, 1980). The 60-year-old captain, who was an officer of the company, was well known for disregarding checklists and operating more as a solo pilot than a team member. On the night of the accident, he flew below the glideslope on the approach and crashed more than a mile short of the runway, despite having received callouts from the first officer regarding his altitude. The captain was visibly upset before the flight because his duty day had been extended to include two additional flights. He was probably also suffering from considerable fatigue since he had been on duty for more than 14 hours and was making his fourteenth approach for landing. Under these difficult night conditions, and when the pilot flying is fatigued, the role of the co-pilot as a monitor of conditions and a source of information on the flight path is critical. The first officer on this flight was very junior and still in a probationary status, so it is likely that he was less assertive in questioning his superior than a more experienced crew member might have been.

Personal invulnerability as a professional attribute   One of the striking concomitants of the cultures of surgeons, anesthesiologists and pilots is a sense of personal competence and a denial of human weakness, specifically vulnerability to the ubiquitous effects of stress. Figure 2.3 shows the percentage of doctors and pilots from our sample who endorse unrealistic attitudes about their performance capabilities when faced with various kinds of stressors. Given the great responsibility borne by members of these professions, it is likely that some of these attitudes may be rooted in psychological denial processes to avoid anxiety about performance failure under such conditions. The primary acquisition of these unrealistic norms, though, is doubtless

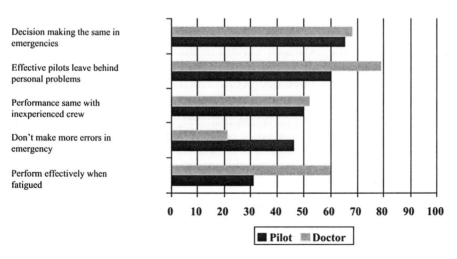

Figure 2.3   Percentages of pilots and doctors endorsing unrealistic attitudes about their personal capabilities

through professional socialization, reflecting norms that have built up over time.

The historical roots of these attitudes are clearly evident in aviation. In the early days, it was a ridiculously dangerous endeavor; those who reflected on their own vulnerability and likely death would probably choose another vocation. The historical tradition of the single pilot also added to the sense of personal conquest. Military authorities were also motivated to inculcate beliefs in immortality into their combat pilots. The primary goal of the wartime military is mission accomplishment, not the survival of pilots. No air force wants its pilots evaluating the threat to their personal well-being while engaged in a dogfight. Even in peacetime, the attitudes would continue and extend to civil aviation, since the military is a primary and prestigious source of pilots.

Unlike the military in combat situations, airlines have a primary concern with safety, not only because safety is an important societal value, but also because the general public may avoid airlines it considers 'too risky'.[5] Nevertheless, organizations may support unrealistic self-perceptions for economic reasons. When CRM training was initiated, one carrier omitted any consideration of psychological stress and the effects of stressors, such as fatigue and personal problems, from its training program. When pressed to explain why this topic was not included, it was finally admitted that senior management feared that too many pilots would call in sick if these issues were raised in training.[6]

Box 2.2   The mariner: steeped in tradition and denial

We have recently begun to collect data in another domain, the merchant marine.[7] Using a variant of the Flight Management Attitudes Questionnaire (FMAQ) designed for the maritime environment, data have been collected from more than 1500 mari-

---

5 The fate of Valujet provides an illustrative example. A disastrous crash led to widespread publicity about safety practices and an order suspending operations until dangerous conditions were corrected. After making major changes in operations and training and resuming operations, the organization was never able to regain its market and merged with another airline so its name could be changed.

6 This was the personal experience of one of us (RLH) in the mid-1980s. We are happy to report that this airline now addresses this topic aggressively in its training.

7 Research with ships' crews was conducted in collaboration with the Danish Maritime Institute and the Risoe Institute. Particular thanks are due to Henning Bogh Andersen, Guillermo Garay and Peter Sorensen, who have collaborated on all aspects of the research.

ners of three nationalities: Danish, Filipino and Indian. Seafaring has a much longer history than flying and many of the traditions of aviation have been borrowed from the sea.[8] The social and power distance between a ship's captain and an ordinary sailor is vast and the authority of the captain absolute. The ship at sea is a total environment in the sense that participants not only work but also live in its surroundings and may be separated from their families for extended periods of time. Given that this restricted environment includes living and social interactions as well as work, it is essential that it have formal governance and a high level of control for the master. As a very old profession, it is not surprising, then, to find that the merchant marine officer corps has a strong professional culture.

Perhaps because of the long tradition of the sea, the maritime world has been slow to embrace concepts of teamwork and open communication and associated psychological training that are universal in aviation. This is a matter of concern, as investigations of maritime accidents have identified the same interpersonal problems that led to the adoption of CRM in aviation.

Seagoing officers share with doctors and pilots a love of their jobs (which are also well paid). They take pride in their calling and, despite relations with their companies, are satisfied with their chosen line of work. They also share the same negative aspects of professional culture reflected in denial of personal vulnerability to stressors. Indeed, overall scores on our stress index are lower for mariners than for pilots and doctors, as shown in Figure 2.4.

Although the denial of vulnerability appears to be a universal phenomenon, professional differences are found. In this case we find that the stress recognition scores of Danish mariners from two shipping companies are significantly lower than those of Danish pilots.

Plausible, if not admirable, reasons for unrealistic attitudes can be found in medicine. Although not at personal risk, medical staff who work in the operating room often face the reality that patients die or suffer permanent damage during surgery. Too much thinking upon the consequences of professional acts could have a chilling effect on the physicians' willingness to undertake difficult procedures. Denial of the effects of fatigue is a special case that relates to organizational practices. Particularly during residency training, young physicians have historically worked extremely long shifts and may be required to deal with emergency situations after being on duty for long per-

8 Pan American World Airways began flying with seaplanes and quite literally adopted the traditions of the sea. Not only did its pilots wear nautical-looking uniforms, all its aircraft were called 'Clippers'.

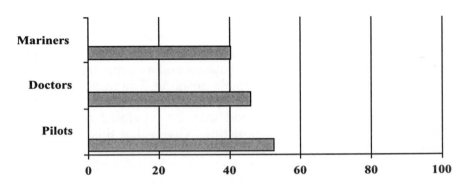

Figure 2.4   Scores on the stress recognition index of pilots from 22 countries and doctors and merchant mariners from three countries

iods. Believing that one is still capable of effective performance when fatigued is an understandable defense mechanism when faced with organizational practices that are inconsistent with safety.[9]

Norms can change   As Figure 2.3 indicated, doctors' attitudes are even less realistic than those of pilots. One might expect that physicians would receive more formal training in psychology and human capabilities and would be more sensitive to their personal limitations. The answer, again, is in the organizational context, as illustrated by attitudes about the effects of fatigue. Pilots fly under strict regulations that limit their duty time to avoid excessive fatigue. In the USA, for example, flight time is limited to eight hours in any 24-hour period, 30 hours in seven days and 100 hours in a month. In contrast, doctors' duty hours have seldom been regulated and the defensive processes discussed above have doubtless helped perpetuate a denial of fatigue's consequences. However, the major reason for the professional difference is undoubtedly the impact of CRM training on pilots' attitudes. Training is increasingly focusing on human error and the limitations of human performance. This is illustrated in data shown in Figure 2.5. The figure contrasts the attitudes of a sample of doctors with no exposure to CRM-like training with the attitudes of pilots from a major airline who were exposed to annual CRM training. The percentage of pilots holding that their performance is

9   In a widely publicized incident in New York, a young woman, Libby Zion, died in a prestigious hospital (Robins, 1996). Among other circumstances, she received a drug that interacted with medication she was taking. The resident in attendance had been on duty for more than 40 hours. One of the positive outcomes of the tragedy was a reduction in working hours for residents in New York.

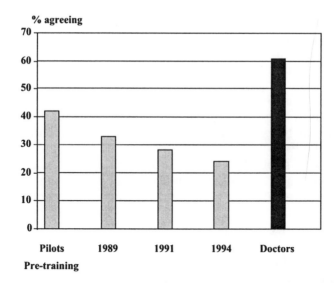

Note: Data are from pilots at a US major airline before initial CRM and after recurrent training, and doctors without training.

Figure 2.5   Percentage agreement with item 'Even when fatigued I perform effectively during critical periods'

unaffected by fatigue dropped steadily over the years, from 42 per cent prior to the initiation of CRM to 23 per cent six years later.[10] It will be of great interest to see if emerging training programs in medicine can effect a similar improvement in attitudes.

Professional Subcultures and Status Hierarchies in Aviation and Medicine

Neither aviation nor medicine has a monolithic culture, despite the existence of common bonds among all members of each. In the case of aviation, subcultural differentiation tends to develop as a function of the type of flying. Military pilots feel more sense of community with other military aviators than with civilian pilots and, among the military, bonds are stronger among those in the same service flying the same type of aircraft. For example, fighter pilots often distinguish themselves from those who fly bombers, transports or helicopters. Among civilian pilots, those who fly for major airlines

10   These represent cross-sectional survey data collected by our group in this organization from the onset of CRM training.

identify more with those who fly for similar organizations than with general aviation or commuter airline pilots. There are also implicit, informal status differences associated with the type of experience of pilots. Those military veterans who flew jet fighters (especially those who can boast of operating from aircraft carriers) have an ascribed status as *ipso facto* 'good sticks' or technically outstanding pilots. Similarly, those who fly for the most prestigious (and highest paying) major airlines are perceived as having particularly strong qualifications.[11]

In medicine, subcultures tend to develop around specialties. The three specialties in our research population, anesthesia, surgery and nursing, require different skills and training. The members of each group differentiate between themselves and members of the others. Stereotypes held by medical personnel about other specialties are strong and occasionally pejorative. As we noted in Chapter 1, many of the errors and conflicts observed in the operating room are at the point of intersection between different groups. There are also status differentials between the specialties. In the minds of the public (and their own), surgeons occupy the most exalted position in medicine, using their skills under great pressure to save lives. Anesthesiologists, although their role is vital in maintaining patients' vital signs and in pain management during and after surgery, are less visible and less recognized by laypersons. Awareness of this status differential is clearly evident in OR interactions and in descriptions by each group. An even larger status differential is found between the two physician groups and nurses, although surgery and anesthesia are among the most prestigious nursing specialties. Interestingly, there is a growing trend in the USA for qualified nurse anesthetists rather than MDs to provide anesthesia in the operating room. In the case of managed care in US medicine, this alternative is being chosen because of the lower costs entailed by using a nurse instead of a licensed physician. This shift in care delivery is increasing the status of nurse anesthetists while lowering that of anesthesiologists.

There are also large status differentials *within* specialties in medicine. In many teaching hospitals, for example, the operating room is staffed by residents, who are MDs in training for the specialties of surgery and anesthesiology, and attendings, who are fully certified members of the specialty. In teaching hospitals associated with medi-

---

11   We are not suggesting that these stereotypes are accurate depictions of the qualifications of pilots with differing backgrounds. However, the dominance of ex-military pilots in airlines for many years and the fact that graduates of military training were given the choice of flight assignments by performance in 'undergraduate' training can lead to observable differences. Historically, the 'best and the brightest' chose fighters over transports or bombers or helicopters, perpetuating the stereotype.

cal schools, the attendings are frequently also faculty. Hospitals that are not associated with medical schools also have residency programs, but they are often less prestigious.[12] The status gap between residents and attendings is very large and the differential often makes residents unwilling to challenge the errors of their superiors.

Among airline pilots, status differentials are between the captain and the co-pilot (or first officer) and flight engineer, if the aircraft has a crew of three, and cabin crews (flight attendants). The captain is by regulation the pilot in command, with total legal responsibility for safety and all other aspects of flight. In addition to visible emblems of authority (four stripes and embroidery on caps), captains receive much higher pay than junior crew members.[13] The exalted role of the captain can be traced back to the early days of aviation when open planes were flown by a single pilot. As aircraft became more complex and passenger service was initiated, a co-pilot was added to the crew. The role of the co-pilot in early civil aviation was not that of a team member, but rather a back-up. Many captains did not allow their co-pilots to fly the aircraft. Their function was analogous to that of a fire extinguisher – something to be employed infrequently under special circumstances (Gann, 1961). Even today, in the minds of some older captains, this is the role of the co-pilot.

When flight attendants (FAs) were first hired for commercial aviation in the USA, they were required to be registered nurses and were viewed as professionals filling an important role in passenger support. As airplanes became more sophisticated and pressurized to fly over weather, the professional requirements were relaxed. While introductions over the public address system still stress that the primary role of the FA is safety, they are viewed by many as primarily on board for passenger service.

Overall, professional cultures have their advantages and disadvantages in terms of performance. Although they are not immutable, there is both institutional and individual resistance to change. In our discussion of applications of psychological findings in Chapters 5 and 6, we will discuss strategies for changing cultures. The final component of professional culture that must be addressed is the personalities that members bring with them when they become socialized into professions.

---

12 We recognize that there are many variants on staffing in different countries and do not imply that there is a universal staffing policy. It is, however, true that, where there are residency programs, the status differentials are large.
13 In many US airlines, co-pilot pay is approximately 65 per cent of the captain's.

Gender

Men versus Women in Aviation

As we noted earlier, pilots have traditionally been male. The growth of aviation after World War I was sparked by the availability of used warplanes and veteran pilots – all male. In addition, the 'macho' image of aviation was congruent with male stereotypes. However, the accomplishments of daring female aviators such as Amelia Earhart have shown that men are not the only ones capable of mastering the skies. The propensity of airlines to hire pilots from the ranks of military veterans perpetuated sexual segregation. Women were banned from flying combat aircraft in the USA until the 1990s and were thus disadvantaged in competition for scarce airline jobs. Outside the USA, aspiring women pilots have not had the ability to use the threat of anti-discriminatory legislation as a means of getting organizations to consider them. At the end of 1996, only 3 per cent of the airline pilots in the USA were females.

Our worldwide data collection efforts with the Flight Management Attitudes Questionnaire have netted more than 15 000 surveys from pilots. Of those, only 248 came from females, and almost exclusively from Western countries. The fact that women have only recently begun to be hired regularly by the airlines is shown in their positions, which are determined by seniority. While half of the males in the sample were captains, less than a third of the women held this position. We were also interested in whether attitudes about stress, personal vulnerability and cockpit management differed as a function of gender. The results showed that women's attitudes were strikingly similar to those of men. They held equally unrealistic appraisals of their capabilities under stress and comparable attitudes about command. A significant difference was found on only one item – the need for written procedures for all situations. While 70 per cent of males disagreed with this, only 58 per cent of females did. Thus females showed a slightly greater propensity to desire formal, written procedures.

Box 2.3   Pornography in the cockpit

In 1979, when I started flying as an observer in the cockpits of commercial airline flights, I was initiated into the 'boys' club' of the cockpit. I had flown enough flights with an airline to become known as someone who was working on aviation safety rather than a 'pointy-headed academic'. On the night of my initiation, I picked up a flight in Austin, Texas, and flew to Dallas and then on to several other destinations. After conversa-

tions on the ground and at cruise altitude, I apparently passed the litmus test. While we were on the ground in Dallas waiting for passengers to board, I was asked if I knew what was under the caps that covered screws securing various panels on the face of the cockpit. When I admitted my ignorance, the captain, with a big grin, pulled off one on the center of the console and showed me the underside, which contained a black and white photo of a small, but significant, portion of female anatomy. It was then revealed to me that similar pictures could be found in the cockpits of airplanes flying for every carrier in the USA.

Recently, a female captain for a major US airline was awarded $875 000 in back salary and damages by a jury. She had sued the airline because it failed to keep pornography out of the cockpit after her complaints. During the course of the litigation, which extended over three years, she was removed from flying duty. As part of the settlement, she can resume flying.

We have asked our colleague, Captain Dr Sharon Jones, to address her experiences with pornography and harassment while flying for both regional and major US airlines. Her comments follow. (Robert Helmreich)

Have I seen pornography in the cockpit? You bet. Do I find it offensive? Of course. Can the portrayal of women solely as sex objects be considered degrading? Certainly. Are women the only people who find these photos distasteful, repugnant or inappropriate for display in a professional workplace? I doubt it. Can their presence constitute sexual harassment? It might. Was gender the primary issue underlying this particular court case? I doubt it. Is a courtroom verdict going to reintegrate this woman into the pilot group? Probably not. Has she, as one commentator suggested, done a grand favor for female pilots as a group? The truth is, she may have done more harm than good.

When a practice has been tolerated by as many and for as long as that of planting pornography in cockpits, it is unlikely to be eradicated without resistance. When a minority demands that the majority abandon traditions that historically have been tolerated, if not revered, a power struggle is likely to ensue. This conflict can be self-perpetuating, with intimidation and humiliation escalating whenever they produce whiny or verbally aggressive reactions.

If the target of this intimidation can be made to feel so uncomfortable that she voluntarily departs, then her tormentors emerge victorious and are able to return to established habit patterns. On the other hand, seasoned veterans are likely to become resentful and revolt if they perceive that their desires are being subordinated to those of a relative newcomer or a group member who is distinctively different. Regardless of the degree to which that individual is protected from reprisal (and perhaps in direct relation to the immunity), chances are good that the core group will project their resentment and distrust onto others who resemble the perceived troublemaker.

Most professional pilots are bound by similarities in interests, experience and capability. These commonalities, coupled with demonstrated performance, foster respect and trust among crew members, who depend on each other for their very lives. Predictability is highly valued in this environment, where coordination and cooperation are essential to survival. Therefore, behaviors or characteristics (like gender) that deviate from the norm can create uncomfortable uncertainty about skills, priorities and expectations.

A male crew member's experience with women may be largely limited to the romantic and familial realms. When confronted with a female crew member, he may make inappropriate assumptions about her values and goals based on prior experience. If a woman permits or, heaven forbid, promotes the focus of attention on gender-related differences that are irrelevant to job conduct, she risks ostracism by the pilot group.

What, then, is the solution to this dilemma? There is no one, correct answer. This is not to suggest that women take the advice of one infamous Texas gubernatorial candidate who suggested that, when threatened by certain masculine intimidation techniques, they 'relax and enjoy it'. There are, however, numerous options available to restore professionalism without sacrificing group cohesion.

It is unreasonable to expect that the novelty of a female crew member will create no consequences. Insisting that male pilots ignore a female's gender is futile. It is natural for a woman to seek some acknowledgment and respect for her achievements, but in return she should be willing to understand and accept some initial confusion and hesitance on the part of her male colleagues. I once saw a woman who had developed a flair for putting everyone at ease with her initial briefing, in which she stated that she understood that most pilots had little experience flying with women, but insisted that everything would be OK because she had tons of experience flying with men.

Female crew members can and should take the initiative to set standards of behavior. They can establish common ground by redirecting attention away from issues stereotypically associated with male–female relationships and toward indicators of shared professional values and experiences. The female pilot must be willing to take responsibility for her own actions, critically evaluating her own performance and soliciting and constructively responding to feedback from others. She can stress the professional nature of relationships by carefully censoring her own communications and limiting them to operationally pertinent matters.

If she is offended by someone's actions, her response to this must be firm and consistent without being confrontational, judgmental or overly critical. The offensive action must be kept in perspective and not allowed to overshadow primary operational goals unless it is truly interfering with their attainment. Offering alternatives is often preferable to outright condemnation. A woman can demonstrate her willingness to engage in stress-relieving, bonding interactions such as joking as long as such humor does not involve ridicule of others. She can indicate an understanding that there is a time and a place for everything, but suggest that an aircraft is no place to be distracted from operational duties by potentially controversial material.

If a woman is convinced that her own behavior is beyond reproach and that she has made a reasonable effort to no avail, she is justified in seeking assistance. However, non-safety-related issues are better addressed through the professional standards committee of the pilots' union than through managerial channels. Because it frequently falls to managers to mete out punishment, pilots may be less than forthright in their communications with them and may resent the implication of wrongdoing attached to a command performance. Members of professional standards, on the other hand, are usually highly respected, credible colleagues who present themselves as compassionate, empathetic mediators and guidance counselors. They represent the consensual position on boundaries of acceptability and can frequently coerce those who have strayed beyond them back into the mainstream.

I recognize the discipline, energy expenditure and discomfort associated with this proposed course of action. I must humbly admit that my own approach to this problem has changed throughout my career and will, I hope, continue to mature as I do. When I became a regional airline pilot at the age of 23, my greatest need was acceptance, which I found I could obtain by de-emphasizing my femininity. By being even more brash than most of my male colleagues, I had hoped to convince them that I was more similar to them than to their wives, mothers and daughters. This technique, though not optimal, proved somewhat adaptive. It also produced consequences that I neither intended nor relished.

First, I violated expectations of females to such an extent that managers, passengers and pilots were caught off-guard and made uncomfortable. After being told by a supervisor who had heard me use a curse word that there were, whether or not I liked it, separate standards to which men and women were held by most of the world, I realized I could not stop people from looking at me and seeing a woman, no matter what uniform I wore. Second, my behavior created a perception that I was amenable to advances, of which I found myself fending off more than my share.

As I have gotten older, a number of things have happened. I am confident of my own capabilities and am rarely called upon to prove them to others, having obtained a position and level of experience that command respect. I have discovered that skepticism regarding my capabilities was a by-product, not simply of my gender, but also of my age; I am actually grateful for the results produced by a few extra pounds and a head full of gray hair. I no longer resent that my gender is more instantaneously ascertained and easily understood than my profession; I have learned to accept that comments about the rarity of females in the profession generally express admiration rather than disdain.

I do occasionally encounter a lack of professionalism in the workplace, but my self-esteem, confidence and experience now permit me to handle these situations both more effectively and with greater grace than I previously did. For example, it has at times been necessary for me to explicitly state that I consider a gender-related comment or form of address to be inappropriate. Furthermore, when I find pornographic material in the cockpit, I simply throw it away as I would any other piece of trash. Of course, I make sure that this is done in full view of other crew members, so that they can ascertain that (a) this is not of interest to me and (b) this is not the tool for getting a reaction out of me, if that happens to be their goal. I can honestly say that there have never been any negative repercussions from either of these actions. (Sharon Jones)

Men versus Women in Medicine

Medicine has a similar, but not so striking, masculine image. Women interested in medical careers have often been directed into nursing rather than medical schools. Not surprisingly, women have increased their numbers and visibility in medicine more rapidly than in aviation. The current head of the American Medical Association is female and, for the first time in the USA, women outnumber men in the entering classes in medical schools. However, it can be argued that the growing percentage of women in medicine is an indicator of the declining prestige of the profession (Spence *et al.*, 1985).[14] As changes such as managed care in the USA erode the autonomy, prestige and

14   A similar pattern occurred in psychology in the 1980s, with women constituting the majority of both undergraduate and graduate students. Of course, it can be argued that psychology never had the level of prestige associated with medicine.

even income of doctors, male college graduates may turn to other professions. As a cross-cultural example, medicine in the former Soviet Union was historically the province of women, but the relative status of medicine was much lower than in the USA.

Women are 37 per cent of our medical sample. However, there are large differences as a function of specialty that appear to mirror prestige rankings, as shown in Figure 2.6. Females are in the majority in the two nursing specialties, consistent with nursing's feminine tradition. In contrast, women filled 19 per cent of the positions in anesthesia and 12.7 per cent of the positions in surgery. Similar to aviation, the situation appears to be changing, in that 29 per cent of anesthesiology residents were women, as were 18 per cent of surgical residents. As with pilots, we looked at gender differences in attitudes about stress, leadership and organizational climate, and found that males and females responded identically.

In summary, women and men who self-select into these professions appear to have common attitudes and values. The exclusion of women has been a matter of discrimination rather than qualification.

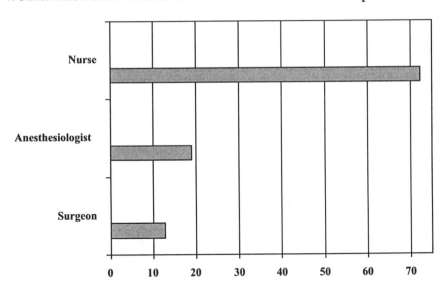

Figure 2.6 **Percentages of women in medical specialties in six hospitals**

'I want to be a pilot/doctor when I grow up': **Personality and Professional Self-selection**

There is ample folk wisdom about personality and vocational choice: 'People with nurturing, caring personalities choose education and nursing as vocations'; 'Those with high degrees of competitiveness and arrogance become titans of industry'; 'Introverted individuals with high levels of achievement motivation become scholars'; 'Those with high achievement needs and a high propensity for risk taking become astronauts and pilots'. Everyone's Aunt Sadie is aware of the above and that personality governs our behavior and plays a central role in our vocational choices. Academic psychology has lacked some of Aunt Sadie's perspicacity, and debates have raged about whether the concept of personality is even a viable one (for example, Mischel, 1968).[15] Fortunately, personality research and the concept of personality have undergone rehabilitation, and academic psychologists have joined Aunt Sadie in recognizing the importance of personality for an understanding of human behavior. The combination of personalities that forms a group can be a major determinant of its character and behavior.

When considering contextual factors that may influence professional culture and performance, the role of personality should be included. It is certainly plausible to hypothesize that some of the stereotypes associated with professions have their origins in the personalities of those who self-select into these vocations. In aviation, there has been a persisting myth of a 'pilot personality' that distinguishes 'Sky Gods' from ordinary mortals. Empirically, though, a unique personality profile that distinguishes pilots from the general public and other vocations has not been validated. However, as we noted in Chapter 1, personality factors are robust predictors of performance. Within occupations as diverse as corporate manager and research scientist, as well as astronaut and aviator, a similar pattern of traits has predicted performance. Those who succeed in endeavors which require teamwork as well as expertise and individual effort possess high levels of both achievement-related traits and interpersonal sensitivity (Chidester *et al.*, 1992; Gibson, 1990; Helmreich *et al.*, 1980).

What then is the role of personality in shaping the professional cultures of aviation and medicine? To explore this issue, William Hines (1996) contrasted the attributes of astronauts (as a highly selected, super-pilot category), pilots, anesthesiologists and surgeons. The trait measures employed were those that have been related to performance in aviation and space (Rose *et al.*, 1994). Hines looked at factor analytically derived scales related to achievement and interpersonal relations that measure constructs validated as influencing work behavior. Scales included 'expressivity', defined by traits in-

---

15   The source of the dispute seems to have been rooted in the fact that single traits measured by personality tests were not robust predictors of behavior in single-event laboratory experiments.

cluding warmth, helpfulness to others, kindness and awareness of the feelings of others, 'verbal aggression', defined by traits such as complaining and nagging, and 'negative instrumentality', represented by negative traits including hostile, dictatorial and egotistical. These scales were derived from a measure of normal personality, the Personal Attributes Questionnaire (Spence & Helmreich, 1978; Spence *et al.*, 1979). In addition, several scales assessing components of achievement motivation were administered (Helmreich & Spence, 1978; Spence *et al.*, 1987). These included a general measure of motivation labeled 'Achievement Striving'; a scale measuring 'Mastery', operationalized as the desire to conquer new and challenging tasks, and 'Competitiveness', defining a motivation to best others in all activities.

Figure 2.7 shows the profile of male pilots contrasted with male college students, who can be considered representative of the college-educated male population. Notably, the male pilots score lower than the student average on Competitiveness and Negative Instrumentality which are negative predictors of performance in this environment and higher on the positive attributes. One of the interesting findings to come out of studies of the personalities of high-performing groups such as scientists and pilots is that few sex differences are found in personality characteristics. However, on many of the same traits, highly significant sex differences are found in unselected, student samples. At least in stereotypically masculine endeavors such as science and medicine, the modal woman scores more like a man (Helmreich *et al.*, 1980). Our data are similar in showing few sex differences. Competitiveness is the notable excep-

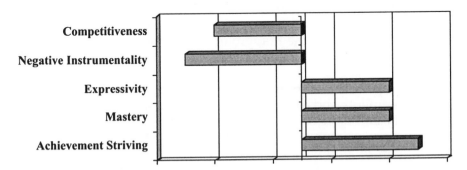

Figure 2.7 Profile of male pilot norms contrasted with male students on performance-related personality attributes (the length of the bars shows the difference in the mean scale scores below or above student average set at zero)

tion, where women score significantly lower than men. It should be noted that competitiveness has proved to be a *negative* predictor of performance in many situations.

It is noteworthy that those who have passed through highly selective screening processes and rigorous training show a profile that differs significantly from that of the average college student. Pilots score higher on positive trait clusters defining achievement motivation and an interpersonal orientation. They also score lower than college students on Negative Instrumentality and Competitiveness. Astronauts differed from pilots by having even higher scores on Achievement Striving and showing slightly more Negative Instrumentality. The attributes of arrogance and hostility associated with Negative Instrumentality and the destructiveness of an overly competitive orientation associated with the latter would clearly impede effective team functioning.

It is also noteworthy that, within the pilot profession, variations in the trait constellations just described were validated as predicting performance in the simulator study described in Chapter 1. Chidester *et al.* (1990) found that crews led by captains with the constellation of high achievement motivation, high interpersonal sensitivity and low scores on the negative scales consistently made fewer errors and were rated as superior by expert observers across the five legs of flight. Crews with captains who were low on all the positive attributes were consistently poor on all flights. An interesting pattern of performance was shown by crews led by a captain who was high on negative instrumental attributes and low on interpersonal sensitivity (that is, individuals with high task orientation who were autocratic, domineering and low in interpersonal skills). On the first flight segments the performance of these crews was poor and comparable to those led by captains lacking in both instrumental and interpersonal skills. However, performance later improved until it was nearly as good as the first group. The researchers hypothesized that crews learned to work with these motivated, but difficult, captains.

The sample of doctors was more similar to the student sample than to the pilots and astronauts. They scored higher than students in Mastery and Expressivity, but were comparable to the students in Achievement Striving and Verbal Aggression. Their scores on Negative Instrumentality were intermediate between pilots and students, but they scored lowest of all groups in Competitiveness. The profile was positive, but not quite as striking as that of the pilots and astronauts. Unfortunately, no performance data are available for the medical sample.

The astronaut, pilot, and medical groups also completed an abbreviated version of the NEO Personality Inventory that measures five components of personality: neuroticism, extraversion, openness to experience, agreeableness and conscientiousness. (McCrae & Costa, 1987). On these measures, astronauts and pilots scored higher in conscientiousness and agreeableness, and lower in neuroticism than did doctors. Astronauts were also more extroverted than either pilots or medical personnel.

We also looked at differences within the medical specialties to see if personality factors might differentiate between the groups. On the NEO measure, there were no differences between nurses, anesthesiologists and surgeons. The groups did differ, however, on some trait dimensions. Surgeons scored highest in achievement striving, followed by anesthesiologists and then nurses. Competitiveness showed a similar pattern, with surgeons again having the highest levels. We also looked at another trait, dominance, which has been shown to influence interpersonal relationships (Nyquist & Spence, 1986). Surgeons again scored as most dominant, although they did not score as high as astronauts.

Overall, the personality findings tell us that these selective professions attract (or select) individuals with high motivation and interpersonal skills and a relative absence of negative attributes. They do not show us a profile of particular professions, but there are variations in profiles that appear to be logical reflections of selection and self-selection. Astronauts, for example, are subjected to intense psychological selection and those we studied had been selected from enormous applicant pools with a rejection rate over 97 per cent. It is not surprising then to find that they score lowest on a measure of psychopathology and highest in motivation. Surgeons score highest on motivational measures, but also are more competitive and dominant than their colleagues. The latter attributes could be associated with friction among groups in the OR.

Summing up Professional Culture

As demanding professions, both aviation and medicine acquire new personnel through processes of selection and self-selection. Screening of applicants in both aviation and medicine concentrates heavily on aptitude and intelligence and both can be described as selective in their recruitment. There is not much evidence for distinct professional personality in either discipline, but it is a safe generalization that members of both are above average in motivation and interpersonal skills.

Space programs and many airlines rely on personality assessment as part of the selection process. Interest in selecting candidates with positive personality attributes including strong interpersonal skills is growing in medicine, but extensive validation using reliable performance measures will be needed. As we have indicated, self-selection also plays a major role in both professions and entry into both requires dedication and perseverance. It is also probably true that those who choose to fly have a more romanticized and perhaps deeper commitment.

Once applicants are selected, both professions require a lengthy training/socialization process that demands at least superficial conformity and provides a clear sense of identity in terms of norms and values. Both groups foster a 'we versus them' stance in terms of differentiating their members from the general public. In the case of medicine, this also serves as a strategy to protect members from allegations of error and malpractice.

Professional culture is shaped by history, the attributes of the professional tasks and by the associated risks and responsibilities as well as by characteristics of its members. Professional culture is dynamic rather than static. A number of circumstances or interventions, ranging from training practices to role models, can modify established norms and values. However, professional cultures have considerable inertia and change requires both strong interventions and time. In the next chapter we examine another factor that individuals and teams bring to the workplace – their national culture.

3 National Culture

As Chapter 2 has discussed (and with apologies to Gertrude Stein), in many ways 'a pilot is a pilot is a pilot'. The professional pilot culture exerts a powerful influence upon pilots' attitudes and behaviors, but there are other influences which also play a role in shaping pilots' attitudes. This chapter will deal with the influence of national culture on pilots' attitudes.[1]

The effect of national culture on pilot training and skills was not a topic of investigation prior to the advent of Crew Resource Management (CRM), probably because the training was perceived and delivered as a set of standardized, universal technical skills. But CRM alerted the industry to the human-to-human interactions which are an integral part of any team performance and, in so doing, it alerted us to the psychological processes inherent in group work. As CRM was introduced and accepted in the aviation industry in the USA, and news of its relevance and success traveled overseas, more and more non-US airlines became interested in this new safety and efficiency initiative. CRM training that was developed in the USA was sent overseas, where it received 'mixed reviews' – the concepts seemed to make more sense in some countries and airlines than in others.

At about the same time that well-intentioned American trainers were baffling Korean pilots with concepts such as assertion in the cockpit, we received a set of questionnaires from some Taiwanese pilots. These pilots had completed the Cockpit Management Attitudes Questionnaire (CMAQ: Helmreich, 1984) and returned it to us for analysis. While we cannot claim to have had the foresight to see that CRM training would need to be modified before being exported from the USA, we did have the good sense to recognize an anomaly

1 Although we are collecting medical data worldwide, the database is not yet as extensive as the pilot set. Consequently, we will focus exclusively on pilots in this chapter, with the expectation that the medical data may well replicate the findings at a later date.

when it presented itself. The Taiwanese data did not 'behave' like other data – the factor structure could not be replicated, and items did not correlate as expected. This led to our first cross-cultural study (Merritt & Helmreich, 1996), in which we found significant differences between US and Asian pilots. This was our 'first clue' that behavior in the cockpit could be influenced by things other than professional standards, and it led us to the pursuit of national culture. We set out to collect empirical data which would help identify the differences and similarities amongst pilots of different countries and cultures. In order to do this, we needed to expand the existing CMAQ questionnaire to include culture-tapping items, and to do this we reviewed the cross-cultural psychological literature.

Cross-cultural Psychology

A broad definition of cross-cultural psychology is 'any field of research in which cultural variables are considered in order to clarify our understanding of a psychological process' (Lloyd, 1972, p.18). While related disciplines such as anthropology study culture as the central phenomenon, cross-cultural psychology studies cultural variation only to the extent that it affects different psychological phenomena. In our case, we were interested in how being a member of a different national culture might affect how one did one's job in the cockpit.

Cross-cultural psychology is as young a discipline as aviation human factors, in that it, too, emerged in the post-World War II era (Jahoda, 1992), and journals to support the new discipline, such as the *Journal of Cross-Cultural Psychology* and the *International Journal of Intercultural Relations*, were first published in the 1970s. The discipline encompasses many domains of traditional psychology, including cognitive, developmental, educational, organizational, physiological and social psychology (Kağitçibasi & Berry, 1989; Bond & Smith, 1996).

A review of the 1990s organizational and social psychological literature showed that cross-cultural studies using pilots or doctors were virtually non-existent; however, there were cross-cultural studies about leadership, communication, perceptions of risk, stress and decision-making, which could have relevance for team performance. For example, there was agreement in the literature from the USA, India and Japan that an effective leader is someone who is both task- (instrumental) and relationship- (expressive) oriented (Bond, 1991; Misumi, 1985; Sinha, 1981; Stogdill & Coons, 1957). However, the specifics of effective leadership behavior do vary cross-culturally (Smith & Peterson, 1988): the same leader behavior which is seen as

harsh and inconsiderate in one culture can be interpreted as paternalistic and encouraging in another. Bond and Smith (1996) concluded
that cultural differences will become apparent only when more
specific measures of leadership style are employed.[2]

Communication styles also differ culturally. The preferred communication style in some countries is direct and specific ('say what
you mean, and mean what you say'), while in others it is indirect and
relies on the context to carry its full meaning (for example, when a
'yes' means only 'I hear you' because I do not want to argue or
disagree with you) (Ting-Toomey, 1988; 1994). Preferred modes of
conflict resolution, from avoidance to compromise to confrontation,
also derive from these underlying preferences for harmony (Tang &
Kirkbride, 1986). See Box 3.1 for an example of cross-cultural communication at cross-purposes.

Box 3.1. What do we mean when we say YES?

A senior captain, an expatriate from the West, walked into the
(Malaysian) scheduler's department and asked him to roster him
off on the 6th of June to celebrate his cat's birthday. This has been
an annual ritual for him. On this date he gathers a few of his
friends who are cat lovers over to his house to help them celebrate
his cat's birthday. They would bring along their cats and they
would spend all evening discussing cats, talking cats, feeding cats,
grooming cats, and so on.

The scheduler was fairly busy preparing the next month's roster, looked up and said YES to the captain's request. All was well.
The party was organized and all were invited. When the roster
came out he found himself on a long trip to Dubai and Europe. He
was upset, the wife was upset and there was some name calling
along the lines of being incompetent to having no integrity. There
was bad blood all around.

What did the scheduler mean when he said YES? Perhaps here
the scheduler was too busy with his roster so the best way to get the
captain out of his face was to say YES. In the East it is not polite to
say NO, especially to one so senior. Perhaps also the occasion does

---

2 We discovered this 'general versus specific' difference in one of our first round
   table discussions with members of a South American airline and representatives
   of the American training group who had been contracted to deliver their CRM
   training. When we asked if the different leadership styles would pose a problem, both parties hurried to assure us that there was no problem, because the
   crew understood their roles and everyone knew the captain was in command.
   As we discovered later, the specifics of those command roles varied widely
   from North America to South America.

not fit the severity and seriousness of the scheduler – celebrating a cat's birthday. This captain must be off his rocker! The fact of the matter is the captain and his wife love their cat, maybe because they do not have any children. What is for certain is that there was a problem. (Captain Azmi Radzi, Malaysia Airlines)

The influence of national culture on social interactions is pervasive, yet it is often unseen by members within that culture, and seen as unpredictable and 'nonsensical' from the outsider's perspective. Consequently, the potential for misunderstandings in cross-cultural encounters is enormous: it ranges from a misreading of emotions (Ekman, 1973) to an escalation of conflict because of an inappropriate apology or intervention (Barnlund & Yoshioka, 1990). Such misunderstandings were the basis of the early, failed CRM courses. Consider that so much of CRM is based on communication and command styles, and it is no wonder that American-style CRM courses were not successful in some Asian and South American countries. But, at the same time, CRM seemed to travel pretty well to some countries, such as Australia and England. The question before us was multilayered: (a) to what extent are pilots' work-related attitudes and values universal, and to what extent are they different; (b) if they are different, are there specific domains in which they differ; and (c) if there are differences at the national level, can they be understood in a systematic fashion, that is, can we cluster pilots from different countries by their attitudes?

With regard to this latter issue, a landmark study conducted by Geert Hofstede (1980; 1991) truly inspired us. This study, now considered 'the gold standard' in cross-cultural research (Bond, 1996), has become a central part of our work with national culture.

Hofstede and National Culture

Hofstede worked as part of an international research team collecting survey data from the employees of IBM during the period 1967–73. In all, a total of 117 000 questionnaires from 88 000 different respondents in 66 countries were collected during the two major survey rounds. Hofstede calculated country scores as the mean of the scores for the seven occupational categories in the marketing and service division of the corporation. This included managers from the country head office, branch managers, technical experts, sales representatives, two levels of service technicians and administrative personnel. Each of the seven categories carried equal weight in the computation, regardless of the actual number of respondents. The data from countries which were surveyed twice within the four-year period allowed a test of stability of the between-country differences, which in turn led to further refinement of the item pool. Hofstede analyzed the reduced set of items and derived four dimensions of national culture, which he called Power Distance, Individualism–Collectivism, Uncertainty Avoidance and Masculinity–Femininity.

Power distance

Power distance (PD) is conceptualized as the extent to which the less powerful expect and accept that power is distributed unequally. On an individual level, it is a measure of the interpersonal power or influence between superior and subordinate, as perceived by the subordinate. In low power distance countries there is limited dependence of subordinates on bosses and a preference for consultation. Subordinates feel more comfortable approaching and, if necessary, contradicting their superiors. Conversely, in high power distance countries, there is considerable dependence of subordinates on superiors, and subordinates are unlikely to approach or question their superiors directly. Using Hofstede's PD index scores, the countries which are lowest in power distance are Austria, Israel, Ireland and Scandinavia. Countries with high power distance include Malaysia, the Philippines, Panama, Mexico and Venezuela. The USA is ranked 38 out of 50 countries, suggesting moderate to low power distance. Box 3.2 gives a simple example of power distance in the cockpit.

Box 3.2   Power distance in the cockpit

A low PD captain meets a high PD co-pilot
'Call me Jim,' said the Australian to his young Malaysian second officer (SO) just back from his ab initio training. 'OK, sir,' replied the SO. 'No, no, just Jim.' 'OK, sir, Jim.' Finally when the SO called him 'Jim,' the captain smiled. 'I have broken the ice,' he thought.

The SO was confused. He was brought up to be polite, and one of the ways of being polite was never to call your superior by his first name. It was clearly spelt out in the Operations Manual that the captains are to be called 'Captain' or 'Sir'. It took some time before the young SO realized that this was quite acceptable. Even though the captain may be comfortable on a first name basis, clearly the SO was not.

A high PD captain meets a low PD first officer
The more serious situation arises when we have the opposite. The Malaysian captain now feels that the Western expatriate first officer is rude, not acknowledging his position by calling him by his

---

first name. At best the situation in the cockpit is cold, at worst it may bring hostility. In any case there is a breakdown in communication and teamwork. (Captain Azmi Radzi, Malaysia Airlines)

Hofstede studied power distance at the occupational level as well as the country level. On the basis of comparisons across 38 occupations, he concluded that occupations with the lowest status and education level (unskilled and semi-skilled workers) had the highest PD scores while those with high status and education had the lowest PD scores. Comparing these occupational differences across countries, Hofstede noted an interactive effect. In low PD countries, the occupational differences were markedly different, with the lower status positions having higher PD scores than the high status positions. In high PD countries, however, the occupational differences were relatively small, with all occupations having high PD scores. This effect was replicated in a recent study conducted with surgical teams in Switzerland. In this low PD country, the surgeons perceived the lowest power distance in their work relationships, followed by the anesthesiologists, while the surgical and anesthesia nurses perceived a significantly higher level of power distance between themselves and the doctors (Helmreich & Schaefer, 1994).

Individualism–Collectivism

Individualism–collectivism contrasts goals reflecting independence from the organization with goals not stressing independence. Using Hofstede's individualism index, the USA is ranked first, with a score of 91, followed closely by Australia and Great Britain. Countries with low individualism scores (high collectivism) include many Central and South American countries (for example, Brazil, with 38) and many Asian countries (such as Taiwan, with 17, Korea, with 18, the Philippines, with 32, and Malaysia, with 26).

Individualists consider the implications of their behavior within a narrowly defined area of personal costs and benefits. Social interaction and group involvement are conceptualized in terms of costs, rewards and outcomes (Thibaut & Kelley, 1959; Radloff & Helmreich, 1968). Independence and self-sufficiency are valued, with individual achievement and recognition being preferred to group-based rewards (Spence, 1985). Self-reliance is a strength, while seeking help implies weakness, and mistakes are evaluated by personal standards (Hui & Triandis, 1986; Triandis, McCusker & Hui, 1990; Sampson, 1977). There is some speculation that extreme forms of individualism are associated with higher crime rates, suicide and stress-related diseases (Triandis *et al.*, 1986; Triandis *et al.*, 1988).

Just as the unit of interest in individualist cultures is the individual, the unit of interest in collectivist cultures is the collective or in-group. People in collectivist cultures consider the implications of their behavior in a framework of concern that extends beyond their immediate family. Behavior is linked to the in-group, that is, the extended family or organization. They value loyalty and harmony within the group, and children are taught obedience and filial piety from an early age. One's destiny is decided to a large extent by group membership and, because place and position are largely predetermined and outside the influence of the individual, there is a stronger acceptance of fate.

Resources, responsibilities and outcomes are shared with other in-group members in collectivist cultures (Bond & Hwang, 1986; Hui & Triandis, 1986). There is a motivating sense of shame not to disgrace the other group members with one's weakness or failure, because mistakes are apportioned at the group level (Bond, 1991). There is also speculation that collectivism is associated with lower stress (Triandis *et al.*, 1988). Reasons include greater social support from one's in-group, fewer self-attributions for failure – a corollary of fatalistic thinking – and an emphasis on stability and harmony which reduces the incidence of confrontations.

Uncertainty Avoidance

Uncertainty Avoidance (UA) can be defined as the extent to which the members of a culture feel threatened by uncertain or unknown situations (Hofstede, 1991). Hofstede argues that countries with high UA will have more people who feel under stress at work, more people who want rules to be respected and more people who want to have a long-term stable career, though the same people may not want all three. One person may react in one way, such as feeling more nervous, while another may become insistent that rules be respected. Hofstede argues that UA is based on country scores rather than individual correlations; hence reactions need not be found within the same persons, but only statistically more often in the same society.

Hofstede sees the need for rules in a high UA country as an emotional need, a need to resolve ambiguity quickly and leave as little as possible to chance. The result of such discomfort can be strict adherence to ineffectual rules (rules for rules' sake) or hasty, unreasoned action aimed at alleviating the emotional discomfort associated with the uncertainty. People in high UA cultures are more driven to keep busy, and are often more precise, whereas people in low UA countries are not so driven, and tend to be more relaxed in their work.

Using Hofstede's UA index scores, which range from eight to 112, the countries which are high in uncertainty avoidance are those of

Latin America, Latin Europe and the Mediterranean. The common stereotype associated with these Romance countries is emotional and expressive, with large sweeping gestures and raised voices. Medium to high are the scores of the German-speaking countries with their predilection for rules, and medium to low are the Anglo and Nordic countries, plus the Asian countries with the exception of Japan and Korea. The USA, with a score of 46, is ranked 43 out of 50 countries, suggesting low uncertainty avoidance.

Masculinity–Femininity

Hofstede conceptualizes masculinity at the national level as pertaining to societies in which the gender roles are clearly distinct; that is, men are supposed to be assertive, tough and focused on extrinsic achievement (high earnings, promotions, material success) and women are supposed to be modest, tender and concerned with quality of life. Femininity pertains to societies in which social gender roles overlap, and there is greater concern for quality of life. In Hofstede's study the four most feminine countries were Sweden, Norway, the Netherlands and Denmark. The most masculine country was Japan, noted for its strong achievement orientation, followed by some continental European countries (Italy, Austria, West Germany) and some Latin American countries (Mexico, Colombia, Venezuela). The USA and Australia were ranked 15 and 16 in Hofstede's study of 50 countries, suggesting moderate to high masculine cultures.

Political priorities are opposed in these two societal systems. In masculine (versus feminine) countries, there is reward for the strong versus solidarity for the weak, economic growth versus protection of the environment, and arms spending versus aid to poor countries. For example, the correlation between defense spending expressed as a percentage of gross national product (GNP) and a country's masculinity index score is strong and positive, while the correlation between overseas aid as a percentage of GNP and the masculinity index score is –.81. These ecological correlations are two examples of the way in which Hofstede validated his interpretation of the dimensions.

Hofstede's Legacy

Apart from the sheer size of the study and the number of countries surveyed, the reason that Hofstede's study has become so important and achieved such acceptance is that there are a number of external correlates which validate the four dimensions of national culture. Hofstede considered economic, geographic and demographic indicators, including GNP, rate of economic growth, latitude of the capital city, size, density and growth rate of the population, defense spending, overseas aid, identity card obligation, press freedom, percentage of professional women, maximum speed limits, public opinion surveys and various large-scale sociological and psychological studies. For example, the dimension of individualism and the GNP indicator were correlated +0.82 for the countries in the studies; that is, the more individualistic countries were also the wealthiest. After controlling for the effect of GNP, individualism and power distance did emerge as separate factors, lending further support to Hofstede's conceptual distinction between the two dimensions.

Three large studies have been conducted in the field since Hofstede, and have acted as a validity check on his conceptualizations of the dimensions. The first originated in Hong Kong (Chinese Culture Connection, 1987): Chinese researchers compiled a set of values (thereby reflecting an Eastern rather than a Western point of origin for the values), which formed the basis of a questionnaire which was administered to university students in 23 countries. Using a statistical approach similar to that of Hofstede, the research team was able to replicate three of the dimensions (uncertainty avoidance was not replicated), while locating another, which they named 'Confucian dynamism' to reflect a long-term, future-oriented perspective adopted by many Confucian cultures in Asia.

The second large study originated in Israel (Schwartz, 1992; 1995; Schwartz & Bilsky, 1987; 1990). Using data from teachers and students in 40 countries, Schwartz consistently locates 10 values in a multidimensional space which aligns with Hofstede's dimensions: self-direction, stimulation and hedonism align with individualism while, on the opposite pole, the values of security, tradition and conformity align with collectivism. Masculinity–femininity appears as achievement opposed to universalism, and power distance is represented as power opposed to benevolence. While these values are not a clear replication of Hofstede's dimensions, nonetheless there is strong overlap between the two studies.

The third large study involves the work of Fons Trompenaars (1994), a Dutch researcher who completed his PhD in Management in the USA. Trompenaars surveyed more than 8000 managers from 43 countries, including many ex-communist bloc countries, using a questionnaire which addresses seven hypothesized dimensions of cultural values. Recent analyses of Trompenaars' data (Smith *et al.*, 1995; Smith *et al.*, 1996) have found considerable overlap with Hofstede's dimensions of power distance and individualism–collectivism, Schwartz's dimensions of egalitarian commitment and integration, and the Chinese Culture Connection's Confucian work dynamism. Hofstede's dimensions of uncertainty avoidance and masculinity–femininity were not readily apparent in the data, a fact that

Trompenaars attributes in part to the different theoretical sources from which the items were generated.

The legacy of Hofstede's work cannot be underestimated. His study remains the largest single investigation of cross-cultural work values. His impressive interdisciplinary approach to understanding and ex-plicating the dimensions has provided fertile ground for other researchers to pursue and test. His quantification of the dimensions has been invaluable. By providing scores for the countries on each of the dimensions, Hofstede created a four-dimensional 'map' of national culture which clustered countries into groups with similar values. Hofstede's study is considered a 'conceptual eureka!' (Bond, 1994) for providing cross-cultural psychologists with a structure which could unify their diverse studies.

Integration and Expectations

On the basis of the literature review, and Hofstede's work in particu-lar, we had reason to believe that systematic differences in human factors-related attitudes existed. Even so, we had to ask ourselves to what extent Hofstede's dimensions of national culture, derived from a cross-section of occupations in a large multinational company in the late 1960s and early 1970s, would be applicable to this specific subject population, that is, commercial airline pilots flying in the 1990s. Pilots are typically at the technological and modernized fore-front of their country's workforce (many are trained or travel overseas as part of their jobs) and it seemed likely that pilots, working in such a highly regulated, high-technology environment, might transcend national influences in favor of a universal standard of behavior. Was professional culture sufficient to explain pilots' behavior, as some might advocate, or was there some aspect of behavior that might also be attributed to one's national heritage?

A related interest was the impact of modernization and technol-ogy. Some authors argue the convergence hypothesis – that people of all modernizing societies are becoming similar to each other in their psychological characteristics (for example, Dawson, 1967; Inkeles & Smith, 1974; Levy, 1966). Some common elements of modernism as defined by these authors include independence from traditional auth-ority figures, ambition for oneself and one's children, low integration with extended relatives, egalitarian attitudes toward family role struc-ture, activism (abandonment of passivity and fatalism), interest in civic affairs and an emphasis on the future (Segall *et al.*, 1990). Cast in Hofstede's terminology, these characteristics reflect greater individu-alism and lower power distance. Other authors have argued that modernization does not eradicate culture, and that traditional characteristics will remain unchanged and coexist with the modern ones (Bond & King, 1985; Kağitçibasi, 1994; Yang, 1988). Pilots function in a very technically advanced, modern, working environment. It will be interesting to see if the predicted shift toward individualism and low power distance suggested by the convergence hypothesis is evident in these pilot groups. Also interesting would be any systematic differences in attitudes toward technology itself: for example, do pilots from more technologically advanced countries have the same attitudes toward aircraft automation as pilots from countries with less exposure to modern technology?

If we might be allowed a generalization here, pilots are pragmatic and tend to be distrustful of psychology. To present conclusions from studies conducted with students and expect any transference of credibility would not be sufficient. We knew we had to collect data from pilots themselves to show that national culture was influential in work attitudes and values. In 1992, we set out to collect data from commercial pilots worldwide with the intention of reporting our findings simply and without bias.

A Global Study of Pilots' Work-related Attitudes and Values

Under the sponsorship of NASA and the FAA, we set out to collect as many data as we could from different airlines around the world. We started by contacting people that we had worked with in the past, asking them to participate in the study. Initial response was very positive. In addition, we attended seminars for the International Civil Aviation Organization and the International Air Transport Association, and talked with many airline personnel from around the world. To encourage participation, and to honor our responsibilities as researchers, we analyzed the data received from every airline and prepared a proprietary report for each airline which included cross-airline comparisons and recommendations for training.

The Questionnaire

Starting with our existing survey instrument, the Cockpit Management Attitudes Questionnaire (Helmreich, 1984), and with Professor Hofstede's permission, we added 16 items from the Values Survey Module (Hofstede, 1982). We also included a section on attitudes toward automation, and wrote new items which we hoped would capture Hofstede's dimensions within the aviation environment. The weakness we acknowledge here is that the items were written by Anglo researchers, so they may unwittingly reflect an Anglo bias (we address this issue in more detail in Appendix A). The result was the

Flight Management Attitudes Questionnaire (FMAQ: Helmreich *et al.*, 1993; a copy is contained in Appendix C). The FMAQ1.0 is an exploratory, cross-cultural 82-item questionnaire designed to measure pilots' attitudes toward command, communication, stress, rules, automation, organizational climate and work values. The work values items are scaled on a five-point Likert scale ('very little or no importance' to 'utmost importance'). The attitudinal items, unless otherwise specified, are scaled on a five-point Likert scale ('strongly disagree' to 'strongly agree').

Data Collection and Sample

Data collection took place during the period 1993–7. Because we were interested in casting as wide a cultural net as possible, all airlines were encouraged to participate, and we worked to the schedules of the participating airlines wherever possible. In some cases, airlines would come back to us as much as two years after the initial contact, saying that they could now participate. From our data collection experience we have learned a valuable lesson in cross-cultural research: that data collection must proceed at the participants' pace, not ours. Establishing and maintaining contact with various airline personnel has been a time-consuming, but ultimately very rewarding, process for us. Again, we would like to thank formally all the pilots and all our friends, new and old, who contributed their time to the project. As of August 1997, we had received data from more than 15 000 pilots in 36 airlines in 23 countries (see Table 3.1).

Airlines who participated in the project took responsibility for the distribution and collection of the questionnaires. Seven airlines (from Argentina, Brazil, Germany, Italy, Korea, Mexico and Taiwan) undertook a translation of the questionnaire for their pilots – other airlines deemed it unnecessary. (As English is the official language of aviation, many airlines conduct their operations and training in English.) The translations and back-translations were done by bilingual aviation personnel to ensure equivalence of technical terms.

All commercial airline pilots were eligible for the larger study; however, because of the global scarcity of female pilots, only males were used in the analyses. For the cross-cultural analyses, we created the most culturally distinct groups by selecting only those pilots whose present nationality and nationality at birth matched that of the airline for which they flew. (The one minor exception to this rule was the British pilots who flew in what was then British Hong Kong. At the time, the British pilots were the majority and the company was run by British managers.) For the analyses involving multicultural airlines (to be discussed in a Chapter 7), these rules were relaxed.

Table 3.1   FMAQ respondents, by country

Country of airline	Number of airlines	Number of pilots
Argentina	1	39
Australia	2	640
Brazil	2	467
British HKG	1	557
Denmark	1	243
Germany	1	240
Gk. Cyprus	1	65
Ireland	1	420
Italy	1	517
Japan	1	51
Korea	1	176
Malaysia	1	801
Mexico	1	167
Morocco	1	60
New Zealand	1	485
Norway	1	216
Philippines	1	120
S. Africa	1	238
Sweden	1	443
Switzerland	2	211
Taiwan	2	499
UAE	1	145
USA	10	8 654
Total	36	15 454

To fully understand the results of our analyses, it is necessary to also understand some of the complexities of cross-cultural research methodology, including issues of culture-sensitive data sampling, awareness of item and culture-level response biases, decisions regarding the appropriate level of analysis and the range of analyses necessary to understand the similarities, differences and unique concepts amongst respondents of different national cultures. Appendix A discusses these issues as they relate to our data set and outlines our solutions to the problems that we encountered. The appendix is not overly technical in detail, and the reader is encouraged to peruse it to develop a better appreciation of the material. Nonetheless, it is possible to read the rest of the chapter without recourse to the appendix.

Results

Looking for Similarities: when Skewness is Meaningful

As part of standard data cleansing and preparation for more complex analyses, descriptive analyses were run on every item in the survey, for every country in the study. In particular, skewed items were investigated for strong floor or ceiling effects.[3] We noticed that many of the same items appeared skewed across most or all of the countries. It is standard practice in many psychological analyses to consider skewed items a 'nuisance' or failed variables, and to omit them from further analyses, because skewed items do not have any variability and can wreak havoc upon any correlation-based analyses. But what if the same items garnered the same high levels of agreement or disagreement across all airline groups? Then we would have evidence of universal consensus by pilots, regardless of national background. Suddenly, our skewed variables took on a whole new importance as indicators of universal pilot attitudes.

We adopted a decision rule from Triandis, Bontempo, Leung & Hui (1990) which stated that one cannot expect 100 per cent agreement or disagreement with any item because there will always be some 'noise' in the method and/or the responses, but 85 per cent could be considered strong evidence of group consensus. Consequently, we reviewed the frequency distributions of all the items across 33 airline groups (in 22 countries) to determine which items were universally or near-universally endorsed or rejected.[4] Table 3.2 lists the 11 items which met these criteria.

The items which attracted the strongest agreement were all related to communication and coordination, with one exception ('I like my job', an item discussed in the previous chapter, and to be discussed again in Chapter 4). There was strong consensus that the pre-flight briefing is important, that communication and coordination are as important as technical skills, that the pilot flying should verbalize plans, and that crew members should monitor each other for signs of stress. There was also strong acknowledgment that the captain's responsibilities include coordination of cockpit and cabin crew. The pilots from Japan and Korea were notable for having considerably lower levels of agreement with the item, 'If I perceive

3   Items which garner very strong disagreement, producing scores which could not be much lower, show a 'floor' effect, while items with very strong agreement produce scores so high they have a 'ceiling' effect.
4   We could have run one set of frequencies for all the 15 000 pilots, but, with the sample sizes varying so widely from one country to another, we would not have gained a true picture of consensus in every country. Hence frequencies were run for every airline group.

Table 3.2 Attitudinal items with strong floor and ceiling effects

Items with strong agreement	Agreement among 33 airline groups (%)
The pilot flying the aircraft should verbalize plans for procedures/ maneuvers and should be sure that the information is understood and acknowledged by other crew	All 33 gps: 85% or more agreed
The pre-flight briefing is important for safety and for effective crew management	All 33 gps: 85% or more agreed
The captain's responsibilities include coordination between cockpit and cabin crew	All 33 gps: 85% or more agreed
Good communication and crew coordination are as important as technical proficiency for the safety of flight	All 33 gps: 85% or more agreed
I expect to be consulted on matters that affect the performance of my duties	32 gps: 85% or more agreed; Japan 76%
Crew members should monitor each other for signs of stress or fatigue	31 gps: 85% or more agreed; Italy 82%, Mexico 82%
If I perceive a problem with the flight, I will speak up, regardless of who might be affected	29 gps: 85% or more agreed; Taiwan 84%, Brazil (1) 81%, Japan 49%, Korea 36%
I like my job	29 gps: 85% or more agreed; 4 USA gps: 83%, 83%, 79%, 77%

Items with strong disagreement	Disagreement among 33 airline groups (%)
Captains who encourage suggestions from crew members are weak leaders	30 gps: 85% or more disagreed; Argentina 79%, Mexico 82%, Morocco 73%
Junior crew members should not question the captain's or senior crew members' decisions	29 gps: 85% or more disagreed; Brazil (1) 78%, Brazil (2) 77%, Mexico 74%, Philippines 80%
It is better to agree with other crew members than to voice a different opinion	29 gps: 85% or more disagreed; Taiwan 83%, Japan 78%, Korea 69%, Mexico 72%

a problem, I will speak up, regardless of who might be affected' (49 per cent and 36 per cent, respectively), otherwise pilots tended to say they would speak up, and that they expected consultation regarding the performance of their duties. Box 3.3 highlights some more differences between Japanese and US pilots from the Japanese perspective.

Box 3.3   Japanese and American pilots

Yamamori and Mito (1993) offer insights into differences between Japanese and American pilots based on their experience with training in both countries.

From our experience of working with American pilots ... we feel that American pilots are more task-oriented than Japanese pilots. Their behavior contrasted with the behavior of Japanese pilots at our seminar in Japan, where the Japanese tended to behave in a more group-oriented fashion. As a result of this observation, we see America as a task-oriented society. Western people seem more aware of themselves as individuals rather than as part of a group. American culture seems to encourage the individual, independent self, while Japanese culture encourages the development of the group-oriented, dependent person.

The Japanese sense of modesty is not seen as a virtue in American culture. In team discussions during CRM seminars, we felt that Americans did not easily accept another person's opinion, whereas Japanese tended to accept a person's opinion, whether right or wrong, in order to preserve harmony within the group. Because they are competitive and tend to view situations in terms of winning or losing, Americans will sometimes aggressively support their own opinion, even if they know they are not entirely correct. In contrast, Japanese will usually become silent and non-supportive of their own ideas if they see some opposition to them. Another important point is that Japanese are often conformists who need to identify with a group. Japanese will rarely try to stand out and be creative in a group situation. This is because we want to achieve a sense of harmony. It is part of our history and our culture. About 1400 years ago, a famous Japanese prince called Shotoku Taishi said, 'Harmony is to be respected.' His words and this thought are still in the Japanese mind today.

Of course, the Japanese are also competitive people. However, they differ from Americans in that their competition is directed toward outside groups or organizations. While the Japanese are very competitive toward each other in their own minds, they will never express that competition verbally.

> In Japanese society, acceptance is highly valued and is achieved through a person's effort for his group. His efforts, whether useful or not, are seen as having merit and will earn him respect and promotion, even if he has little real ability. Although we saw these differences in our cultures, we realized that, in the cockpit situation, neither the Japanese way of behavior nor the American way is the best way. We do not think that any culture, whether Japanese, American, or any other, fits in with the cockpit environment.
>
> There are many situations where authority must be shown in the cockpit. There are also times when cockpit authority must be questioned or challenged. And it is in this kind of challenge situation that crew members react differently on the basis of their cultural background. Authority is rarely challenged in a group-oriented society. But, as we in the airline industry know, this kind of attitude has led to many fatal accidents. On the other hand, in a task-oriented society, those in authority may fail to listen to the opinion of others when their authority is challenged. This, too, has led to fatal accidents. (Yamamori & Mito, 1993, pp.213–14)

The three items which attracted the strongest disagreement were also concerned with communication. Most pilots disagreed that captains who encouraged suggestions from the crew were weak leaders, and most believed that it was okay for junior crew members to question the captain's decisions. There was a small cluster of countries for which the level of disagreement was not as pronounced as in other countries (disagreement levels in the 70–80 per cent range). These countries were Mexico, Argentina, Brazil, Morocco and the Philippines. The final item, 'It is better to agree than voice a different opinion' (which is conceptually related to 'If I perceive a problem I will speak up ...'), attracted less disagreement from the pilots of Japan, Korea, Mexico and Taiwan.

These preliminary results are informative for three reasons. First, we were able to determine that there is universal recognition that communication and coordination in the cockpit are important – a very positive outcome, and one that reflects favorably on the professional pilot culture. Also pilots appear strongly individualistic in wanting to be consulted about their duties and in wanting to talk freely with their peers and superiors as they see fit.[5] Third, these analyses provided our first hint of national differences. In line with other cross-cultural communication research, the Japanese and Korean pilots were notable for showing greater concern for harmony

---

5   These may seem like universal traits, but consider other occupations: consultation and free exchange of information are not common across all strata of the working world.

in the cockpit (less willing to disagree openly, less willing to speak up if a problem is detected). A more speculative finding was the loose clustering of the geographically distant countries of Mexico, Morocco, the Philippines, Argentina and Brazil on some command items. These countries do share a history of imperialist colonization from Mediterranean Europe (from Spain, Portugal and France) which may account for some commonalities.[6] We were quite pleased with our serendipitous 'first look' at the data. We established two areas of strong commonality amongst pilots in 22 countries (the importance of communication and the preference for consultation) and we had our first glimpse of national differences.

Captain Robert Bumgarner, a US pilot who has worked for oriental airlines for more than five years, has conducted some local research with his fellow pilots in Taiwan. The convergence between his results and ours can be seen in Box 3.4.

Box 3.4   From national culture to cockpit culture

National culture influences, but does not necessarily control, pilot behavior in the cockpit. Certainly, it shapes expectations about interpersonal relationships. But, as all pilots know, they share a professional culture that overrides and transcends the influence of national culture in many important ways. For example, pilots from collectivist cultures, such as those in Asia and South America, exhibit individualistic behavior to a much higher degree than is common to their national culture – it's required by the job. More importantly, because airline pilots deal day in and day out with life-threatening situations, they are forced to be better communicators and more team-oriented than most of their countrymen. Flying brings with it certain behavioral necessities and traditions that create a culture unique to pilots around the world.

This shared set of professional beliefs and practices make the transition to Asian airline operations easier for the Western expatriate, at least during the time he is operating an aircraft. The question is, to what degree do Asian pilots share similar expectations about cockpit behaviors and in which specific areas are they likely to exhibit characteristics common to their native national culture?

In an effort to determine how similar pilot thinking really is, I conducted an informal survey during CRM training at a multicultural Taiwanese airline. This airline employed pilots from more than 30 national cultures, but almost all of its first officers

---

6   If this idea seems too 'far-fetched', recall that the USA, Australia, New Zealand and Ireland are also geographically distant yet are bound by their common legacy of British imperialism, as later analyses will demonstrate.

were Taiwanese ab initio pilots. Over a period of one year, I presented each of the pilots who attended the course with a series of 16 statements relating to how pilots like to be treated by their colleagues. I then asked them to indicate the statements with which they agreed. Of the 218 pilots tested (about half Asian), more than 90 per cent agreed with the following statements:

- I want to be told when I make a mistake so I don't make it again.
- I want you to tell me if you disagree with me.
- I want my boss to ask for and listen to my input and concerns.
- I like it when others tell me what is on their mind.
- I like it when people call me by my first name.
- I want my subordinates to think of me as their partner rather than as their boss.
- I like being treated as an equal.
- I like people to look me in the eye when they talk to me.
- I prefer people to say what they mean and mean what they say, even if it's unpleasant.
- I like direct, honest answers to my questions of other people.

Although I had expected more agreement than disagreement, I was surprised to learn that almost all the Asian pilots wanted to be called by their 'first' name, that they wanted to be looked in the eye when you talk to them, that they wanted to be told when they made a mistake so they would not make it again (what about face?), and that they wanted others to tell them what is on their mind. More surprising still was their preference that subordinates treat them like a partner rather than as a boss. These responses provide a comforting foundation for cockpit relationships.

There were only four statements in the survey with which more than 25 per cent of the pilots disagreed:

- I want the freedom to accomplish work assignments in my own way (29 per cent).
- I like being seen as an individual, not just one of the group (41 per cent).
- It feels good when I am noticed and singled out for praise (45 per cent).
- It's my accomplishments at work that matter most, not just my efforts to accomplish assigned tasks (47 per cent).

Here you see the effects of Asian culture in the responses of the pilots. Asian pilots are generally collectivist or group-oriented, so they are uncomfortable when they are singled out in front of others for praise or scorn, they believe that, as long as an employee does his or her best, the results are not so important, they do not like to express personal beliefs or complaints at public meetings, so don't expect them to act like Western F/Os at flight safety meetings, and they are uncomfortable deviating from approved operating procedures, so when you do it, they will not like it. These attitudes lurk behind the comforting facade of common viewpoints like tigers in jungle foliage. And the unaware Westerner who strays too far from SOPs, who criticizes one of his colleagues in public, or who denigrates one of his first officers for the way he operates, even though he has tried to do his best, will discover that these tigers bite. (Captain Robert Bumgarner, China Airlines, an expatriate US pilot)

Work Values Items: What do Pilots Want?

One section of the FMAQ includes several items from Hofstede's survey and addresses the importance of different work values. Respondents are asked to imagine their ideal job, not their present job, and then to rate the importance of various attributes of that ideal job. These attributes, 13 in all, include security of employment, free time and independence from the organization, opportunities for advancement and high earnings, attributes of the task related to rules and routines, and good relationships with co-workers and superiors. As with the skewed items, these items also provided an opportunity to consider both the extent of professional similarities and the range of national differences.

Pilots were asked to rate the work values on a scale from '1 = no importance' to '5 = of utmost importance'. Item scores could not be compared directly because of cultural response biases (a detailed discussion of this issue appears in Appendix A) so we used ranks. The mean scores of the captains' ratings and the first and second officers' ratings within each country were averaged, and then converted to ranks, with '1 = highest ranking, most important attribute' down to '13 = lowest ranking, least important attribute'. The full matrix of these country-level rankings of the 13 items is given in Table B.1 in Appendix B.

Table 3.3 is a summary table which highlights both the similarities and differences in the rankings. The work values items are listed in the table in descending order of importance for the 22 country sample as a whole, and the columns are organized from highest to lowest rank (most to least important) across the page. Each cell then represents the number of countries who gave that ranking for that item.

Table 3.3 Work values items ranked by pilots in 22 countries

Work values Items[a]	MOST IMPORTANT — RANKINGS — LEAST IMPORTANT												
	1	2	3	4	5	6	7	8	9	10	11	12	13
Security of employment	9[b]	9	1	1	1	1	1						
Sufficient time for personal/family life	10	4	1	3	1	1	1	1					
Live in desirable area	1	3	8	5	3		2						
Work with cooperative others		4	4	6	4	3	1						
Good relations with co-workers		1	4	2	4	8	2	1					
Opportunity for advancement	2	1	1	2	3	1	7	2					1
Challenging tasks/sense of accomplishment			2	2	2	3	1	6	1	2	2	2	1
Opportunity for high earnings				1	2	3	6	8	1		2	1	1
Find the correct answer/one truth			1			1	1		5	4	8	2	1
Job with no surprises			1					3	3	5	4	4	1
Warm relations with superior				1	1			1	7	8	4	1	1
Changing routine					1			1	4	3	2	3	9
Observe strict time limits						1			1		2	9	9

Notes:

a   The work values items have been listed in descending order of importance across the 22 countries. That is, 'Security of employment' attracted the highest mean ranking amongst the 22 groups, while 'observing strict time limits' attracted the lowest mean ranking.

b   The numbers in the cells represent the number of countries whose pilots' rank orderings fit that cell; for example, pilots from nine countries rated 'security of employment' their most important work value. Empty cells indicate no rankings. (Rows and columns both sum to 22, the number of countries in the study.)

For example, pilots from nine countries ranked 'security of employment' as the most important attribute in their ideal job (top left in the table) and pilots from another nine countries ranked it second most important, while no group ranked it lower than seventh in their list of 13. At the other end of the spectrum (bottom right in the table), pilots from 18 countries listed the need to observe strict time limits for work projects as the least or second-least important attribute,[7] and no country ranked it higher than sixth. Notice how the frequencies of rankings for the most part follow the diagonal from top left to bottom right – this is an indication of the general similarity of the rankings across the different countries. The three most important attributes for most pilots are security of employment, sufficient time for family and personal life, and the opportunity to live in a desirable area. Next, there is a concern for working relationships with co-workers (although note how concern for a good relationship with one's superior is rated much lower), followed by rewards (both intrinsic and extrinsic) and then task specifics stated in varying levels of flexibility and order (for example, changing routine, strict time limits, the one answer).

At the same time, take note of the outliers (those scores which fall outside the diagonal) as indicators of national differences. For example, pilots from one country ranked high earnings as the least important attribute, and pilots from another country ranked a warm relationship with their supervisor as their least important attribute. Table B.1 in Appendix B allows the interested reader to identify the ways in which each country conforms and differs from the general pattern of endorsement.

Following on from the general exploration of values, we next used hierarchical cluster analysis to see if pilots of different countries could be clustered together according to their work values. This was the first test of 'national culture' and not just 'national differences', in that the analysis looked for underlying patterns which could unify the data. The results were informative. The first countries to cluster together, that is to share a similar pattern of endorsement of the 13 work values, were the Anglo cluster of Australia, USA, New Zealand, Ireland and the British pilots in Hong Kong. As mentioned earlier, although these countries are geographically distant, they do have a common heritage of British imperialism. Two other clusters were easily identified – a Scandinavian cluster of Norway, Sweden and Denmark, and a Germanic-influenced cluster of South Africa,[8] Germany and Switzerland (both airlines in the Swiss sample were

---

7   Let us hope this does not also relate to on-time performance.
8   The pilots from South Africa also clustered with the Anglo pilots in some solutions, an interesting statistical representation of their mixed heritage.

German-speaking). The South American and some Asian countries (Argentina, Mexico, Brazil, Japan, the Philippines and Malaysia) were the next to cluster, though not as tightly.[9] It is likely that, if we had more countries from each continent, for example Venezuela, Chile and Colombia from South America, the two groups would be more distinctly separated. For now these countries share some similarities, even if it is only the extent to which they differ from the Western countries. A fifth cluster was formed by Korea and Taiwan. The country which was so unique in its pattern of endorsement that it did not cluster with any other countries was Italy. (This difference can be seen most clearly in Table B.1 in Appendix B: Italy's rankings were often at odds with the majority.)

We used the cluster solution to combine pilots from 20 countries into six clusters of culturally similar countries. Recall that this clustering was based on empirical analyses of pilots' responses to a set of ideal work values. That the 20 groups form recognizable cultural groups is testament to the reality of national culture.

The Anglo, Scandinavian and Germanic groups gave similar rankings to most items but differed slightly in their endorsement of the opportunity for high earnings and the opportunity for advancement. When compared with the pilots of the South American/Asian cluster and the Korea/Taiwan cluster, the Western pilots (Anglos, Scandinavians, Germanics) were notable for placing a higher value on a changing work routine with new, unfamiliar tasks, a job with challenging tasks which allowed for a sense of personal accomplishment, and a job that provided sufficient time for personal and family life. Conversely, the Western pilots had the lowest ratings for a job with no surprises, a job with strict time limits and the need to find the one set answer. They also placed the least importance on a warm relationship with their superior. The Korean/Taiwanese pilots were notable for placing the highest value on observing strict time limits and finding the one set answer, and the lowest value on a job with challenging tasks and the need for sufficient time for personal or family life. The South American/Asian pilots had the highest value for a job with no surprises and the lowest value for a job with a changing routine, but they also had the highest value for a warm relationship with their direct superior and the opportunity for advancement.

In sum, there was near-universal endorsement of security of employment and the importance of working relationships. Western pilots showed the greatest preference for flexibility (changing work routine,

9   The pilots of Morocco and Cyprus also fell into this cluster. We believe this was a forced fit, an empirical contrivance, and so we excluded these pilots from the cluster in subsequent analyses.

no set time limits or single solutions, challenging tasks), the Korean/Taiwanese pilots showed the greatest preference for order (time limits, one way to do a job) and the South American/Asian pilots showed the greatest preference for predictability (no surprises, unchanging routine). Table 3.4 uses four scales derived from country-level factor analysis of the work values items to summarize the results.

Apart from the specifics of the results, which are interesting in themselves, the actual cluster analysis itself should be highlighted as a major finding. It is difficult to maintain denial of national culture when the results align the countries so neatly into recognizable cultural clusters. The Anglo cluster is particularly impressive – that pilots from such disparate corners of the world could have common work values bears witness to the power of historically derived cultural values. At the same time, we acknowledge that not all countries fit as neatly into clusters, but that may be due to the limitations of the current sample. For example, if we had the data from other, Spanish influenced, South American countries we could identify a 'cleaner' South American cluster. Nonetheless, the work values items unequivocally illustrate the presence and influence of national culture.

Table 3.4   Work values scales and effect sizes for six clusters

Scale	F	Effect Size	Anglo	Scandia	Germanic	S. Amer. & Asia	Korea & Taiwan	Italy
Relations	10	0.01	73.6	73.5	75.7	75.7	75.1	75.2
Rewards	332	0.25	80.7	73.3	74.9	78.0	61.9	60.0
Independence	267	0.22	85.3	85.7	82.0	74.8	74.5	81.2
Order	472	0.33	50.8	55.2	55.0	67.2	75.5	69.1

Notes:
Relations = work with cooperative others, warm relations with superior, good working relations with co-workers.
Rewards = high earnings, advancement.
Independence = sufficient time for personal/family life, living in desirable area, personal sense of accomplishment from challenging tasks.
Order = strict time limits, job with no surprises, the one solution.
Scores were calculated using Schwartz's transform for cultural response bias, rather than ranks. Range for all scales is 0–100.

Attitudes toward Communication, Command, Stress and Rules

In all, 44 items on the FMAQ were written to address issues of command, communication, rules and procedures, and the limits of human performance. Before analyzing for more complex patterns, we ran descriptive analyses on every item in every country, and ran one-way Analysis of Variance (ANOVA) using country as the independent variable.[10] Some items were identified as poorly or ambiguously written, and were dropped from further analyses. Table B.2 (Appendix B) records item means and country-level effect sizes for the items which were retained.

Communication Five of the six communication items have already been discussed in the section on skewed items. These items attracted strong agreement across all pilot groups. There was almost universal consensus that pre-flight briefings are important, that the pilot flying should verbalize plans and check for understanding, that communication and coordination are as important as technical skills, and that crew members should speak up and voice a different opinion if they perceive a problem (these last two items attracted less endorsement from the Japanese and Korean pilots) (see Table 3.2). The final item, 'A debriefing and critique of procedures after each flight is an important part of developing and maintaining effective crew coordination' drew very strong differences of opinion (see Figure 3.1) across national lines. The pilots of the Anglo and Western countries all had lower mean scores than did the pilots of other countries. The reason for this difference is not obvious. It may be that pilots from individualistic countries are reluctant to publicly evaluate their own performance, or it may be that pilots from high power distance countries expect a debriefing and critique from the captain.

Command Eight items addressing command roles and command interactions were combined to form a composite score, from which to measure differences in attitudes toward command. The items were as follows: the captain should take control and fly the aircraft in emergencies; the first officer should never assume command; success in flight is primarily due to the captain's technical proficiency; I rely on superiors to tell me what to do in an emergency; crew shouldn't question the captain's decisions; captains don't need to encourage crew questions, captains who encourage crew suggestions are weak leaders; and subordinates are afraid to disagree. Low scores on the scale reflect low power distance as conceptualized by Hofstede, that is, there is less distance between the captain and the crew, and communication is openly initiated from both directions. High scores on the scale reflect less communication initiated by junior crew and greater unquestioned reliance on the captain.

Differences among the five Anglo countries were minor and, with the exception of Cyprus and Italy, the differences among the 11 Anglo

10 To balance the other samples in the analysis, a random sample of 420 pilots was selected from the larger USA sample for use in these analyses.

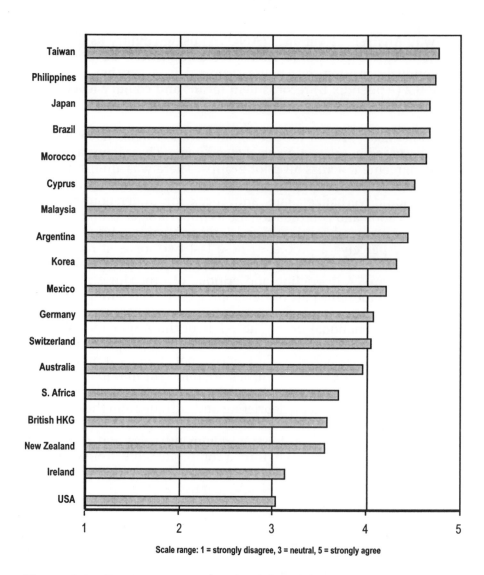

Scale range: 1 = strongly disagree, 3 = neutral, 5 = strongly agree

Figure 3.1   Country means for the debriefing item

and other Western countries were also minor (effect sizes less than .04 for the eight-item composite).[11] Across the 22 countries, however, the differences in attitudes toward command produced an effect size of .37. That is, more than one-third of the variance in pilots' attitudes

11   Effect sizes can range from zero to one; higher scores indicate a stronger effect for the variable of interest. In this case, an effect size of .04 indicates there is almost no meaningful difference between the pilots of the Western countries with regard to command roles and interactions.

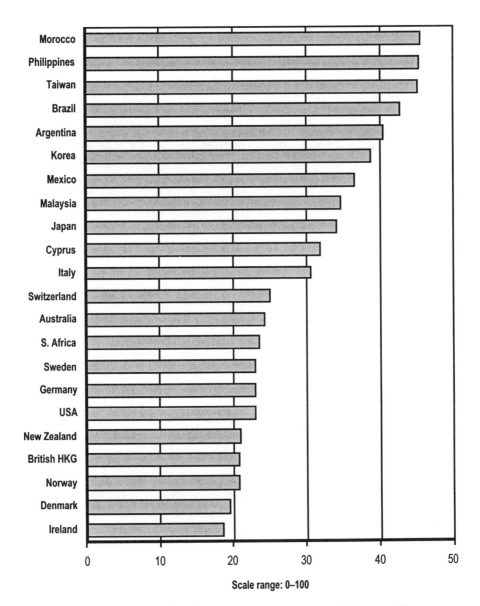

Scale range: 0–100

Figure 3.2   Command scale: mean scores across 22 countries

toward command can be accounted for by broad national differences, particularly between the Western and non-Western pilots (see Figure 3.2).

Pilots from the Anglo, Scandinavian and Germanic groups were all lower on the scale than the South American and Asian groups.

The pilots from Morocco, the Philippines and Taiwan had the highest scores, followed by Brazil, Argentina, Korea and Mexico.

To keep the meaning of these differences in perspective, it is important to understand the range of possible scores on this scale. The lowest possible score (smallest power distance) is zero and the highest, or most hierarchical, is 100. The average scores for the Western countries range from 19 to 25 (32 with Italy and Cyprus included), while the non-Western pilot averages range from 34 to 46. In other words, even though differences are pronounced and divide the countries into two recognizably different groups, the highest country score is still lower than the mid-point on the scale. In effect, the pilots from the Western countries have *very low* scores, while the pilots from non-Western countries have *low to average* scores.

Performance under stress   Attitudes toward stress and the limits of human performance did not display the same level of cultural differences as the command items. Of the 12 items which address performance under stress, five relate to what crew members *should* do: for example, crew members should monitor others for signs of stress, should alert others when overloaded, should mention their own stress to others before or during a flight.

Converted to a 0–100-point scale, the country-level means ranged from 65 to 88, indicating relatively positive attitudes. Six other items related to crew members' evaluations of their own performance: for example, *I* am less effective when stressed or fatigued, *my* decision-making ability is just as good in an emergency (reverse-scored), personal problems can adversely affect *my* performance. When these items were converted to a 0–100-point scale, with high scores reflecting a realistic appraisal of one's abilities under conditions of stress, the country-level means ranged from 36 to 66. In other words, while pilots in most countries recognize what others should do regarding their stress, they are more than a little reluctant to acknowledge their own limitations. The effect size for differences across the pilots of the 22 countries on this scale was less than .1, indicating a rather small difference when compared with the effect size of .37 for the command scale. Also scores did not fall into a neat Western/non-Western dichotomy (see Figure 3.3).

The last stress item asks whether a truly professional crew member can leave personal problems behind when flying. This time, the item asks the respondent to consider the professional (ideal) standard for handling stress. The average level of agreement across the 22 countries for this item was 67 per cent and, with the exception of four countries, agreement in every country was more than 50 per cent, the highest endorsement being 97 per cent agreement amongst the Fili-

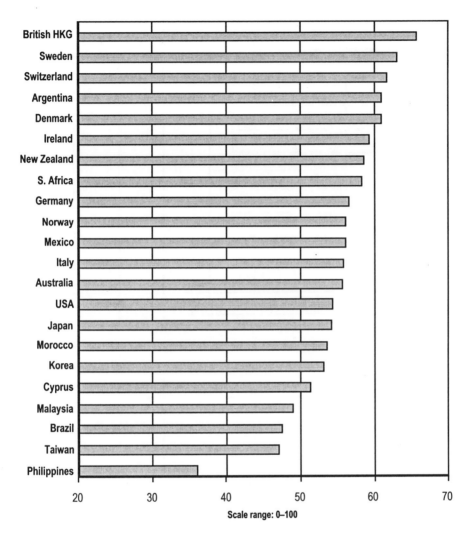

Figure 3.3 'My performance under stress': mean scores across 22 countries

pino pilots (see Figure 3.4). This item highlights the fact that a clear majority of pilots believe that the professional standard, the standard to aspire to, is one of invulnerability to stress.

To fully understand the significance of this item, consider that there was a significant negative correlation between this item and the six-item self-stress scale at the individual level ($r = -.36$ across 5000 pilots); that is, the more respondents endorsed the professional standard as one of invulnerability, the less likely they were to have

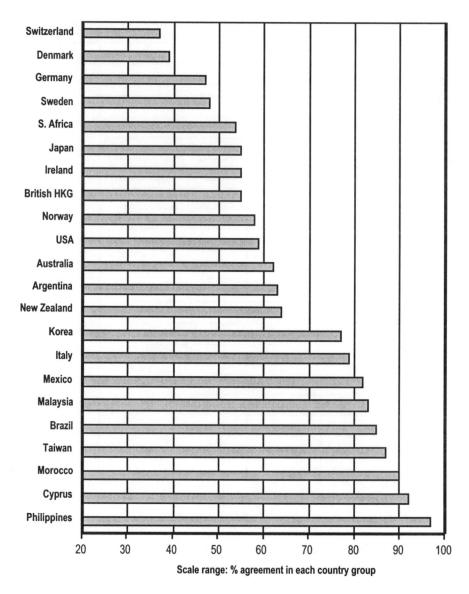

Figure 3.4   'A true professional can leave personal problems
behind when flying': percentage agreement across 22
countries

realistic standards about their own performance. Put simply, attitudes about performance under stress are clearly influenced by the
professional norm and, as stated in Chapter 2, the professional pilot
culture seems to encourage unrealistic attitudes toward stress.

The correlation at the country level was even stronger (–.80). That is, the more pilots of a country endorsed the professional standard as being invulnerable, the more their country scores on the self-scale also reflected unrealistic attitudes. This result provides interesting evidence that pilots' perceptions of their professional culture may also be influenced by their national culture. For example, pilots who come from more 'macho' national cultures may perceive pilot performance as more 'bullet-proof' than other pilots.

Rules and procedures   Two items regarding rules and procedures also proved interesting at the national level. The item, 'the organization's rules should not be broken, even when the employee thinks it is in the best interest of the company', served to separate the Korean and Taiwanese pilots, who agreed with the item, from all other pilots, who tended to be neutral or disagreed. The second item, 'written procedures are required for all in-flight situations', also showed the Korean and Taiwanese pilots with the strongest endorsement, followed by the other non-Western and Germanic countries. As Figure 3.5 shows, the Anglo,[12] Italian and Scandinavian pilots all had mean scores less than three on the five-point scale, indicating disagreement, while the other countries all had means higher than the mid-point, indicating general agreement.

These attitudes towards rules and procedures are conceptually linked to the work values items regarding order and routine (strict time limits, the one solution, a job with no surprises).[13] We used Schwartz's (1992) transform to neutralize the cultural response biases in the values items, and then combined the five items to form a 'Rules & Order' scale (important to observe strict limits, to have a job with no surprises, to find the truth, the one correct solution; the organization's rules should not be broken; written procedures are required for all in-flight solutions), which proved to have an effect size as strong as that observed with the command scale (η^2 = .34 for 22 countries. See Figure 3.6). The pilots of Taiwan and Korea had the highest scores on this scale, the Anglo pilots had the lowest.[14]

12   Again, the pilots of South Africa are located between the Germanic pilots and the Anglo pilots.
13   At the country level, the three-item scale was correlated +.75 with 'written procedures are required ...' and +.56 with 'organization's rules should not be broken'.
14   In trying to understand the Korean and Taiwanese pilots' stronger preferences for rules and order, we speculate that it might be due to their unique military situations. Other airlines recruit their pilots from the military and we do not see this effect; however, both Korea and Taiwan have serious present perceived threats (North Korea and mainland China) which may keep the military on an even tighter regimen of control. This 'tighter' approach to flying may carry over to civilian flight.

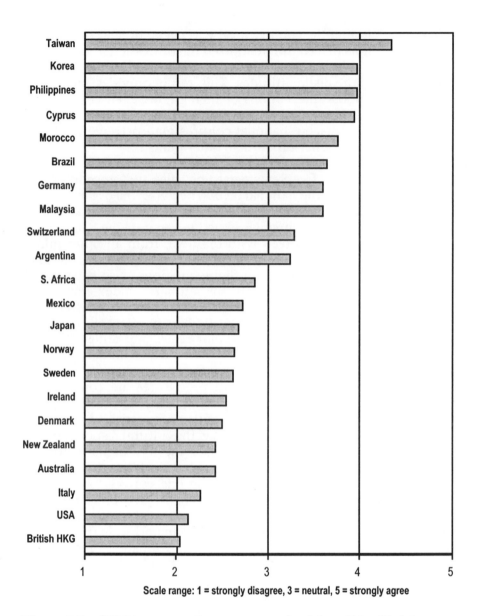

Figure 3.5   'Written procedures are required for all in-flight situations': mean scores across 22 countries

To summarize this section, attitudes toward communication and consultation were generally positive and undifferentiated across the 22 countries, and attitudes towards human performance under stress tended to be more realistic when applied to others than to oneself.

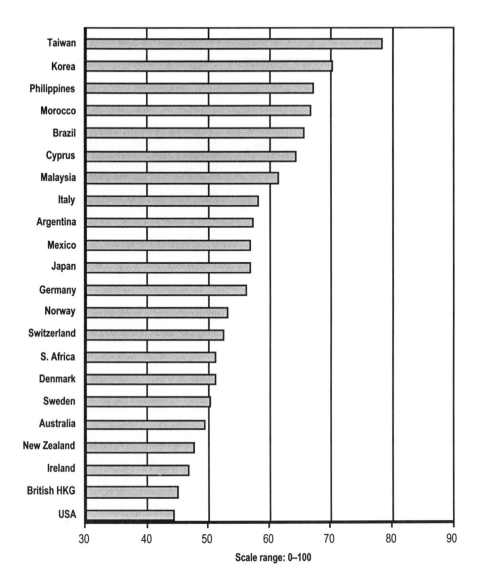

Figure 3.6   Rules and order scale: mean scores across 22 countries

This pattern held across the 22 countries, indicating a professional norm. At the same time, pilots of some countries endorsed a more unrealistic professional standard, suggesting that perceptions of the professional culture can be affected by national culture. The strongest differences between pilots of different countries were observed with regard to command roles and interactions, and attitudes toward order, rules and set routines. In both cases, the mean scores aligned by cultural cluster; that is, Anglo pilots (from five countries) shared similar views, just as the pilots from the three Scandinavian countries shared similar views, and so on.

Technology: Friend or Foe?

In the FMAQ, 15 items address attitudes toward automation. To analyze these data we selected the subset of pilots who said they flew automated aircraft. Defined as aircraft equipped with a flight management computer (FMC) capable of both lateral and vertical navigation, some examples of automated aircraft include the Airbus A300-600, A310, A320, A330 and A340; selected Boeing 737-300 and later series, 747-400, 757, 767 and 777; McDonnell-Douglas MD11 and selected MD80 series; and the Fokker F100. The automation database consisted of 2820[15] pilots from 18 nations: Australia, Brazil, Denmark, Greek Cyprus, Germany, Ireland, Italy, South Korea, Malaysia, Mexico, New Zealand, Norway, the Philippines, Sweden, South Africa, Switzerland, Taiwan and the USA. (There were insufficient numbers from Japan, Argentina, Morocco and British Hong Kong to be included.)

We analyzed the data with ANOVAs, as we had with the previous data, and also used level of agreement as the basis of analysis. The second approach, which rendered results similar to the analyses of variance, was used to circumvent cultural response biases. For these analyses, we reduced the original five-point scale to a simpler three-point categorization: 'disagree', 'neutral' and 'agree'. This transformation neutralized the response bias without sacrificing the intent and meaning of the responses. The proportion of pilots responding in each category ('disagree', 'neutral' and 'agree') was calculated for each automation item for each national group (for pilots of automated aircraft only). Pearson's chi-square statistic and Cramér's *V*, a measure of associative strength which is conceptually similar to effect size, were then calculated for each item. Additionally, the range of agreement (that is, the difference between the country which had the highest percentage of pilots in agreement and the country with the lowest percentage, or least endorsement) was calculated for every item.

There was a significant association between nationality and responses to all 15 items. Cramér's *V* coefficients showed effect sizes ranging from .13 to .32, indicating a consistent and substantial relationship between nationality and attitudes toward automation. Table 3.5 summarizes the results of the 15 tests of association and their

15   There were more than 2000 US pilots in our automation database. In order to make the USA sample roughly equivalent to that of other countries, we used a random sample of 10 per cent (223 pilots) from the USA data.

effect sizes, and presents the range of percentage endorsement across the 18 nations for each item.

Inspection of the level of endorsement across countries (see Table B.3 in Appendix B) revealed striking differences in levels of agreement. Across the 15 items, the difference in percentage agreement ranged from as little as 21 per cent across the 18 countries (suggesting relatively similar views amongst the pilot groups) to as much as 74 per cent. The average difference in the range of endorsement was 51 per cent, suggesting highly disparate views about automation at the national level.

To fully understand the data, the percentage agreement scores can be viewed in several ways. We can look at items showing the greatest consensus across, and within, nations, as indicators of universal or normative attitudes; we can look at items which have the least consensus across, and within, nations, as indicators of uncertainty or divergent views on automation management; and we can consider item correlations at the national level to better understand the underlying themes in the data.

Table 3.5 Automation items: effect sizes and range of endorsement across 18 countries

Item		Effect size Cramér's V	Range[a] (%)	Range[b] % spread
1	Prefer automation	0.23	36–100	64
2	Access FMC in abnormal conditions	0.21	54–93	39
3	Should always use automation	0.29	42–100	58
4	Avoid 'reprogramming' FMC	0.20	31–68	37
5	Concern re losing skills	0.23	28–77	58
6	Easy to forget FMC ops	0.22	29–80	51
7	More automation is better	0.37	0–74	74
8	Avoid disengaging auto	0.34	3–73	70
9	FMC not fully understood	0.20	24–51	29
10	More verbal required	0.29	28–84	56
11	Disengage for proficiency	0.35	26–88	62
12	More cross-checks required	0.20	52–90	38
13	Co. expects automation use	0.32	27–92	65
14	Ensure FMC op. acknowledged	0.16	74–96	21
15	Feel free to select level	0.13	67–89	41

Notes:
Significant differences (p < .0001) on all items.
a = scores were recorded as the percentage of pilots in each country sample who agreed with the item.
b = the range of endorsement across the 18 countries.

The item which had the greatest consensus across *and* within nations was 'I make sure the other pilot acknowledges programming changes I make in the FMC.' The range of agreement across nations was 74–96 per cent; that is, approximately three-quarters or more of pilots in every national group agreed with this item, suggesting a strong normative attitude.[16] Other items which showed a wider range of consensus across nations but reasonable consensus within nations (that is, approximately 50 per cent or more of the pilots within the national group in agreement) were 'Under abnormal conditions, I can rapidly access the information I need in the FMC' (54–93 per cent), 'I feel free to select the level of automation at any given time' (48–89 per cent) and 'Automated cockpits require more cross-checking of crew member actions' (52–90 per cent). One item showed the reverse pattern: 50 per cent *or less* of pilots in every national group agreed with the item 'There are modes and features of the FMC that I do not fully understand' (22–51 per cent). In other words, the majority of pilots in our database, regardless of national background, were more inclined to say they knew how to utilize the automation effectively, and they knew how to include the other pilot in automation decisions and activities.

These results coincide with earlier results that suggest that pilots are confident of their ability to perform their duties, and that the professional pilot culture acknowledges the importance of communication in the cockpit. But as the data on human performance under stress suggest, pilots may sometimes be too confident in their abilities. Bernard Ziegler, an Airbus Industrie Senior Vice President of Engineering, is quoted as saying that flight management computers may offer too many possibilities and be too complex, with the result that many pilots rely on only 20 per cent of the software features (Hughes, 1995). In a simulation study with pilots who flew automated aircraft, Sarter and Woods (1992; 1994) found that many pilots held incorrect or incomplete notions concerning the FMC and its activities. Laboratory and simulator experiments have also demonstrated that automation use can lead to excessive trust and decreased vigilance (Parasuraman *et al.*, 1993; Wickens, 1992), especially when the automation is very reliable and is used for extended periods (Hilburn *et al.*, 1993). Several dramatic incidents involving pilot passivity when faced with automation failure highlight this concern (for reviews, see Hansman *et al.*, 1995). If these normative data are correct, it is highly unlikely that a majority of pilots really do understand all the modes and features of the FMC. The pilots' responses then are

16 Despite this attitudinal agreement, our line audit data (based on jumpseat observations) indicate that this safeguard is frequently omitted, at least amongst US pilots.

consistent with their sometimes inflated confidence in their personal efficacy, especially under stressful conditions.

The items which showed the least consensus across nations were the automation preference items, 'I look forward to more automation – the more the better' (0–74 per cent) and 'I prefer flying automated aircraft' (36–100 per cent). (Recall that these analyses included only those pilots who flew automated aircraft.) Pilots in some national groups were considerably less enthusiastic about automation than others, saying 'enough already' to the level of automation (for example, no pilots in the Swiss sample said they were looking forward to more automation), while others seemed quite receptive to the idea of more automation (for example, 95 per cent of the Mexican pilots said they preferred flying automated aircraft, and three-quarters of them said they were looking forward to more automation).

When the endorsement levels for the items were correlated at the national level (15 items times 18 nations, automated aircraft pilots) a clear picture emerged. National groups who said they preferred flying automated aircraft also said they were looking forward to more automation ($r = +.75$), they believed they should always use the automation tools provided ($r = +.74$), and that they should avoid disengaging the automation ($r = +.69$). They also believed that they could rapidly access the FMC in abnormal conditions ($r = +.80$), they were not concerned about losing manual flying skills ($r = -.83$) and they disagreed that there were modes and features of the FMC that they did not fully understand ($r = -.65$). In other words, a preference for automation is accompanied by (over-) confidence in one's ability to use the automation and (over-) reliance on automation; conversely, wariness about automation is accompanied by concern for flying skills, a willingness to disengage the automation and less reliance, even underreliance, on the systems. Box 3.5 relates a chilling story of overreliance on automation, compounded by national differences, in the maritime environment.

Box 3.5   Seduced by automation: the grounding of the *Royal Majesty*

The grounding of the cruise vessel *Royal Majesty* provides a compelling illustration of the effect of overreliance on automated systems. The 'electronic crew member' in this case was disabled and the failure to check his or her 'health' during a voyage from Bermuda to Boston had disastrous consequences. This description is drawn from the National Transportation Safety Board's investigation of the accident (NTSB, 1997).

The *Royal Majesty* was a modern, highly automated vessel capable of carrying 2000 vacationers. It was equipped with what is called an 'Integrated Bridge System' combining computers with the most modern navigational equipment including receivers for GPS (global positioning satellites) and LORAN (a radio-based navigational system), multiple radars, a Fathometer to display water depth, and an autopilot.

The maritime world is cross-cultural as a result of economic pressures. Many ships, whatever their ownership, fly so-called flags of convenience, meaning that they are registered in a country where operating costs can be minimized. Crews are selected from whatever nationality offers the best exchange rate for the company and the lowest salary costs. The *Royal Majesty* was registered in Panama, but all its officers were Greek, while the automated systems were manufactured in the United States.

On leaving the harbor at Hamilton, Bermuda, the automated navigation system was engaged with the ship to follow a pre-designated course guided by position information from the GPS satellite navigation system. However, less than an hour after leaving port, a sailor apparently tripped over the cable from the GPS antenna to the bridge, disconnecting the antenna. At this point the display on the bridge showed two warnings, *SOL*, indicating that there was not an accurate navigational solution, and *DR*, warning that the vessel was being navigated by dead reckoning (deduced course based on last available information).[17]

For the next 34 hours none of the officers on watch checked to determine that the system was functioning properly and none used another source of navigational information such as LORAN. At 10pm the *Royal Majesty* ran aground on the Rose and Crown Shoal near Nantucket Island. At the time of the grounding the ship was 17 miles off course in an area on the approach to Boston noted for dangerous shoals. At the time of the accident, visibility was 10 miles and lighted buoys were in sight that would have allowed visual navigation. What is striking is the crew's failure to utilize any of the multiple sources of information available to verify their position in dangerous waters. In addition to visual piloting and LORAN, the Fathometer would have told the crew that they were in shallow water, but it was set incorrectly. Finally, no one on the bridge was monitoring the radio as Portuguese fishermen attempted to warn the *Royal Majesty* on the distress channel after recognizing that the ship was in danger.

2045: Fishing vessel *Rachel E* (in English) 'Calling the cruise boat in the position 41 02N, 60 24W. Over.'

---

17   Like most accidents, there was not a single causal factor. The National Transportation Safety Board noted that human factors of the Integrated Bridge System and displays had not been well designed.

> 2046: Fishing vessel *Rachel E* (in English) 'Calling the cruise boat in the position 41 02N, 60 24W. Over.'
> 2046: Fishing vessel *San Marcos* (in Portuguese) 'Maybe nobody on the bridge is paying attention.'
> Fishing vessel *Rachel E* (in Portuguese) 'I don't know. He is not going the right way.' (NTSB, 1997)

A summary scale using the seven items cited above was used to highlight national differences, and rendered an effect size of .28 for differences across the 18 countries. Figure 3.7 shows that the pilots of Ireland, Scandinavia and Switzerland are the most wary of automation, and the most willing to disengage it, while the pilots of Brazil, Mexico, Korea, Cyprus, Taiwan and the Philippines show the strongest preference for and reliance on automation.

To conclude this section on automation, let us consider an issue not yet addressed – the cultural differences inherent in the manufacturers' design philosophies. Some Anglo pilots have told us that they believe the Boeing planes are built more with the pilot in mind, allowing greater pilot discretion and interaction with the systems. Airbus planes, they say, are built to almost fly themselves with minimum 'interference' from the pilots. Consider where these two planes are designed. Boeing is built in the USA, the most individualistic country in the world. Individual freedom and action are sacred, hence the planes are built to give at least the semblance of individual pilot control. At the same time, engineers in the American culture are caricatured as being rather dull and inflexible (as in the Dilbert© cartoons). In France, engineering schools are considered the most elite schools, producing the most elite professionals. The French word for engineer is closer to the English word 'ingenious', meaning 'cleverness or originality in invention or construction'. From this perspective of engineering as elegant function, the Airbus plane is designed to function as perfectly in its role as possible, with minimal influence from outside sources. If we try to imagine the differences in design philosophy, we can say Airbus conceptualizes the plane at the top of the design hierarchy with pilots subordinate, while Boeing conceptualizes the pilot on a more interactive footing with the plane.

Despite these differences, Boeing, Airbus, and all other Western manufacturers share a fundamental design concept. They all favor the side-by-side egalitarian seating of captain and co-pilot, and the co-sharing of controls. This configuration has generally gone unquestioned because it is culturally congruent with low power distance individualistic values. Such a balance of power in the cockpit is not the optimal arrangement for other cultures.

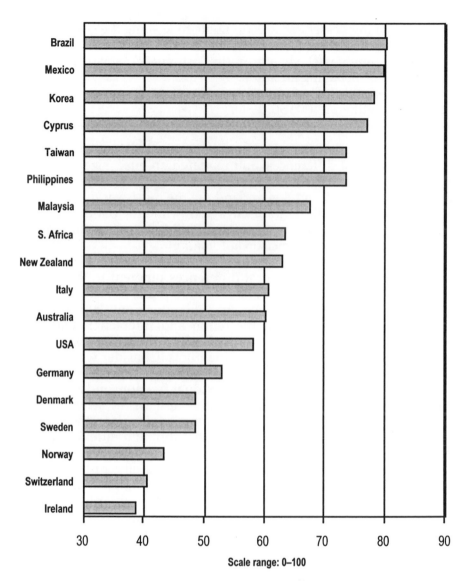

Figure 3.7   Automation: preference and reliance

Looking for Patterns: Meaningful Cultural Differences or Coincidence?

Using the FMAQ to cast a wide data net, we have been able to detect both the similarities and meaningful differences amongst pilots from different countries. Strongest similarities were seen in areas of communication and consultation, the desire for security of employment and good working relationships, and attitudes regarding stress management (unrealistic for self, slightly better for others). Strongest differences were observed with regard to command roles, preference for and reliance on automation, the desire for personal independence from the company, and the degree of flexibility and autonomy preferred in the job. Cluster analysis, a purely empirical approach to the data, consistently aligned the pilot groups into recognizable cultural clusters. This result, in and of itself, validates national culture as a meaningful influence upon pilots' attitudes and values. But can we go further with our analyses? To better understand the roots of some of these differences, we returned to Hofstede's work and tested the relationships between his dimensions of national culture and the attitudes and values of commercial pilots flying in the 1990s.

Box 3.6   Culture in the cockpit: do Hofstede's dimensions replicate?

Power distance index
Hofstede's power distance (PD) index is based upon three items (percentage who choose consultative leadership as their ideal leadership style, percentage who choose autocratic or directive leadership as the typical leadership style, and mean response to 'how often subordinates are afraid to express disagreement'). The formula provided by Hofstede was applied to the aggregated pilot scores.

For the 22 countries in the data set, the correlation between the PD scores for Hofstede's study and the PD scores calculated for the pilots was +.77. With two small exceptions (Malaysia and South Africa both lower by five points), all pilot groups had higher PD scores than Hofstede's original country scores, primarily because the percentage of respondents reporting autocratic or directive leadership as typical was significantly higher in the pilot groups (t = 9.9, df = 21, $p<.001$; average difference between Hofstede and pilot scores = 23 per cent). Pilots in every country perceived that they work for a more autocratic or directive leadership (indicative of high power distance) than other occupational groups reported in Hofstede's earlier study. At the same time, the percentage preferring a consultative leadership (indicative of low power distance) was also significantly higher in the pilot groups (t = 3.1, df = 21, $p<.01$; average difference = 7 per cent).

Individualism–collectivism index
Hofstede's IDV index is based upon four work goal items (important to live in an area desirable to self and family, to have sufficient

time left for personal or family life, to work with people who cooperate and to have good physical working conditions). The last item was omitted from the FMAQ because it was considered functionally inequivalent across the two surveys (the physical cockpit environment is standard across aircraft and airlines, therefore physical working conditions are invariant). Hofstede's formula was adopted here, with an approximation made for the missing item.[18]

Hofstede's original country scores were correlated +.69 with the index based on raw scores (see Table B.4, Appendix B, for these and the other index scores for Hofstede's original sample and the pilots' scores) and +.76 with the index based on within-subject standardized scores (used to counter cultural response bias). Using the index which was calculated with the raw scores, the range of scores was 44 (114–58; s.d. = 12.9). Hofstede's country scores by comparison have a range of 74 (17–91, s.d. = 25.0) and the highest score is still lower than the lowest score observed in the pilots' data. The elevated scores and restriction of range for the pilot-derived IDV scores suggest that pilot scores for individualism are elevated and more convergent, relative to Hofstede's original country scores. These results support the modernization hypothesis that countries are moving toward greater individualism, at least for pilots.

Uncertainty avoidance index
Hofstede's formula for the UA index is based upon three items (how often do you feel nervous or tense at work?; the organization's rules should not be broken, even when it is in the company's best interests; and the percentage who say they plan to work for the company for five years or less). The third item was omitted from the FMAQ for not having functional equivalence – the volatility of the aviation industry and the financial disincentives for changing employers make security of employment paramount to most pilots. The UA index was calculated with two approximations made for the missing item. In one composite, every country was given a constant (the average percentage reported in Hofstede's 40-country study). A second approximation took the actual percentage figure reported in Hofstede's data for each of the 22

18   The missing item (good physical conditions) was intended to tap the Collectivist end of the dimension and it was noted that Hofstede's scores for the missing item were on average +.69 of the scores for the other Collectivist item in the index formula across all 40 countries in *Culture's Consequences*. This information was incorporated into the formula for the pilots to allow some variance in the approximated item, the variance determined both by the individual country and the other collectivist item in the formula.

countries. Clearly this number, taken as it is from Hofstede's original calculations and inserted directly into the formula, should
greatly enhance the possibility of a favorable replication.

Hofstede's country scores for UA were correlated +.23 with the
composites which substituted a constant and +.45 with the composites which used precise substitution. There were no significant
differences between the pilots' country scores and Hofstede's country scores for the item 'organization's rules should not be broken',
however, there was a significant difference for the other item,
'how often do you feel nervous or tense at work?' ($t = 9.4$, $df = 21$,
$p<.001$). With one minor exception, all pilot groups said they were
less nervous or tense at work than their IBM counterparts across
seven occupations, which means that either the IBM corporation
of the 1960s and 1970s was a high-stress, life-threatening work
environment for manual laborers, clerks, technicians and managers,
or pilots appear incredibly cavalier about the stress involved in the
commercial aviation environment. (Could this be another reflection of the professional pilot culture?)

Masculinity–femininity index
As with the IDV index, Hofstede's MAS index is based upon four
work goal items: important to work with people who cooperate
with others (FEM), to have security of employment (FEM), to have
opportunity for high earnings (MAS) and opportunity for advancement to higher jobs (MAS). Two item composites were calculated.
The first was based on Hofstede's formula for raw scores, and
correlated +.17 with the country scores from Hofstede's study; the
second was based on the within-subject standardization procedure and correlated +.19 with the country scores from Hofstede's
study.

The poor correlation between Hofstede's data and the pilots'
scores can be traced to a reversal of preferences between the two
data sets. For example, in Hofstede's data, the 'feminine' item
regarding security of employment was ranked the least important
of the four items in 14 of the 22 countries (and second to least
important in five other countries). By comparison, security of employment was given the highest ranking by the pilots in 17 countries
(and second most important in the other five countries). Conversely, the 'masculine' item regarding opportunity for high
earnings was ranked first or second most important in 14 of the 22
countries in Hofstede's data, but was ranked least important by 16
of the 22 pilot groups (and second to least important by another
five groups). This reversal of preferences in the pilot groups (high
scores for the feminine items, low scores for the masculine items)
produced lower MAS scores for all but one country (pilots' coun-

try-level scores were an average 37 points *lower* than in Hofstede's sample) and accounts for the poor replication.

This failure to directly replicate this index highlights the importance of occupational context. The pilot profession is globally a financially rewarding profession, and the promotional structure is unambiguously presented (from junior officer to captain, to check captain/airman (senior pilot designated to evaluate performance of pilots) or management). Therefore pilots have already self-selected into a profession which offers high earnings and opportunity for advancement (and it is easier to say such things are relatively unimportant when one already has them). At the same time, security of employment is paramount to pilots because a change in employer will often produce a drop in seniority (that is, income) and bidding privileges (the monthly flight schedules are determined by pilots' preferences, with senior pilots receiving first option). Finally, working with cooperative others (in the cockpit, Air Traffic Control and on the ground) is a necessary prerequisite to safe flight. These occupational attributes restricted the range of possible scores among the pilots and doubtless contributed to the failed replication of Hofstede's MAS index. It is possible that combining the pilots' scores with those of flight attendants and ground and gate personnel might render a more balanced national average closer to Hofstede's scores.

We conducted two sets of analyses. The first was a direct replication of Hofstede's methodology. Hofstede's items were applied as prescribed by his formulae (Hofstede, 1982) and the resultant pilot-derived country-level scores were correlated with Hofstede's original country scores for each dimension. To summarize the direct replication, the best correlations between Hofstede's index scores and the pilot-derived scores were as follows: power distance (+.77), individualism–collectivism (+.76), uncertainty avoidance (+.45) and masculinity–femininity (+.19). That is, imposing empirical constraints of item and scalar equivalence on data from another time and profession (commercial pilots 25 years later), the dimensions of individualism–collectivism and power distance could be successfully replicated in the pilots' domain, the UA index was weaker but still present, and the MAS index failed to replicate, primarily because of differences in occupational context. See Box 3.6 for a description of the items and results for the direct replication.

In the second, more conceptual analysis, we removed the constraint of item equivalence across time and populations and correlated the country-level composites and scale scores derived from our analyses with Hofstede's country scores on his four dimensions to discern the level of conceptual overlap between the two studies. We wanted to see if the pilots' work-related attitudes and values could be related to underlying dimensions of national culture, as identified by Hofstede. Table 3.6 highlights the correlations, many of which are significant and may require some explanation.

Table 3.6   Country-level correlations between Hofstede's data and the pilot data

Pilot composites	Hofstede's data			
	IDV	PD	UA	MAS
Independence	.92**	−.81**	−.56**	−.14
Command	−.86**	.79**	.51*	.12
Like/prefer Automation	−.74**	.74**	.63**	.22
Rules & Order	−.88**	.67**	.47*	−.10
My stress	.60**	−.71**	−.23	−.12
Relations	−.24	.10	.11	.07
Rewards	.32	−.04	−.23	.15
Others' stress	.07	−.09	−.30	−.27

Note: Hofstede's dimensions were correlated in this sample of 22 countries as follows: IDV and PD, $r = -.78$; IDV and UA, $r = -.48$; IDV and MAS, $r = +.02$; PD and UA, $r = +.29$; PD and MAS, $r = +.21$; UA and MAS, $r = +.38$.
** $p < .01$; * $p < .05$.

Of the eight composite scores derived from the work values and attitudes items, five were significantly correlated with Hofstede's IDV and PD index scores. In addition, four of those same composites were also correlated with the UA index, but not as strongly. No composites (or single items) were correlated with the MAS index, lending support to the notion that this dimension may not be relevant in the pilot environment.

Although it is tempting to discuss the data sequentially by each dimension, talking in turn about individualism–collectivism, power distance and uncertainty avoidance, the reality and the true richness of the data lie in their multicollinearity. The strong intercorrelations amongst and between the dimensions and the scales present a richer, more complex picture than previously suggested by a reading of Hofstede and other cross-cultural psychologists who focused exclusively on individualism–collectivism (Kim *et al.*, 1994; Markus & Kitayama, 1991).

In our data, pilots from countries with high individualism (the Anglos, Scandinavians and Germanics) were more likely to endorse sufficient time for personal and family life, and living in a desirable area – both indicative of personal independence from the organization. But, more interesting, these pilots were also more likely to eschew hierarchical command styles, they showed less preference for and reliance on automation, they were more likely to reject rules and procedures seen as inflexible and they were more likely to have (slightly) more realistic attitudes toward managing their own stress. Pilots from the high power distance countries endorsed the more hierarchical command style, as expected, but they also showed a stronger preference for automation and for rules and procedures. Finally, high uncertainty avoidance was associated with a preference for rules and procedures, as expected, but it was more notably associated with a preference for and reliance on automation and more hierarchy in command.

These complex relationships highlight the interrelatedness of the dimensions and their manifestation in the aviation environment. The preference for hierarchical command may reflect a willingness and expectation to rely on superiors, but such behavior also reflects a strategy for avoiding uncertainty in that clearly delineated command roles leave no doubt as to who is expected to carry out which duties in an unexpected situation. Similarly, clearly set rules and procedures reduce uncertainty, but they also preserve and protect the command hierarchy by ensuring that task expectations are set and that no one transgresses their set roles. Box 3.7 relates these ideas to the crash of Avianca Flight 052.

Box 3.7   Avianca flight 052: national culture in the aviation system

On 25 January 1990, an Avianca flight ran out of fuel and crashed while attempting a second approach to New York's John F. Kennedy Airport (Helmreich, 1994; National Transportation Safety Board, 1991). The Boeing 707 departed from Medellin, Colombia, and encountered poor weather during its transit up the US coast. The weather at New York was also marginal at best. The flight was placed in holding patterns by air traffic control three times for a total of 1 hour and 17 minutes.

While in the third holding pattern, the flight crew informed air traffic control (ATC) that they could not hold longer than five more minutes and lacked fuel to reach their scheduled alternate airport, Boston. However, the crew did not declare an emergency.[19]

---

19   By declaring an emergency, a flight receives expedited handling. In the absence of the formal declaration, ATC was under no obligation to provide any special handling for the flight.

A landing at New York was attempted, but the runway was not seen and the approach was aborted. The crew accepted a lengthy flight path before attempting a second landing and ran out of fuel and crashed about 16 miles from the airport. The pilots and a number of passengers were killed in the accident.

Several behaviors of the crew that contributed to the accident may be explicable in terms of national culture. Some time before the crash, the flight engineer was aware of the dangerously low fuel.[20] Why did the crew persevere in attempting to reach New York, when there were many airports along the route where they could have landed uneventfully? Why were the junior crew members not more forthcoming in communicating the emergency? Why wasn't the crew more assertive in advocating that the captain either declare an emergency and receive instant clearance to land or divert to another airport with acceptable weather? After failing in the first attempt to land, the crew accepted a vector that took the flight more than 15 miles away from the airport. Why didn't the flight crew demand a clearance for an immediate second approach?

Both uncertainty avoidance (UA) and power distance (PD) appear to be relevant to the situation. Those high in UA are likely to be more committed to a course of action once chosen and less flexible in considering other alternatives. The captain of Avianca 052 appears to have been committed to reaching New York. The issue of fuel was not considered even during the extended holding periods, nor was the possibility of diverting.[21]

The effects of PD are more striking. The flight engineer, although clearly aware of the crisis situation, only communicated the urgency of the situation non-verbally to the steward. Although the Ground Proximity Warning System (GPWS) sounded 15 times during the approach (indicating that the flight was below the glidepath for the approach), none of the junior crew members expressed concerns. More striking was the behavior of the flight engineer when the captain executed the missed approach. Instead of communicating directly the criticality of the situation, he attempted to show the gravity of the situation indirectly by reading from the aircraft operating manual the instructions for executing a missed approach with minimal fuel on board.

---

20 At one point, the steward came to the cockpit to inquire about the status of the flight. The flight engineer (sitting behind the captain) pointed to the empty fuel gauge and made the gesture of cutting the throat to indicate the perilous situation.

21 By the time the flight first communicated concern over their fuel (but without declaring an emergency), their fuel was insufficient to reach their scheduled alternate, Boston.

The air traffic controllers had no reason to believe that the flight was *in extremis* since the crew had not declared an emergency. After the missed approach, the controller said, 'I'm gunna bring you about 15 miles Northeast and then turn you back onto the approach. Is that fine with you and your fuel?' The first officer replied, without asking the captain for confirmation, 'I guess so. Thank you very much.' When the captain asked what ATC had said, the first officer only replied, 'The guy is angry.' The most parsimonious explanation for the behavior of Avianca 052 with ATC is again in terms of PD. Similar to the dynamics within the cockpit, the relation between the flight and ATC was one of subordinate to superior. The crew would not question the actions and decisions of the controller.

In retrospect, this accident seems to illustrate how cultural characteristics within and between cultures can combine with tragic results.

The preference for and reliance on automation can also be interpreted in one of two ways. Either automation is perceived as a relatively senior, expert crew member which was bought and endorsed by airline management, and which should therefore be followed without question (the relationship between automation and power distance) or the automation's 'expertness' acts as a form of certainty, in that it can make many sophisticated decisions and reduce uncertainty in the flight environment (the relationship between automation and uncertainty avoidance). On the flip side of this argument, the reluctance to rely on automation can be interpreted in one of three ways. The automation can be seen as having too much authority, which would be anathema to low power distance pilots, it can be seen as reducing one's flexibility and autonomy in flight, which would irritate individualistic pilots, or it can be seen as overly deterministic and rigid, an annoyance to low UA pilots. In other words, the same overt behaviors may derive from different underlying rationales. We do not wish to imply that there are no differences between the dimensions as conceptualized by Hofstede, but rather to highlight that the same outcome can originate from different cultural orientations.

On Closer Investigation: What we Miss with large-scale Studies

The results from the replication study and the individual-level analyses were empirically quite impressive. Using a distinctly different population from a distinctly different time period, correlations as high as .92 were observed with Hofstede's dimensions of national culture, and yet the results were strangely unsatisfying. Knowing the ranks of the countries on different scales and indexes created a general expectation for behavior, but a valid criticism of these large-scale, cross-cultural studies is that interesting intra- and intercultural effects are overlooked in favor of the broad brushstroke differences across all countries. For example, we have been talking of the Anglo and Scandinavian countries as having the lowest power distance scores, and the Philippines, Brazil, Morocco and Taiwan as having the highest scores. Does this mean that pilots from the Philippines, Brazil, Morocco and Taiwan all endorse the same command style? The answer to that question can be found upon closer investigation. Indeed, by studying the results of the inter- and intracultural analyses more closely,[22] the command styles endorsed by the pilots of the Philippines, Brazil and Taiwan could be distinguished by the relative priorities given to rules (Taiwan), rank (Brazil) and relationships (Philippines).

Taiwan had the highest score on the Rules & Order scale, and was notable for its relatively high ranking of strict time limits and a preference for finding the one correct answer or solution. The Taiwanese pilots also had the highest mean scores for the rules items (written procedures are needed for all in-flight situations; the organization's rules should not be broken) further developing their profile as the country with the most pronounced preference for precision and the one, exact way.[23] Taiwan is a country in transition. Unlike the isolationist countries of Japan and Korea, Taiwan has aggressively embraced Western modernism, disrupting some traditional patterns in the process. Working with this airline, we learned that the younger, better educated officers were more computer-literate and had better English skills than the pilots who came from the military. As a result, these officers often viewed the older, military-trained captains as 'dinosaurs', yet they still said they would not challenge these captains, because they did not want them to lose face. The junior officers who had been trained overseas rather than in the military had attitudes toward command which were more similar to those of the expatriate captains that the company had begun to employ, rather than to those of their own Taiwanese captains. These first officers even said they preferred to fly with the expats rather than their own

22 As part of our agreement with every airline, we prepared a full report on their pilots' attitudes. These intracultural explorations often alert us to idiosyncrasies which large-scale investigations overlook.
23 We experienced this phenomenon first hand, on a Taiwanese aircraft. The service in Business Class was extremely elaborate, involving many, many procedures, but all highly routinized and inflexibly delivered, to the point of annoyance rather than pleasure, at least to us Anglos.

nationality because the expats gave them more freedom to do their job. It may be that, in this rapidly expanding, rapidly changing country, rules and procedures provide a reassuring continuity that a culture in transition can no longer provide. If the procedures are clearly set and followed, then no one's face need be threatened.

Although their individual and country-level scores were similarly distinct from the Anglos and Scandinavians, the Brazilian pilots present quite a different profile from the pilots of Taiwan. Not only did the Brazilian pilots rank the opportunity for advancement to higher level jobs as their most important work value (the Taiwanese pilots ranked advancement second to last), they also had the highest mean scores for the items 'Senior staff deserve extra benefits and privileges' and 'Junior crew shouldn't question the Captain's or senior crew members' decisions.' A logically consistent profile emerges for these pilots: everyone seeks advancement to higher level jobs, because everyone accepts that seniors deserve extra benefits and privilege. Conversely, junior rank has no privileges, and therefore little voice.

The Filipino pilots present yet another profile of command. One of the earliest conceptual refinements to the concept of individualism–collectivism was the recognition that collectivists' in-group behavior differed from their out-of-group behavior (Bond & Hwang, 1986; Hui & Triandis, 1986), but it was never clear from the literature whether the cockpit would elicit in-group or out-of-group behavior. This question has been answered by the Filipino pilots. They endorse a more benign, hierarchical command, one which is characterized by paternal captains encouraging crew member questions and subordinates being less afraid to disagree. The Filipino pilots bring their in-group behavior into the cockpit and the organization: the Filipinos have the highest mean score for the item 'Working here is like being part of a large family', which suggests that the company may well represent the in-group for many Filipino pilots.

These thumbnail descriptions highlight the true uniqueness of national cultures and the motivations underlying behaviors which may appear similar to an outsider. Only by looking at each culture in turn, and comparing and contrasting it with other cultures, can we really appreciate the uniqueness of that culture. (The same can be said for the Anglo cultures – there are differences between American, English, and Australian pilots which broad analyses will not uncover.) Chapter 6 will address the need to understand the local context in some depth (including national and organizational influences) before effective culture-sensitive interventions can be developed.

Future Directions for the FMAQ

Work with the FMAQ and national culture is a continuous process, and we continue to collect data from new countries. We have expanded our research to include multinational airlines because they provide a fascinating context for understanding the interplay and potential conflicts between national cultures (Chapter 7 is dedicated to this topic). The FMAQ was modified in 1996 and the skewed items were dropped. In addition, the new FMAQ now includes many organizational items. The paradigm in aviation safety is shifting from overly simplistic, blame-oriented, diagnoses of pilot error to more comprehensive analyses of the system, its safeguards and its failures (See Chapter 5; also Helmreich, 1994; Johnston, 1996; Paries, 1996; Reason, 1990). The FMAQ has been modified to reflect this changing paradigm. Variants of the FMAQ are also being developed for use with other professionals, both within and outside aviation. Our aim is to test the generality of our aviation findings with professionals in other high-stress, high-accountability, team-oriented environments – one such group being the astronauts who will be working together in the multinational space station.

Conclusions

At some point empirical researchers have to forgo the security of simply reporting their results and actually reflect on their meaning. To that end, we would like to finish this chapter by integrating and interpreting the data with some of our own speculations and 'hunches'. We openly acknowledge our Anglo bias, but that is the inescapable nature of national culture. As best we can, we will endeavor to be as balanced as our world views will permit.

National culture is a product of heritage. Religion, history, language, climate, population density, availability of raw materials and resources, political movements and wealth all play a role in the development of unique national characteristics. This confluence of influences has produced some intriguing and defining differences across the globe, to which any world traveler can attest. While Anglo pilots may cluster together in these data, this is certainly not meant to imply that all Anglo pilots are alike or even that all pilots of one culture are alike. As members of our own culture, we can always discern the more subtle differences amongst ourselves. An accent can reveal the town or geographic region, and clothing styles can alert the observer to the social and economic background of other members. These subtleties are not so apparent to the outsider, yet it is often the outsider who can see the broad similarities which we cannot. Similarly, in the analyses for this chapter, the subtleties of within-culture differences have been over-looked in favor of the broad brushstroke differences. The data have been used to derive empirically 'national stereotypes' which can give broad guidance on global differences in pilot attitudes. In Chapter 4, we will begin to look more closely at differences within national culture by focusing on organizational cultures. For now we will conclude by discussing what we have learned so far.

National differences were most notably observed in the areas of command, the endorsement of rules and procedures, and attitudes toward automation. A conceptual replication of Hofstede's work indicated that, within the pilot data, the dimensions of individualism (IDV), power distance (PD) and uncertainty avoidance (UA) were significantly intercorrelated, suggesting that the same behavior could be the result of one, or an interaction of more than one, dimension.

At the broadest level of national differences, pilots can be distinguished by their expectations and preferences for autonomy and flexibility versus dependence and order. The first is reflected in the egalitarianism of low PD, the independence of high IDV and the flexibility of low UA, while the latter is reflected in the set order of high PD cockpits and the strong adherence to rules in high UA cockpits. To balance this thinking, consider that pilots from high PD and UA countries are more likely to follow orders and adhere to standard operating procedures, because they are more likely to understand their role in the system and defer to those with greater seniority or authority. Pilots from individualistic countries will try to express their independence and 'I'-ness with greater autonomy, greater flexibility and greater discretionary use of company procedures.

The point that we wish to stress here is that every national culture has its strengths and weaknesses with regard to optimal flight management. The extreme of either viewpoint would be detrimental. Being too rigid to adapt to contingencies is as ineffectual as being too undisciplined to follow Standard Operating Procedures (SOPs), just as a too tightly controlled cockpit can be as dangerous as a too loosely controlled cockpit. By understanding the cultural perspectives of other countries, pilots can be introduced to other ways of managing their cockpits and a 'best practices' approach can be developed. In the ideal cockpit, a pilot will follow SOPs yet retain the expertise to know when deviation from those SOPs might be necessary and will know when to follow orders and when to question them.

We cannot leave this chapter without clarifying a misperception. Some authors have correlated national culture with accident rates and concluded that pilots in certain countries are safer than others. We take umbrage with the simplicity of this statement. The resources allocated to the aviation infrastructure vary widely around the globe.

While pilots in Europe enjoy some of the most sophisticated Air Traffic Control support, pilots in parts of Africa and Asia are faced with little or no support; indeed, the runways may not even be lit for lack of electricity or stolen equipment. Accident rates are a function of the entire aviation environment, including government regulation and oversight, and the allocation of resources for infrastructure and support, not just pilot proficiency.

To imply that a pilot's national culture propels him or her toward greater or lesser safety is implausible, simplistic and ethnocentric. An Australian pilot once said to us, 'We have no accidents, so why don't they all just fly like us?' When you consider that the entire population of Australia is less than 20 million and could reside in Manila or Mexico City, yet Australia is the size of the continental USA, that Australia has some very benign weather, and that Australia is a wealthy, industrialized country with a strong regulatory and aviation infrastructure, then you have to concede that factors other than the admittedly very fine efforts of the pilots have contributed to Australia's outstanding safety record.

Here is a simple thought with which to end the chapter. We believe that every national culture values the safety of its members and that every airline is dedicated to improving the safety of its operations, to the extent that existing resources will permit. To that end, training and other interventions will be more successful if the underlying values of the national culture are honored and incorporated, rather than denigrated or ignored. We will return to culture-sensitive training in Chapter 6.

4 Organizational Culture

We did line audits at both airlines and organized a day for a full debriefing with observers and Management at each airline. The difference between the two airlines was extraordinary. At airline X, they asked us if we had observed anything that posed an immediate safety threat. Four observers raised their hands and commented on the same problem: not being able to get weather for the next destination in some foreign cities. The Vice President of Flight Operations said, 'That should be fixed,' left the room, dealt with it immediately and returned to the meeting. The meeting continued with discussions of who would be responsible for addressing the problems that were noted. The Management group were sincere and swift in their efforts to redress the problems raised by the audit.

At airline Y, many of the airline observers worked on the project on their own time because they believed their airline was in trouble and were committed to improving its operational safety and efficiency. At the debriefing, several safety concerns were raised by the observers, to which the senior managers in attendance said, 'This is nothing we haven't heard before.' When issues of standardization were raised, the Management group continued their defensive and hostile stance by focusing on pilot uniforms as an example of poor standardization. The meeting went downhill from there. I tell you, I know which airline I'd rather work for. (Expert observer from the Aerospace Crew Research Project, and veteran of six line audits)

We begin this chapter with a question for our readers. Do you think that *your* perceptions of your employer or organization affect *your* level of commitment and job performance? Some of you may agree completely. Some may hesitate, remembering an instance where annoyance with the company or Management translated into less than 100 per cent performance, and others may argue that, regardless of the environment, professionalism should, and does, transcend organizational difficulties. While the latter is the most reassuring answer from a safety perspective, is it true? In many ways this question echoes the issues raised in Chapter 3, namely to what extent are pilots (and other high-risk, high-consequence professionals) influenced by factors other than the norms and standards of their professional culture? In this chapter we explore the influence of organizational culture on performance.

We noted in Chapter 2 that a strong majority of pilots and medical professionals like their jobs, but does this necessarily imply that they also like their organizations? Apparently not, for, among our pilot data, the percentage that agreed they were proud to work for their organization ranged from as little as 26 per cent in one US regional airline to an overwhelming 97 per cent in a major US carrier (see Figure 4.1). Does pride in the company, or the lack thereof, affect one's performance? This and other questions prompted our research into organizational culture.

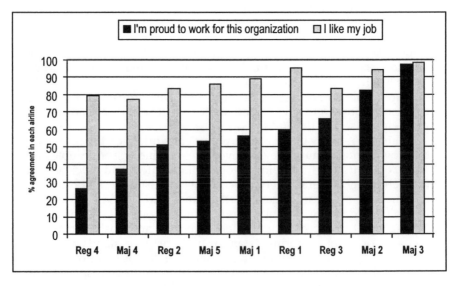

Figure 4.1   Liking the job and liking the company in nine US airlines

In this chapter we describe our approach to the study of organizational culture as a hybrid of the managerial, anthropological and psychological approaches. We compare two US airlines on various parameters to highlight the best and the worst organizational cultures that we have seen in nine US-based airlines. We also discuss organizational subcultures and list some strategies for strengthening an organization's culture.

The Study of Organizational Culture

Defining Organizational Culture

Definitions of organizational culture tend to vary according to the academic discipline from which they originated (Trice & Beyer, 1993). Business schools tend to define organizational culture as a phenomenon which can be managed and manipulated (Deal & Kennedy, 1982; Peters & Waterman, 1982). Sociologists and anthropologists adopt a more ethnographic approach stressing that each organization is a unique, historically derived, subjective phenomenon beyond simple manipulation (Frost *et al.*, 1991; Pettigrew, 1979; Smircich, 1982) and organizational psychologists with an empirical background seek to reduce the phenomenon to its subcomponents (Cooke & Rousseau, 1988; Xenikou & Furnham, 1996). Box 4.1 provides a simple analogy between tribes and organizations to illustrate the anthropological approach.

Box 4.1   Tribes and organizations

Borrowing from anthropology, we can say that organizational members are like members of a tribe. The elders of the tribe are entrusted to lead wisely, to set the rules for the rest of the tribe to follow, and to set an example that others can respect (senior management). Members of the tribe may be easily identifiable by their unique apparel (uniforms), their dialect (publications, press releases and local in-house jargon), their distinctive weapons and tools (the company's products and technology) and their housing arrangements (the style of the company's headquarters, and its distance from other offices). There are rituals which celebrate initiation into the tribe and rites of passage which establish one's place in the tribe (recruitment, promotion, 'an office with a view'). Finally, revered members are entrusted to remember and recount the myths and legends of the tribe's origin, the early hardships, the battles, the heroes and the victories which have shaped the tribe's history and identity. Tribes which survive have a strong sense of their culture – of who they were and who they have become.

We define organizational culture as the values, beliefs, assumptions, rituals, symbols and behaviors that define a group, especially in relation to other groups or organizations. There are two important and distinct layers of culture. The surface structure, or visible, outer layer of culture consists of observable behaviors and recognizable physical manifestations such as members' uniforms,[1] symbols and logos, organizational routines and rituals, and printed documents. The deep structure, or inner layer of culture, consists of the values (put simply, what is important to us and what is not), the beliefs and the often subconscious assumptions which underlie the surface structure and provide the logic which guides the members' behaviors. It is necessary to 'read' and understand both layers if we are to influence the culture (Schein, 1992; 1996). Because we are studying performance in high-risk, high-technology industries, we chose to confine our research to those elements of organizational culture which we believed would affect performance and safety. From this perspective, organizational culture is viewed as an independent variable,[2] and individual performance remains the dependent variable of interest.

In common with the business school approach, we agree that one reason to study organizational culture is to find a way to manage it. Organizational culture is locally determined and more amenable to influence than national culture, which is monolithic and resistant to change. It is the organizational culture which ultimately channels the effects of national and professional cultures toward standard practices, and it is the organizational culture which shapes members' attitudes toward safety and productivity.

In common with the anthropological approach, we agree that each organizational culture is unique and socially constructed. From this standpoint, interventions that work in one organization may not be successful in another, because of complex organizational dynamics. We also acknowledge that, while it is necessary to 'unpackage' a culture into its important elements (the empirical psychological approach), we also believe that adopting a purely reductionist approach could be self-defeating (losing sight of the culture while counting the 'trees').

Cultural Strength

The cultural strength of an organization has been variously defined as coherence (Deal & Kennedy, 1982), homogeneity (Ouchi & Price, 1978), stability and intensity (Schein, 1992), congruence (Schall, 1983)

---

1   At Southwest Airlines, the flight attendants have several choices of uniform, including shorts and athletic shoes. Not only does the uniform project the company's image of fun and casual but still efficient service, it also provides the flight attendants with the most practical shoes in the case of an emergency evacuation, and it sends a message to the flight attendants that the company cares about their on-the-job comfort.
2   This is the main point of contention between business theorists and anthropologists: the latter fear that culture will be reduced to a Management tool for 'pernicious social effects' (Siehl & Martin, 1990, p.273).

and internalized control (DiTomaso, 1987). Cultural strength relates to whom and how many accept the dominant values, how strongly or intensely the values are held and how long the values have been dominant (Gordon & DiTomaso, 1992). What is interesting about this conceptualization is that it does not seem to matter what the values and beliefs are, only that everyone agrees on them. Using these definitions, several companies can have strong cultures without holding similar philosophies. For example, British Airways and American Airlines are conservative, financially stable, large and very 'navy blue' in their image, while Southwest Airlines and Virgin Atlantic are also financially successful, but smaller, with a more adventurous, people-oriented, 'colorful' image. All four airlines have strong organizational cultures and all are very successful.

Does cultural strength actually have an impact on organizational performance? Using a clever operationalization of cultural strength (the consistency, rather than the content, of employees' responses to survey items about organizational culture), two longitudinal studies have shown that a strong culture is predictive of organizational performance as measured by short-term profits and growth in assets (Denison, 1990; Gordon & DiTomaso, 1992).

Methodological Approaches

Each academic approach to organizational culture favors a different form of methodological inquiry, from the purely idiographic case study of the anthropologists to the strictly empirical analysis of quantitative psychologists. We believe that some of the best work has been conducted with a combination of the qualitative and quantitative methods (for example, Denison & Mishra, 1995; Hofstede *et al.*, 1990; Siehl & Martin, 1990) and, in this vein, we use a mixed methodology of questionnaires, observations and interviews to help us 'read' organizational practices, norms and values. The human factors attitude questionnaires for pilots and medical personnel (FMAQ, ORMAQ – Operating Room Management Attitudes Questionnaire) were expanded in 1994 to include organizationally specific items about safety practices, interactions with other employee groups (including Management and the training department), perceptions of Management communication and feedback, and some open-ended questions which prompt respondents to give their opinions about perceived weaknesses in the organization and suggestions for improvements. Many of these items were originally suggested by members of organizations who were helping us customize the survey for their particular needs. We have since developed a set of core organizational items, but always invite the organization to add any items which are relevant to their unique circumstances.

In addition to the attitude questionnaire, a behavioral observation checklist is used to systematically audit on-line behaviors in daily operations. (The derivation and form of the behavioral checklist will be discussed in greater detail in Chapter 5, and research findings based on audits at five airlines will be presented.) Members of our research group train and calibrate members of the organization in the use of the checklist, followed by a period (usually six to eight weeks) of on-line, non-jeopardy observations in order to gain an understanding of system-wide daily operations. In the interviews, participants are encouraged to voice opinions which we, the outsiders, might have otherwise overlooked.

While data from the behavioral checklists provide information about the performance norms and safety practices within the organization, the attitude questionnaires, interviews and open-ended questions probe the underlying beliefs and values. Once all the information has been collected and analyzed, a meeting of all interested parties (Management, trainers, employees, researchers) is then scheduled to discuss the findings. Once the culture is known unto itself via this multilayered analysis, interventions can be designed which utilize the organization's strengths and remediate its perceived weaknesses.

How Good can it be? How Bad can it get?

When we first started to collect data on organizational norms and practices, we had no pre-existing data for comparison purposes, and hence no way of knowing how standard or deviant the organizational attitudes were. An example that comes immediately to mind is pilots' attitudes toward Management. In our first couple of surveys, we were shocked at some of the responses regarding Management. In one airline, only 28 per cent of the pilots agreed that they trusted Senior Management. That number seemed disastrously low, but it turned out to be the highest level of endorsement for Senior Management across four US airlines in our database.[3] In one airline, where we received more than 1200 survey responses, exactly 15 pilots said they trusted Senior Management – that translates to 1.3 per cent! Even when pilots agreed that Senior Management was doing a good job, they still said they distrusted them. (In each airline, the percentage who agreed that Senior Management was doing a good job was always higher than the percentage who said they trusted Senior Management.) On the basis of these and other responses to Manage-

---

3   This particular item was not used in the Southwest Airlines survey. If it was, we are sure the percentage for that pilot group would be much higher.

ment items in our expanding database, we are now speculating as to whether a lack of respect for Management might not be another indicator of professional culture. For example, could it be that, once people reach a certain level of professional status, they resent any and all forms of (Management) imposed control?[4]

Further to this point, we acknowledge that we are viewing organizational culture through the lens of one, sometimes two, employee groups. (In our airline research, flight attendants and maintenance personnel have sometimes been involved in organizational surveys. In the medical environment, we collect data across specialties and occupations). It is very possible that other employee groups may perceive the organization and its Management quite differently. Ideally, information should be collected across several employee levels, including the managers themselves, to derive a balanced view of the company. Nonetheless, subjective perceptions rather than 'hard facts' shape an organizational culture and, by studying the perceptions of our professional groups, we gain an important understanding of how these groups perform their work in the full organizational context. We are also able to see what things these groups would like changed or upheld.

We currently have five major airlines and four regional US airlines in our organizational database. We also have some non-US airlines in this database; however, to avoid confounding national and organizational cultures, we will concentrate on the US airlines as the largest data source within one national culture. From the US database, we have selected two airlines. One exemplifies a healthy, positive environment, the other reflects some alarming organizational norms and practices. Table 4.1 summarizes some of the differences captured by the questionnaire. (Neither of these airlines conducted a line audit so we will rely on the survey data for this comparison.) It is important to remember in the ensuing discussion that both organizations are from the USA, and as such are embedded in a highly individualistic, relatively low power distance society. Perceptions of Management, the preferred level of organizational communication and feedback, and perceptions of safe practices may all be influenced by national culture. (See Box 4.2 for examples of the way in which national culture can influence organizational culture.) Organizational norms in other countries may be different from those we are about to discuss.

---

4   Of course, it could be that all airline Management is inept, but that would seem to stretch the bounds of probability a little too far.

Box 4.2 The influence of national culture upon organizational culture

It was a relatively new airline, much smaller than the major carriers, and its owner was well known for being creative with his airline's image. This airline is one of the most luxurious and profitable carriers of the region and its culture is totally geared toward passenger comfort and satisfaction. As well as offering full à la carte meal service on flights as short as one and one-half hours, the owner of this airline, as a trademark, had decreed that captains would personally greet and shake the hand of every passenger as they boarded the aircraft. I had a hard time making my point that pre-flight activities and checklist reading should not be interrupted for the sake of shaking passengers' hands. I guess I might have another opportunity to address this issue when they start receiving their wide bodies next year – that's going to be a lot of hand-shaking. (Antonio Schuck, aviation training consultant)

This story comes from Brazil, a high power distance country where, as we saw in Chapter 3, privileges and benefits are important and expected. But what impact would such a gesture have in a low power distance country such as Denmark or Ireland? It might seem foolish or pretentious – it would certainly be surprising – to have the captain greet each passenger personally and shake his or her hand.

In the USA, many organizations are advocating 'employee empowerment'. Every employee is 'granted' whatever power they need to solve a problem and satisfy a customer. This strategy, which is aimed at making every employee feel important enough to handle any situation that may arise, may be the ultimate low power distance strategy. Southwest Airlines, which actively promotes individualism and empowerment amongst its employees, has gone as far as having a 'classless aircraft'. There are no business or first class seats on Southwest aircraft, there is no meal service, and all passengers are treated the same.[5] Such an egalitarian, no-frills strategy may be totally unacceptable in a high power distance country.

Another trend in US organizations is 'downsizing' – a euphemistic term for laying off employees in order to streamline organizational priorities. This individualistic approach to Management (individuals as commodities to be disposed of when no longer 'viable') has encouraged an 'everyone for themselves' attitude amongst employees and seriously diminished organizational commitment and loyalty. Compare such an approach to that

---

5　A Southwest captain corrected us here: '*All* our passengers are first class passengers', he said.

adopted by Philippine Airlines, whose pilots we identified in Chapter 3 as valuing collective, familial relations.

Philippine Airlines was originally owned by a family of Spanish descent, but the government took it over in the 1960s. During Marcos' regime, the airline was routinely stripped of its resources. Following the People Power Revolution in the 1980s, Cory Aquino installed a new president, and then another, but the government was called in to bail out the airline on several occasions. During that time of transition and financial hardship, the PAL pilots elected to work fewer hours per month (from an industry average of 80 hours down to 30 hours or less) rather than have the company lay anyone off. The company was privatized in the 1990s and the new owner, Mr Tan, has invested a lot of his own money in the company's future. The good news is that many of the pilots are still with the company and can contribute their expertise to its new expansion. This organizational approach to financial hardship reflects the national culture of the Philippines, just as downsizing reflects an individualistic approach.

In sum, the values embedded in the national culture are likely to find expression in the organizational culture.

In Airline A, 87 per cent of pilots agreed that morale is high, compared with a demoralizing 3 per cent in Airline B.[6] Virtually all of the pilots (97 per cent) in Airline A said they were proud to work for their company, compared with only one-quarter of the pilots (26 per cent) in Airline B. How can there be such differences when both groups are essentially performing the same tasks in the same air space subject to the same regulations? We believe that these items reflect the organizational climate, the affective component of an organization's culture. Put simply, organizational climate is the sum of the members' emotional feelings and reactions to working for the company. The issue to explore more closely is the extent to which these feelings of pride or antipathy affect performance. We will return to this point after we present some more data.

Perceptions of Management varied widely between the two groups, 84 per cent of pilots in Airline A being confident that Management would never compromise safety for profit, compared with only 12 per cent in Airline B. The pilots in Airline B are extremely cynical and distrustful of Management, including Flight Operations Management, and these attitudes are having negative consequences on safety practices and norms. While the majority of

6 When we looked more closely at the 3 per cent who said morale was high, it turned out they were all new employees (less than 1.5 years with the company). Given more time, these pilots may also become disillusioned with the company.

Table 4.1   A comparison of organizational attitudes in two US airlines

Item	Percentage agreement Airline A	Percentage agreement Airline B
Organizational climate		
I like my job	98	79
I'm proud to work for this organization	97	26
Pilot morale is high	87	3
Working here is like being part of a large family	82	35
Management perceptions		
Management never compromises safety for profit	84	12
Satisfied with chief pilot availability	63	26
Management deals well with problem pilots	44	15
Flight Operations listens and cares	—[a]	17
Senior Management is doing a good job	—	3
Management supports pilots	73	—
Safety norms and practices		
I know the correct safety channels to direct queries	85	57
I'm encouraged to report unsafe conditions	–	38
My safety suggestions would be acted on	68	19
Fairness of checking	78	63
Crews I fly with adhere to Standard Op. Procedures	93	76

Note:
[a]   The two airlines did not use all the same items in their surveys, but the content areas overlapped.

pilots in both airlines agreed that they knew the proper safety channels to direct their queries (85 per cent and 57 per cent, respectively), only 19 per cent of the pilots in Airline B (compared with 68 per cent in Airline A) were confident that their safety suggestions would ever be acted upon.

There is one item in Table 4.1, the last item, which we believe is more telling than any other, because it links attitudes with important behaviors. In Airline A, 93 per cent of pilots agreed that their fellow crew members adhere to the company's Standard Operating Procedures (SOPs). In Airline B, that number is only 76 per cent. Recall the question that started this chapter: do people's perceptions of their organization and Management affect their performance? Some people argue that true professionals should not and do not allow organizational difficulties to affect their performance. But in Airline B we see a demoralized and cynical pilot group which believes that Management will compromise the crews' safety for profit, that Flight

Operations Management has no interest in their line-flying concerns and that their own suggestions for improving safety will be ignored by an uncaring Senior Management. As a result, there is greater willingness to deviate from company mandated procedures, even when those procedures are designed to maximize safety.

There are three possible psychological explanations for this phenomenon. First, the pilots may be adopting an 'if you don't care about the airline, why should we' attitude. It is difficult to maintain your own high standards when you perceive others doing less. Second, the pilots may be transferring their distrust of Management to any procedures mandated by Management, and may prefer to use their own judgment instead of following Management-set procedures. The third explanation is an 'acting out' theory which suggests that the pilots are escalating their 'bad' behaviors as a form of rebellion and a simultaneous desire to be noticed and heard.[7] One way to draw Management's attention to pilots' concerns is to make those concerns more visible.

Whatever the psychological reasoning, enough pilots in Airline B are sufficiently dissatisfied with their company to be prepared to deliberately transgress company standards, thereby increasing the likelihood of a safety threat. In a way, it is a credit to the strength of the professional culture that the number is not lower, but, in truth, the number may not be lower because pilots' personal safety, and the safety of strangers, are implicated in any pilot work activity. Pilots who are dissatisfied with Management may still fly safely, for their own survival and that of the passengers, as much as from a sense of professionalism. This is not to say that some pilots may not find other ways to express their organizational dissatisfaction, such as tardy and absentee behavior, poor cooperation with other employee groups and 'work-to-rules'.

There is another organizational feature which distinguishes Airline A from Airline B. Pilots at both airlines were asked to rate the level of teamwork and cooperation that they experience with other employee groups at their airline. As Figure 4.2 clearly shows, the pilots at Airline A consistently report much greater cooperation and teamwork with flight attendants, ground personnel and maintenance, dispatch and ramp personnel than do the pilots at Airline B.

It does not take a rocket scientist (or a psychologist) to deduce which of these two airlines has the better on-time performance record and the faster turn-time at the gate. Successful commercial aviation operations are dependent upon the coordinated activities of several employee groups, from the ticket and gate agents to ramp personnel,

---

7   This theory may make more sense to readers who have teenagers, or who remember their own teenage years.

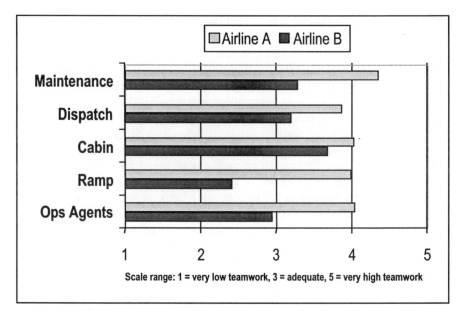

Figure 4.2 Teamwork with other employee groups

dispatchers, caterers, cabin and the cockpit. (See Box 4.3 for an example of some effective, if extreme, teamwork between the cabin and the cockpit.) Having said that, Airline A consistently wins awards for its on-time performance, Airline B does not. Airline A attracts a greater and more loyal customer base than Airline B because of the awards it wins for on-time performance and customer service (a product directly related to employee subgroup teamwork and cooperation). In other words, not only does Airline A appear to have pilots and Management who are more committed to the conduct and maintenance of safe operations, Airline A is also more efficient and more profitable in its operations.

Box 4.3 Now that's teamwork!

An Australian flight attendant was operating on a Lockheed Constellation where, in spite of smoking being illegal, he witnessed one of the First Class passengers lighting up an after-dinner cigar. Politely, he asked the gentleman to extinguish the offending item, pointing out the no-smoking sign. The passenger retorted that, as the chairman of a large American mining company, he would be damned if a flight attendant was going to tell him to stop smoking. Further polite attempts failed and despairingly the flight attendant decided to consult the captain. Once he had told his sorry tale, the captain told him to inform the passenger that, 'if he didn't put it out, he would come back there and insert it where it hurts'. The flight attendant did exactly what he was told and, fortunately, the captain did not have to execute his threat.

The passenger made a formal complaint and, when the flight attendant was called to account for himself, he explained that he was merely doing what the captain had told him to do. The captain backed him up completely and pointed out that the passenger was in breach of the Civil Aviation Regulations and threatening the safety of his aircraft. Although it was agreed that this was probably not the image of customer care they wanted to project (at least not in First Class), no one was punished and the flight attendant went on to become part of Senior Management. (Graham Braithwaite, British human factors and safety researcher working in Australia)

There is one potential weakness that we perceive at Airline A and it is by virtue of its own success. Analogous to 'group think' (Janis, 1972), a company can become blinded by its own success, and resistant to outside scrutiny or ongoing internal analyses. 'Don't mess with a winning formula' and 'If it ain't broke, don't fix it' can encourage complacency rather than vigilance. In a related vein, only 44 per cent of the pilots at Airline A agreed that 'Management deals well with problem pilots'. In such a well-knit, familial organization, it may be unpleasant or awkward to seek out and discipline deviant members. Only organizational vigilance (such as setting and enforcing standards) will ensure that Airline A remains safe and productive.

This comparison of two airlines speaks to the heart of our argument about organizational cultures in high-risk, high-technology industries. We do not wish to enter the chicken-and-egg debate of whether a happy worker is a productive worker, or a productive worker is a happy worker, but we do believe that 'an unhappy worker can be a very disruptive element'. If organizational difficulties become too great, even professionals will be tempted to perform below their true standard.

As we stated earlier, we are not interested in organizational climate or commitment per se. What we are interested in is how these phenomena can affect on-line performance and safety. These results demonstrate that the effect can be positive, as we observed in Airline A, or it can be poisonous, as we saw in Airline B. The effects of a healthy, safety-oriented, organizational culture can be observed in better defenses against potential safety threats in the system, and they can be felt economically, in terms of greater efficiency and productivity.

Organizational Subcultures: Are we Singing from the Same Song Sheet?

Up to now we have discussed organizational culture as a unitary concept, but the reality is that people bring their history and multiple cultural memberships with them to their job, hence an organization consists of many subcultures based on profession, previous work history, location, gender, age and nationality, to name a few. Working at a different base, or in a location far from the central headquarters, can encourage the development of different norms (especially if there is a common grievance or a charismatic personality to help shape those norms: see Box 4.4).

Box 4.4   Home of the weird: Pan Am in Berlin

During the Cold War period following the end of World War II, Pan Am was given exclusive rights among the Western Powers to provide commercial air service between Berlin (which was jointly ruled by the USA, France, England and the Soviet Union) and other destinations in West Germany. Pan Am established a crew base there which attracted pilots whose values and behavior were, to say the least, at variance with the nautical, clipper image of the airline. Our initial attitude survey found the Berlin pilots to be significantly different from the rest of the airline on the majority of attitudes about personal capabilities and cockpit management.

Robert Gandt (1995) in his book, *Skygods*, provides an accurate and amusing picture of life at the Berlin base in a chapter aptly titled 'Where you never have to grow up'. He describes one pilot who routinely clucked like a chicken on the air traffic radio frequencies and carried a plucked rubber chicken dangling from his flight bag. Other pilots eschewed the military white caps and blue jacket with brass buttons that formed part of the required uniform, choosing instead to wear fezzes, berets, babushkas, capes and monocles. Compliance with regulations was also highly idiosyncratic: one pilot was dismissed for letting a flight attendant fly his airplane. One pilot who commuted had two disparate lifestyles, as a teetotalling pillar of the church in Oklahoma and as a hard partying and drinking Sybarite in Berlin. It was with reason that the crew room in Berlin became known as the Cuckoo's Nest. Since the safety and performance record of these deviants was exemplary, they were allowed to go their own way.

Similarly, working with the same group of people in the same fleet or the same hangar can encourage the development of local norms over time. Sometimes these norms can be positive – local solutions to local problems – but sometimes not. For example, we have observed widely different usage of checklists, and adherence to Standard Operating Procedures across fleets from the same airline, suggesting slippage in standards across fleets. (These results will be discussed in more detail in Chapter 5.)

Perhaps the most difficult cultural challenge for any organization is unifying the values, beliefs and practices of employees from merging companies. Owing to the volatility of the aviation industry, mergers and buy-outs have become commonplace. These decisions are usually made on sound financial reasoning, but there is rarely concern for the social consequences. 'The way we do things here' is no longer the same 'here', and members from both organizations struggle to adapt (or resist) the changes. Partners in a merger are rarely equal: usually one company is larger and has more political influence (more members in Senior Management). Consequently, issues of fairness inevitably develop; for example, seniority lists are rarely merged to everyone's satisfaction. Members in the larger, dominant company also tend to pressure members from the smaller company into adopting their way of thinking and acting, and may even assume that the new employees are somehow inferior.[8] But what if the smaller company has the better ideas?

We surveyed pilots and flight attendants approximately one year after the merger of two airlines. The pilots from the smaller airline embraced healthier attitudes toward crew coordination and command than the pilots of the larger airline. Even more interesting, the responses aligned by previous airline affiliation rather than occupation. That is, the pilots in the smaller airline had attitudes that were closer to those of the flight attendants from the same airline than to those of their pilot peers in the larger airline. As we delved further, we discovered that the smaller airline had a more progressive training program which included very effective cabin–cockpit joint emergency procedures training which had strengthened the team concept within the company. Now subsumed (and usurped) by the larger training department, it has been a continual battle for those individuals who chose to remain to change the dominant training philosophies and priorities.

To summarize this section, the existence of subcultures is to be expected and need not be detrimental, as long as these cultures are united by common values and beliefs represented in the organizational culture. An integrated organizational culture can be

8   In one particularly acrimonious merger which led to cries of discrimination in training and fleet assignments, pilots from the smaller airline were characterized as inexperienced, slow-learning 'hillbillies'. This surely is the organizational equivalent of ethnocentrism.

characterized by subgroup cooperation, a strong corporate identity, a positive organizational climate and high employee morale, all of which have a positive impact on service and safety. A discordant organizational culture, on the other hand, is characterized by some or all of the following: a weak or poor corporate identity, subgroup divisiveness, high absenteeism or turnover, a negative organizational climate and poor employee morale, each of which can affect service and overall safety negatively. Figures 4.3 and 4.4 represent the differences between discordant and integrated cultures, with regard to safety, and error management (to be discussed in Chapter 5).

We end this section with a cautionary tale from Edgar Schein of the Massachusetts Institute of Technology (MIT). When talking about organizational subcultures, Schein (1996) makes a simple but useful distinction between the 'operators', the 'engineers' and the 'executives'. The 'operators' are those line personnel who make and/or deliver the products and services that fulfill the organization's basic mission. The individuals in this group are most often the target of training and other interventions designed to make them more efficient and effective. They are also the group who must negotiate the various interdependencies in the company. The 'engineers' design

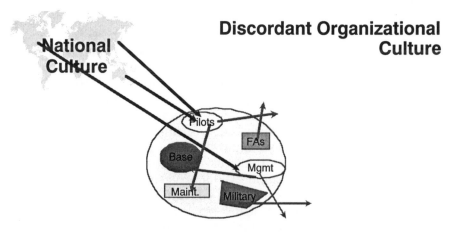

Line pilots are 'divorced' from management
Senior pilots are not good role models
'Blame and punish' approach to error
Inter-group conflict and divisiveness
Safety is uncoordinated and haphazard

Figure 4.3   Discordant organizational culture and safety

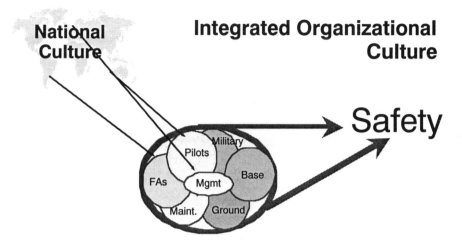

Management provides unifying leadership

Subcultures exist but cooperate

All groups strive toward same goal: **Error Management**

Figure 4.4   Integrated organizational culture and safety

and monitor the core technology and the systems of the organization. The tacit, shared, assumption of this group is that they prefer to
work with systems, machines, routine and rules, designing elegant
solutions which require little or no human involvement. The 'executives' exercise financial accountability and learn to rely on rules,
procedures and systems, most notably reward and control systems,
to ensure that financial criteria remain paramount in the organization's decision making.

When operators interact with engineers, there is invariably tension
and mistrust. The result is usually a call from the operators for more
human-centered technology, or more training to manage the new
technology. Both options require a decision by the executives, who
must base their decisions on financial returns and accountability.
Though unintentionally, the executives and engineers collude to minimize the importance of the human factor in the larger system.

This three-group analysis will immediately appeal to any trainer
who has gone to Management asking for training resources, or any
pilot who has wondered 'What robot designed this aircraft?!' Schein's
argument goes further, however, and points out that, every time we
decry the technocratic values of the engineers or the financial em-

phases of the executives, we are in effect saying, 'Forgo your cultural values and adopt ours. Our culture is right, yours is wrong.' He points out that psychologists, by nature of their discipline, are particularly biased toward the human factor, and that more time should be spent understanding the cultural perspectives of engineers and executives in order to orchestrate organizational unity. In the next chapter we present a model and management strategies which we believe respect the values of all three groups. In creating a safety culture, we also believe that organizational subcultures can be unified. We conclude this chapter with some general principles and strategies for unifying and strengthening organizational cultures as a first step toward creating and sustaining a safety culture.

Strengthening the Organizational Culture: Tell the Story, and Tell it Again

Though definitions vary, most researchers agree that organizational cultures are historically determined and socially constructed (Hofstede *et al.*, 1990), which is to say that they evolve through the telling and retelling of important stories by their members. The following strategies all strengthen organizational culture by articulating the desired values and norms and reinforcing members' behavior appropriately.

The Role of Management

Given the unique role of Management, as the group centrally positioned to influence and unite all other groups, many cultural strategies originate with and/or require the full enthusiasm of Management. Management can direct cultural shift by specifying the desired actions and reinforcing the appropriate norms, but the efforts of Management in this direction must be sincere. While it may be possible for Management to direct people to change their work behavior, it cannot direct people to change their values. And without the underlying values and beliefs in place to guide the behavior, any Management-directed behavior shift will be short-lived.

Senior Management is a part of, not apart from, the culture; that is, it does not look down upon the organization and direct it by edict, rather it influences the culture as a participating element within the culture. It is the actual and not the espoused management practices that are noted by others in the organization. There is no redemption for Management which convinces employees to accept a pay cut for the sake of the company's long-term health and then awards itself bonuses and stock options. When employee groups feel that they cannot trust Management (and amongst pilots this tends to be the norm), they will reject with suspicion any new initiatives, including training and new safety procedures. The first and most important task for Management is to gain and keep the trust of their employees.[9] We will talk more about building trust and credibility in Chapter 6.

It is also Management's responsibility to provide leadership and a common vision that unifies cultural subgroups. Management that uses a 'divide and conquer' strategy with its employee groups gets exactly that, a divided and ultimately defeated organization. In at least two airlines that we are aware of, Management announced pilots' salaries to other employee groups as a strategy to embarrass the pilots at salary negotiation time. The net result of such actions has been complete subgroup divisiveness: ground personnel are not prompt at push-back (when plane is pushed away from gate), gate agents are civil but uncooperative, and the pilots feel isolated and attacked. And everyone mistrusts Management! Figure 4.5 summar-

Strengthen the Organizational Culture: The Role of Management

The Jargon	Straight Talk
Diagnose the present culture(s)	Who are we?
Provide a vision	Who do we want to be?
Articulate the values	Set the rules
Reinforce the desired norms	Stick to the rules
Set an example for others to follow	Walk the walk

Figure 4.5   The role of Management

9   A popular US phrase which encapsulates this view is: 'You gotta walk the walk, not just talk the talk.'

izes and simplifies the role of Management in shaping organizational culture.

Role Models

There are many role models other than Senior Management in an organization. Supervisors, trainers, instructors and line managers should all be active promoters of the culture and its desired outcomes. In order to be a positive role model for the company, these people must understand and internalize organizational values, and then be active and visible supporters of the organization's goals. Then they are in a better position to transmit these values and practices to line personnel and new-hires (new employees). Sincerity cannot be faked, therefore individuals should be carefully screened for these influential positions – seniority or popularity is not enough. We have seen quality training programs fail because of lack of support from these people of influence. These role models should be responsive to all employees who query or challenge the company's standards and norms.

Recruitment and New-member Socialization

The recruitment of new pilots is both influenced by the organization's culture and determines its continuation. For example, some airlines have traditionally only hired former military personnel, sometimes looking for those with a particular background, such as Navy carrier-based fighter pilots. Other airlines, particularly outside the United States, hire non-pilots and train in all aspects of flight from initial licensure to qualification for airline operations. The rationale often proposed for this practice is that it ensures that all have the same values and background. On the other hand, many airlines hire from a variety of sources, including the military, general aviation, regional airlines and failed airlines, and face the challenge of integrating these disparate experiences into the norms and practices of the organization.

One of the most effective ways to transmit organizational values is via recruitment and new-member socialization. Organizations which actively recruit members who exhibit the desired values have already begun the process of successful indoctrination. To that end, choosing applicants for their non-technical skills may be just as important as ensuring their technical competence. New-hires (who by definition are seeking cultural membership) can be quickly and successfully socialized into the organization in very direct fashion. Rather than leaving the new member to discover the organizational norms through observation, trial and error, a mentoring system allows a senior person to explain the culture to the newcomer. By explaining the organization's history, its present focus, its quirks and idiosyncrasies, its successes and challenges, the senior person socializes the newcomer to the airline's culture. The senior person is also available to explain why something is done the way it is, thereby revealing the underlying or implicit structure of the company. Published histories and guidelines also provide the newcomer with the 'company line' – what it means to be a member of the culture. Successful socialization is a cultural shortcut in that it provides the most direct and unambiguous route to strong cultural membership.

Organizational Language and Publications

Company publications and other documents provide another opportunity for Management to strengthen the culture by articulating the values and publishing the norms. For example, does the Management send a divisive 'us and them' message or an integrated 'we' message in its intracompany communications? As Box 4.5 demonstrates, the use of language can be a potent means of encoding values. Both of these excerpts were downloaded from the Internet on the same day, both were company press releases, both were essentially telling the same story of a financially successful quarter, and both contained a quote from the company's CEO.

Box 4.5   Two stories of success

We are extremely pleased with our outstanding third quarter 1997 earnings performance, up 52 per cent from the third quarter 1996. We also enjoyed an excellent cost performance, with third quarter unit costs down 2.1 per cent from last year... Excluding salaries, wages and benefits, which increased primarily due to substantially higher Profitsharing and Employee savings plan contributions, virtually all other unit cost categories were down from year-ago levels. This clearly demonstrates our People's ability and resolve to maintain our dramatic low cost leadership. (Herb Kelleher, Chairman, President and CEO of Southwest Airlines, in a press release dated 23 October 1997)

Delta's record results for the September 1997 quarter continue the financial progress the company has achieved over the past few years. Our solid financial performance in the September 1997 quarter reflects continued strength in the economy, strong business demand, improvements in transatlantic performance and continued cost containment ... Delta's unit cost control during the September 1997 quarter will help sustain our position as the most

---

> efficient major network US carrier. This powerful competitive advantage is a critical ingredient to building a winning organization. (Leo F. Mullin, President and CEO, Delta Airlines, in a press release dated 23 October 1997)

One cannot read the two press releases without gleaning some sense of the guiding values in each company Mr Kelleher publicly attributes the financial success of the company to all the people who work for the company, and unashamedly states that the only increased costs were related to employee profit sharing and benefits, which he considers legitimate. Mr Mullin, on the other hand, publicly attributes the financial success of the company to the economy, business demand, transatlantic performance and continued cost containment: there is no mention of the employees. One could draw the conclusion that the first airline values its people, while the second airline appears to value balance sheets and economic forces. Let us hasten to add that these are only impressions gleaned from a short press release. The reality in each company may be quite different; nonetheless these press releases send an implicit message (intentional or otherwise) to the public, to stockholders and to employees about what is important in that company.

As well as the formal language of the organization, there are also stories and myths about 'heroic founders', employees who 'went the extra mile' or 'how we overcame early adversity' which all reflect and perpetuate the culture. Anecdotes are powerful transmitters of values, extolling the culture with every recounting. *Nuts* by Freiberg and Freiberg (1996) is a book-length collection of stories, photographs and rituals which celebrate the history of Southwest Airlines. There is even a chapter which explicitly states the 13 values on which the Southwest philosophy is built. While this book is a fascinating read in and of itself, it has served an even more important role. A copy of the book was sent to every employee in 1996 to celebrate the airline's twenty-fifth anniversary. The airline has undergone massive expansion in its 25 years; distributing the book to all employees is a clever and sincere way to transmit and share the company's values with all the members, new and old. It is not a coincidence that Southwest Airlines has the lowest attrition rates in the industry. This company has worked hard to make its workers both happy *and* productive.

Create a Winning Team

Making the cultural membership more attractive is another clever way to unite cultural subgroups and create a proud and motivated workforce. While this can be done with financial incentive programs like profit sharing, it can also be achieved with an early success or the presence of a common enemy. Everyone wants to be on a winning team: it encourages greater striving. At the same time, group membership can be strengthened in the face of opposition. The common enemy might be a competitor, or 'hard times' to be survived – something against which the group can strive.

Continental Airlines has emerged from bankruptcy in the 1980s to become an award-winning airline in the last two years. Much of this success has been attributed to the new CEO, Gordon Bethune, who initiated the now famous 'Go Forward Plan', whose tenets are 'fly to win, fund the future, make reliability a reality and work together'. In October 1997, the airline had just completed its tenth consecutive quarter of record pre-tax earnings. (To test our Internet-inspired theory of company values embedded in press releases, we went back and found this in a Continental Airlines press release dated 16 October 1997: 'Our award-winning service has delivered another record quarter both financially and operationally,' said Continental Chairman and CEO Bethune. 'I'm proud of our team.') What is interesting to us about this airline's reversal of fortune is the new-found energy and enthusiasm that we have observed throughout the company. We are currently engaged in innovative projects with the pilots, flight attendants and the safety office.

US Airways is another airline undergoing major cultural change. Under the leadership of Stephen Wolf, the airline has changed its name (from USAir), its logo (to a stylized, gray flag, designed to suggest the US flag), its mission (to be *the* carrier of choice, with international reach) and its standards. When asked what the new logo meant, several employees gave interesting answers. 'It's a flag to rally people, to take us into battle,' said one pilot. 'It's the one color to show that all the previous mergers have produced this one, united airline,' he added. 'It's a reflection of the CEO's style and personality,' said another pilot. 'It's supposed to be subdued. It represents our company in transition. When we finish evolving, perhaps it will change,' said yet another. Despite the variety of answers, everyone who was asked had an opinion, a good indication that people in the company are beginning to internalize the changes.

This airline also had a profitable third quarter in 1997, and this quote was taken from the *US Airways News* magazine (3 November 1997): 'These outstanding results are a tribute to our employees' hard work and professionalism, and their dedication to making US Airways the carrier of choice,' said Chairman Stephen Wolf. 'The strength of their commitment bodes well for our company's future.' The attentive reader will notice that Mr Wolf embedded the company's mission, to be *the* carrier of choice, in this statement. He is articulating the organization's goals as he reinforces his employees' behaviors.

Capitalize on Timing

Cultural change is slow and cannot be cynically manipulated. None-theless, it is possible to capitalize upon propitious moments to advance the desired values and norms. Press releases are often used to herald organizational success, as we have noted. Accidents and incidents, while never desirable, can serve to alert the organization to its weak-nesses and propel change (see Box 4.6). The open discussion of incidents and safety breaches as they occur, and speedy action in response to those incidents, can send a message of sincere concern for safety.

Box 4.6   Delta Airlines: a case study of organizational change

Captains Rueben Black and Robert Byrnes (Byrnes & Black, 1993) have provided a detailed portrait of how a large organization (more than 8000 pilots) can change its culture in response to wrench-ing experiences. After undergoing the trauma of a serious crash at Dallas–Fort Worth International Airport in 1985, Delta faced a series of incidents in the summer of 1987 which, although not resulting in injury or damage, greatly embarrassed the organization and tarnished its reputation (being the butt of comic routines on late night television does not enhance passenger confidence in safety). These incidents included a near mid-air collision over the North Atlantic, the inadvertent shutting down of both engines after take off, and landing at the wrong airport. The airline had also recently merged with another carrier (Western Airlines) with a very differ-ent corporate culture.

Delta had publicly rejected Crew Resource Management (CRM) training in an interview that formed part of a Public Broadcasting System (PBS) special on air safety. A Delta spokesman stated that it was a 'captain's airline' and that training in crew coordination was neither consistent with policy nor needed. However, in the wake of the incidents, Management re-evaluated its policies on flightdeck management and committed itself to formal training in CRM. To accomplish this, no cost or effort was avoided. Research into the attitudes and practices of pilots was conducted and a number of consultants were engaged to assist in curriculum development for new training. Perhaps most critical, Management wholeheartedly embraced a new policy of flight operations based on teamwork and open communication. The process was highly successful. Sur-vey and observational data taken after the policy shift and inauguration of training showed significant shifts in both attitudes and behavior. (Helmreich & Foushee, 1993)

All of the strategies that we have discussed have as their common thread the articulation and sharing of an organization's values, beliefs and practices. In other words, the strategies aim to make explicit and known that which is often implicit, unknown, vague or misunderstood. In telling the story, and telling it again, members vitalize and strengthen their organizational culture.

In Chapters 5 and 6, we discuss the values and practices inherent in safety cultures. We have concluded this chapter with strategies for unifying and strengthening organizational cultures because we believe that a safety culture can be developed and sustained more successfully when the organizational culture is strong. Once the culture has been unified and there is trust between employees and Management, standards and norms for safety can be successfully introduced and upheld throughout the company.

5 Error Management: a Cultural Universal in Aviation and Medicine

Man errs as long as he strives. (Johann Wolfgang von Goethe, Faust, 1832)

Truth lies within a little and certain compass, but error is immense. (Henry St. John, Viscount Bolingbroke, Reflections upon Exile, 1716)

Give me a fruitful error any time, bursting with its own correction. (Vilfredo Pareto, Comment on Kepler, 1870)

We have discussed how the three cultures, professional, national and organizational, influence attitudes and values about work. In this chapter we discuss how these cultures intersect within organizations and can be channeled toward a safety culture. We suggest error management as an essential strategy for achieving a safety culture and describe the need for empirical data to diagnose an organization's health and practices. After considering methodological approaches, we discuss findings from research into crew behavior. We conclude with a discussion of culture and error management in medicine.

Safety Culture as an Organizational Outcome

In high-risk endeavors, such as aviation and medicine, safety is critical. Catastrophes can destroy an organization's reputation and profitability. The elements that form professional, national and organizational cultures can come together to define a safety culture or can create an unsafe operating environment. A safety culture is more than a group of individuals promulgating a set of safety guidelines, it is a group of individuals guided in their behavior by their joint belief in the importance of safety, and their shared understanding that every member willingly upholds the group's safety norms and will support other members to that common end. A safety culture is visibly manifested in safe behaviors at the front lines of organizations. James Reason (1990) describes people in these positions (for example, pilots and operating room staff), as being at the 'sharp end' of organizations.

The Interplay of Cultures

There can be a variety of interrelationships among national, professional and organizational cultures which are ultimately reflected in the behaviors at the 'sharp end', whether safe or unsafe. In Figure 5.1 we sketch a model of interrelationships of elements that can lead to a safety culture and safe behaviors. National culture is the most distal element of the model and the one least amenable to change. It can influence the organizational culture, for example in the forms of communication and leadership practiced, as we discussed in Chapter 3. It can also determine the style of training and the nature of training delivery, as we will see in Chapter 6. National culture further influences the safety culture, for example in high UA cultures, through a reverence for procedures.

The organizational culture, discussed in Chapter 4, has powerful influences on training practices. Financial strain can shape the or-

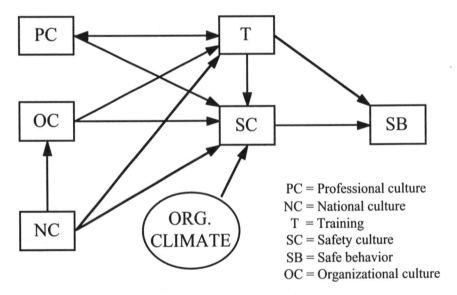

PC = Professional culture
NC = National culture
T = Training
SC = Safety culture
SB = Safe behavior
OC = Organizational culture

Figure 5.1   A model of the intersection of cultures and their outcomes

ganizational culture and can also have an indirect impact by reducing resources available for training and support of the infrastructure. The values and demonstrated commitment of Senior Management regarding safety directly influence the safety culture. If an atmosphere of trust exists between employees and Management then standards and norms for safety can be introduced to all groups. Employees will willingly report safety concerns (a) because they believe it is their responsibility to do so, (b) because they are encouraged by their co-workers to do so, (c) because they are confident that their Management will take immediate and appropriate action to redress the problem, and (d) they know that they will receive continuing feedback from Management on important safety and organizational issues which affect their performance. However, none of these actions can be accomplished if the organization does not have accurate data showing the status of its operations and threats to safety.

Organizational culture and subcultures result in positive and negative behaviors. One notable area is the use of checklists. If respected role models and credible managers stress strict compliance with checklist usage, these behaviors will become second nature. On the other hand, if there are cultural norms of non-compliance, checklists will be disregarded. In a training session at one major airline, a pilot from a fleet notable for its non-compliance commented that 'Checklists are for the lame and weak.' This type of response reflects an attitude toward the possibility of error that is both erroneous and cavalier.

The organizational culture, particularly relations between Management and employees, is the major determinant of the organizational climate. The climate (or morale) of an organization is distinct from the organizational culture and reflects the pride that members feel in working there and their sense of organization as family. We feel that organizational climate can play an important role in shaping the safety culture. Climate certainly can influence motivation and perceived stress. It also influences the efficiency of operations (for example, on-time performance) and the corporate image perceived by the public.

Although it has been hypothesized that a negative organizational climate poses a threat to safety, no empirical evidence has been found to support this view. For example, the FAA conducted several inspections of Eastern Airlines during a period of extreme conflict between Management and labor (including not only pilots but also mechanics and other personnel). Despite a poisonous work environment, no evidence of an increase in safety-related incidents or unsafe practices was found. Nevertheless, we feel that further empirical data may show links both to safe behavior and to the organization's safety culture (see Box 5.1). It is likely that the strong professional culture of aviation provides some defense against the effects of a negative organizational climate, as discussed below.

Box 5.1   Morale and safety

The following comment was written by a flight attendant with more than ten years experience in response to our survey at a major airline.
    Supervisors and management lack respect for the professionalism of flight attendants. They concentrate on the negative instead of improvement, guidance and leadership, thus lowering morale. Many of us don't even care about safety issues. We go there, serve drinks and food, do what we have to do to earn a few dollars and go home.

Our model shows links to and from professional culture. The pride and motivation associated with the profession may influence the safety culture through feelings of responsibility for passenger safety and dedication to executing one's job as effectively as possible. This same pride and motivation come with pilots to training and make them attentive and responsive students. On the other hand, the sense of personal invulnerability we have noted as a professional universal can have a negative influence on the safety culture by making pilots less aware of personal limitations and less accepting of training, such as CRM, that is focused on safe behaviors. We show a path between training and professional culture because we have seen in Chapter 2 that training about human performance limitations can change attitudes about personal vulnerability and, hence, the professional culture.

Behavior at the 'Sharp End'

We use the term 'safe behaviors' to reflect acts that have been found to be critical in avoiding accidents and incidents or in their consequences (Helmreich *et al.*, 1995; see Box 5.2). On the basis of analyses of accidents and incidents, we defined a set of 'behavioral markers' that reflect the positive and negative expression of these acts and can serve as criteria of crew performance (Helmreich *et al.*, 1994). These behaviors are reliably observable in flight and have been further documented in analyses of accidents by the National Transportation Safety Board (Helmreich & Hines, 1997; NTSB, 1994). All of the cultural influences we have discussed are ultimately manifested in the behaviors of flight crews. Figure 5.2 gives examples of the way in which national culture may influence crew behaviors. As the figure indicates, there are behaviors that can be placed on a continuum that

**Figure 5.2   Behaviors related to national culture and their
relationships with safety of flight**

varies from a higher probability of accident or incident to a higher
probability of safe flight. The nature of these behaviors suggests that
no culture is optimally configured for safety. Compliance with Standard Operating Procedures (SOPs) is associated with high uncertainty
avoidance. A strong group orientation is a characteristic of collectivist
cultures while skepticism about the actions and use of automation is
stronger in individualistic cultures. On the negative side, members
of individualistic cultures may be more likely to eschew teamwork
and operate as though they were in solo flight. High power distance
cultures may generate autocratic leaders who do not solicit or accept
ideas or guidance from junior crew members. Finally, pilots from
high PD and collectivist cultures may become overreliant on automation, treating it as an infallible, senior crew member.

Box 5.2   Behavioral markers in accidents and audits

As part of the validation of our performance assessment instrument, the Line/LOS Checklist (LLC: Helmreich *et al.*, 1994), we
evaluated crew behavior in 52 accidents and incidents where hu-

man performance had been determined to be causal (Helmreich *et al.*, 1995).[1] The majority of the accidents included identifiable human error. In several cases, however, crews demonstrated exemplary performance which helped mitigate the severity of accidents. The LLC defines 25 observable behaviors, called behavioral markers; each marker can be coded as representing positive or negative action. The Cockpit Voice Recorder (CVR) transcript was reviewed for the positive or negative presence of each behavioral marker. In each of the accidents and incidents, one or more behavioral markers were identified as contributing to the outcome. In the accidents involving crew error, the range of markers implicated in each was between one and 10. In two accidents involving mechanical failure where the crew's performance was outstanding, 7 and 12 markers were identified as contributing positively to the outcome. The most frequently identified negative marker involved poor leadership, the captain failing to establish a balance between authority and crew participation in decision making. Others included the failure to establish open communications and a team concept, not providing adequate technical briefings, failing to plan ahead for contingencies, and a lack of assertiveness on the part of junior crew members. These data provide strong evidence for both the validity and the importance of these factors in crew performance. Peter Connelly of our research group has also analyzed in depth a series of accidents and similarly demonstrated a close link between behavioral markers and causal factors (Connelly, 1997).

The National Transportation Safety Board conducted a study of US accidents involving crew error (NTSB, 1994). In this study 302 errors were identified in 37 accidents. One of our students, Patrick Williams, was able to match 216 of the errors to behavioral markers, with the remainder involving technical errors not classified by the LLC. Building on the NTSB study, the Flight Safety Foundation has established a project called 'Approach and Landing Accident Reduction'. Robert Helmreich and Ratan Khatwa are co-chairs of a data group that is working to classify behavior in the worldwide aviation accident database. Part of this project will involve identifying the presence of LLC behavioral markers in the accident records. One of the goals of the project is to identify critical behaviors amenable to training interventions.[2]

---

1   Data for the majority of the cases examined came from National Transportation Safety Board accident reports. Others came from personal investigations or incident reports shared by airlines.
2   Other aspects of the project are examining issues surrounding equipment and technical procedures that may also be involved.

As we have pointed out, professional culture can make both positive and negative contributions to crew behavior, as shown in Figure 5.3. Pilots with a strong sense of pride and motivation are likely to be better prepared and highly cognizant of their responsibilities for safe operations. In the same vein, they may be more approachable and more committed to working as part of a team. But the sense of personal invulnerability that we have found so prevalent among pilots can lead to being aloof, to disregarding team-mates, and to taking undue risks.

Figure 5.3   Influences of professional culture on safety

Error Management as a Universal Strategy

Error is an inevitable accompaniment of human endeavor, recognized by philosophers and scientists alike. There is an inherent envelope framing human performance that is determined by the human genome. It includes limits on vision, perception, cognitive capacity, memory and attention. Physiological and environmental conditions such as fatigue and external stressors further limit performance. Human limits can often be reached in 'tightly coupled' industries where activities involve individuals, teams and technology (Perrow, 1984). However, in flight operations, errors can be traced, not only to human failings such as cognitive slips and lapses identified by Reason (1990), but also to maintenance problems, organizationally imposed workload, fatigue, external agencies such as Air Traffic Control (ATC) and, very critically, *chance*. In essence, errors rain down on crews who are surrounded by various defenses, as illustrated in Figure 5.4. The task of organizations and crews is to defend against these errors and to manage those that will inevitably occur. By managing errors, we mean to avoid them whenever possible, but, failing that, to trap those that do occur before they are executed (for example, making an erroneous input to the flight management computer, but catching it before the command is executed). At the next level, effective error management will mitigate the consequences of those errors that do occur. In the worst cases, errors are missed (that is, never detected) or exacerbated, with consequences made more serious by the erroneous corrective actions of the crew. Box 5.3 gives examples of errors and reactions, while Figure 5.5 shows the possible responses to error on the continuum of severity.

Our thinking about error management was particularly influenced by the work of James Reason (1990; 1997). Our approach, however, includes national and professional cultures as well as organizational culture and deals specifically with training as an error-management

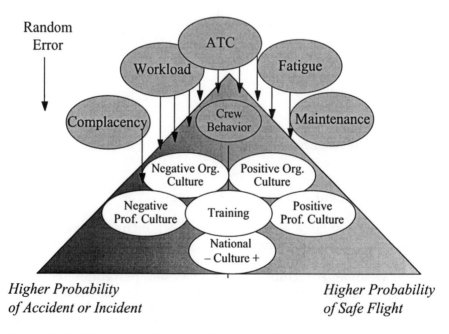

Higher Probability
of Accident or Incident

Higher Probability
of Safe Flight

Figure 5.4   The rain of error and error defenses

strategy. To summarize and extend the universality of error to the universality of error-management strategies, we propose five precepts about error and its management.

Box 5.3   Observations of error

The following are verbatim comments about error and its management made by expert observers during line operations at major US airlines. They illustrate the concepts of avoiding, trapping and mitigating error and provide an example of an error exacerbated.

Error avoidance
No error occurred in an off-normal, potentially error-inducing setting because of active crew strategies and appropriate responses: 'First Officer confused about proper frequency approaching the Take Off position. Captain stopped aircraft and handled situation smoothly, as neither pilot knew if they were cleared for the runway.'

Error trapping
Trapping indicates that an error was discovered and corrected before it became consequential: 'First Officer mis-set altimeter on the In Range Checklist. As the Captain scanned the cockpit, he caught the error and corrected the First Officer's input.'

Error mitigation
Mitigation indicates that appropriate action was taken to lessen the severity of consequences after the error was made: 'Autopilot disengaged unintentionally by First Officer, aircraft lost 300' before Captain caught error. Potential violation, ATC called them to check altitude.'

Error exacerbation
Exacerbation indicates that the crew's actions increased the gravity of the situation: 'Captain specifically asked the First Officer if he identified the ILS; First Officer said yes, when in fact he did not. This goes down as one of the most unprofessional acts I have been witness to in my aviation experience.'

Five Precepts for Error Management

1   In any complex system, human error is inevitable. In systems such as aviation and the operating room, where teams must interact with technology, errors will occur.
2   There are limitations on human performance. All humans have limits imposed by cognitive capabilities such as the capacity of memory.
3   When performance limits are exceeded, humans make more errors. When overloaded or under stress, decision-making ability is

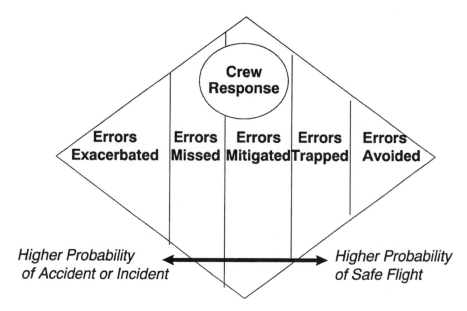

Figure 5.5   Crew response to error

hampered. High levels of workload can exceed cognitive capacity. Similarly, stress and fatigue can severely limit information-processing ability. Under such conditions, humans are also more likely to make errors of *omission* (forgetting items on checklists) and *commission* (setting the altitude incorrectly in the flight management computer).

4   Safety is a universal value.[3] In every culture, members value and strive to increase it. Safety, however, is not a binary condition defined by safe or unsafe practices, but a continuum running from increased to decreased probability of accidents. Although safety is universally valued, national cultures and organizations fall at different points on this continuum. In the case of national culture, the availability of resources and infrastructure may determine the level of safety. Africa, for example, lacks a supportive infrastructure such as a sophisticated air traffic control system and has the poorest safety record in the world. Safety does not come free. Organizations differ in the resources they can devote to safety as well as in perceptions of safety needs.

---

3   We recognize that individuals differ in their propensity to take risks and that some actively seek risky activities. However, at the organizational and national level, safety rather than risk is the shared value.

5 High-risk organizations have a responsibility to develop and maintain a safety culture. Institutions and organizations that bear responsibility for the safety of the general public have an obligation to maximize the safety of their operations and to commit the resources needed for the endeavor. The task is to make sure that individuals and teams accept their responsibility for safety and error management.

Error Management as Individual and Crew Strategy

Individual crew members can contribute to error management at the individual level by recognizing their own limitations and acting accordingly. Avoiding fatigue and practicing stress management techniques can reduce (but not eliminate) the probability of error. Individuals can also contribute to error management by maintaining their technical proficiency and adhering to organizational rules. However, the most important individual contribution can be made by accepting the concept of teamwork and practicing the concepts of CRM. Although the support and delivery of CRM training is an organizational responsibility, its enactment occurs at the crew level.

CRM as Error Management

Airlines around the world began CRM training in response to incontrovertible evidence that 'pilot error' and, specifically, interpersonal failures were implicated in the majority of accidents and incidents in aviation (for example, Cooper *et al.*, 1979). In the vernacular of the early 1980s, when the first programs were introduced, CRM was viewed as a means of eliminating error. (See Box 5.4 for a discussion of the evolution of CRM training.)

Despite its roots in coping with error, by the mid-1990s many participants and trainers had lost sight of the goals of CRM. Informal queries of flight crews with the question, 'What is the purpose of CRM training in your company?' usually elicited responses like 'To help us get along better.' Error reduction or management was not seen as a program goal. Also, as we have stressed, the export of CRM to other national cultures proved to be problematic. The CRM basics of open communication and consultative leadership are not easily accepted in cultures where hierarchical differences between leaders and subordinates are large and expected. We sought to restore the original goals of CRM toward safety and error management as concepts with universal acceptance.

It was in this context that we proposed a fifth generation of CRM training that has the explicit goal of managing human error

(Helmreich *et al.*, 1997a; in press). Fifth-generation CRM is based on recognition of the fact that human error is ubiquitous and inevitable. To be effective, the training must credibly communicate the limits of human performance with regard to physical and mental capacity and the ability to function under stress. The explicit goal of this aspect of training is to change the professional culture by fostering a more realistic awareness of personal limits and capabilities. This is an achievable and critical goal that has as a primary benefit the removal of personal barriers to acceptance of CRM concepts. If pilots recognize the inevitability of error, the idea that behaviors taught in CRM are countermeasures against error becomes both palatable and important.[4] Accepting the inevitability of error also makes it easier to report personal mistakes and mishaps. The goal of error management gives subordinates 'permission' to query their seniors' actions as well as to report problems. While the avoidance of error represents the most effective use of countermeasures, CRM training necessarily stresses that errors will occur despite the best efforts of all involved.

The positive acts shown in Figures 5.2 and 5.3 are examples of the specific behaviors taught in the newest CRM courses as error countermeasures (we discuss the structure and support of error management CRM in Chapter 6). Curricula for CRM can include positive examples of avoiding, trapping and mitigating error, and fatigue countermeasures, conflict resolution, optimal automation use and group decision making (see Helmreich *et al.*, in press, for further discussion of curriculum specifics).

Learning from error   As the quotation from Pareto at the beginning of this chapter suggests, error can also serve as a powerful learning tool. The experience of error and its management gives the individual and the organization valuable information about personal capabilities and system function. Writing of the unintended consequences of automation, Rochlin (1997) argues that both the experience of error and successful error management provide essential preparation for dealing with future, complex situations:

> Human learning takes place through action. Trial-and-error defines limits, but its complement, trial and success, is what builds judgment and confidence. To not be allowed to err is not to be allowed to learn; to not be allowed to try at all is to be deprived of the motivation to learn. This seems like a very poor way to train a human being who is expected to act intelligently and correctly when the automated system fails or breaks down – that is, in a situation that comes predefined as

4   A basic countermeasure is the use of multiple crew members to provide redundancy and monitoring. Checklists are also examples of countermeasures.

requiring experience, judgment and confidence as a guide to action. (Rochlin, 1997, p.126)

If we accept the premise that the commission of error is an important part of learning to deal with complex systems, the implications are that training programs should include situations where trainees err and should provide them with guidance and feedback on coping with these errors. We will discuss this point further in Chapter 6.

Culture and CRM Revisited

It may be useful to revisit the successes and failures of CRM training with the wisdom of hindsight. We can now recognize that the reasons for imperfect acceptance were more complex than we realized at the time. We can also learn important lessons about how to mount new programs. The earliest CRM programs were completely focused on the flight crew in the cockpit. There was no concern with the crew's interface with other elements of the system and, in some cases, only marginal support from senior management. A good example of this is the experience of one component of the Air Force in implementing CRM for its transport pilots. We were asked to help validate the impact of the training and used as primary data the performance ratings made by standardization and evaluation (stan-eval) pilots (the military equivalent of check airmen). Our tabulation of ratings before and after training led to a startling conclusion: CRM training significantly worsened the performance of the crews. On further investigation we found that the Air Force had not provided CRM training for the stan-eval pilots. We also found that what drove the evaluators' ratings down was perceived weak leadership and indecisiveness on the part of those evaluated after receiving training. What triggered these poor ratings was crews doing exactly what they were trained to do – seeking input from all crew members in decision making. The evaluators, however, saw this as a weakness, particularly when the aircraft commander sought the opinion of the enlisted flight engineer. Evaluators saw indecisiveness when crews practiced what they had been taught in CRM training. In effect, the Air Force had set up a system that rapidly erased the message imparted in training. The practice of keeping instructors and instruction in CRM separate from the organizational training department also had unintended negative consequences. Through the isolation of CRM training from the normal instructional/operational environment, the inadvertent communication was that this is not truly operational material and can be disregarded. Indeed, the practice may have given the message that managerial support was weak or ambivalent.

The early weaknesses of CRM programs were in the failure to embed the training in the context of the organizational culture and in not providing a more compelling rationale for the program, at least in recent years. In retrospect, what is surprising is how well accepted CRM training was and how much impact it had when it was presented without the necessary organizational support and infrastructure.

Box 5.4   The evolution of CRM in aviation

CRM training has changed dramatically since its inception in the early 1980s (see Helmreich & Foushee, 1993, and Helmreich, Merritt & Wilhelm, in press, for a more extensive discussion of its evolution). Although developed as means of coping with error, early CRM courses were derived from training programs in organizational development and relied heavily on games and self-diagnostic exercises that were conceptually light years from the environment of the cockpit. One of the most widely used games was called 'Lost on the Moon' – an exercise in prioritizing what essential supplies would be needed if one became stranded there. Although being trapped in some airports may feel like being lost on the moon, the operational relevance is clearly limited.

The original focus was only on the cockpit crew. However, as programs matured and evolved they became more modular and the focus broadened to include cabin crews and other elements of the system in which crews function. CRM programs also became more operational in focus and began to concentrate on specific behaviors (briefings, strategies to enhance situation awareness, conflict resolution, and so on) that enhance team functioning. Many of the later courses also began to address system issues and the influence of culture on team interaction. By our measurement, CRM had passed through four generations by 1995 (Helmreich, Merritt & Wilhelm, in press). As we have noted, many pilots by the mid-1990s had lost sight of the *raison d'être* for CRM. Although we cannot pinpoint a cause, it is possible that broadening the focus had the inadvertent side-effect of clouding its goals.

There has also been something of a backlash against CRM training in the United States. Some critics have assailed it as a form of 'New Age' brainwashing aimed at achieving group harmony. Others have blamed CRM unfairly for failing to eliminate human error accidents and incidents. While CRM is far from a universal panacea for human failings, it is a highly effective and essential aspect of professional training. Recognizing its importance as well as its limitations, our goal has been to develop an organizational strategy of error management that can be as easily accepted in Asia as in Alaska.

Error Management as Organizational Strategy

Simply providing training in CRM as error management will not necessarily lead to significant behavioral change on the flightdeck. A safety culture that supports dealing proactively with error-inducing conditions rather than blaming or punishing individuals who err is also needed. Organizations need to recognize and publicly acknowledge that human performance has its limits and that error is inevitable. Perhaps the strongest action that can support the safety culture is taking a non-punitive stance toward error and establishing policies that encourage pilots to report errors and safety problems. We are not suggesting that any organization should be tolerant of willful violation of its procedures or rules. Rather, we are talking about organizational tolerance for inadvertent error. Taking positive action to address issues raised through such a program gives a strong message about the strength of the safety culture. American Airlines has had success with its Air Safety Action Partnership (ASAP), a joint effort of the FAA, the company and the pilots' union. The program encourages pilots to report error without jeopardy and takes immediate action to address problems identified. Rather than hiding errors, the open sharing of error *and the effective management of error* provide reinforcement of CRM practices. The saying, 'We must learn from our mistakes or be doomed to repeat them', captures the essence of error management in a blame-free culture.

Another organizational practice that requires change for the implementation of fifth-generation CRM is the training and qualification of instructors and check airmen (Tullo, in press). It is essential that training and evaluation focus not only on the avoidance of error, but also on the management of error. Effective management of error should be reinforced just as exemplary, error-free performance is. This is not an easy task, since the historical model in aviation has centered on blame and punishment of error, and organizations operate with considerable inertia.

Looking at the inevitably flawed human operator in a complex system, it is hard to avoid the conclusion that organizations that recognize and manage error will be far more successful than those that deny or fail to recognize it. To manage error, though, requires understanding of it and its roots. This requires in turn that the organization indulge in self-scrutiny and diagnosis.

Diagnosing Organizations

Here we describe techniques for collecting the data organizations need to maintain a safety culture and to practice effective error management. As we pointed out in Chapter 1, there is not an arbitrary distinction between applied and basic research. The same research that supports organizational effectiveness can contribute to theories of human behavior and academic science.

We focus first on the types of data organizations need for self-diagnosis. Seeking data involves the use of two broad research strategies: *reactive methods*, that look back at the roots of mishaps and near-mishaps, and *proactive methods*, that attempt to isolate latent failures and areas where organizational defenses are weak (Reason, 1997). There is also a concern with finding areas where defenses are strong.

Reactive Sources of Diagnostic Data

Accident reports   Most safety initiatives in aviation have been and continue to be reactive, most dramatically in response to accidents. Using a medical metaphor, accident investigation is analogous to a post mortem after the death of a patient. The autopsy reveals the nature of a particular pathology, but not an indication of the prevalence of the precipitating circumstances in the population. Unfortunately, also, many accident investigations look for a primary cause, most often pilot error, and fail to examine organizational and system factors that set the stage for the catastrophe. The Canadian investigation of the Air Ontario accident at Dryden is a shining exception (Helmreich, 1992; Moshansky, 1992). Although the proximal cause was rapidly identified as the crew's failure to de-ice, the investigation turned up latent problems associated with both the organizational culture and training practices and the national regulatory system. Few countries, however, can afford to mount an investigation of this magnitude, and the time lag between the accident and the report was nearly three years.

Incident reports   Incident reports are often touted as a more diagnostic source of system information than accident investigations, since incidents are more common than accidents. In our experience, however, incidents often suffer from being less carefully investigated and frequently fail to probe beyond the proximal cause, usually the pilot. Continuing the medical analogy, the incident is like a broken bone that sends the individual to the doctor. The doctor sets the bone, but rarely considers the root cause(s): was the fracture due to weak bones, poor diet, being a victim of abuse, or high-risk lifestyle? Setting the bone is no guarantee that the patient will not present again next month with another symptom of the same root cause, perhaps this time with a more serious outcome. Isolated incidents, investigated in a cursory fashion, provide little information of value.

NASA runs a very successful incident-reporting system for the Federal Aviation Administration that allows pilots and others in the aviation system to report incidents, including those in which they may have violated rules. This system, the Aviation Safety Reporting System (ASRS), was established in 1975. Reporters to the system are given limited immunity from regulatory action in exchange for sharing their information. Data collected under the system are maintained in a de-identified database that is available to organizations and to the general public. More than 307 000 reports from pilots have been received to date.[5] A similar system called CHIRP (Confidential Human Incident Reporting Procedure) exists in the United Kingdom and another has been opened in Australia. Many useful data have been assembled by ASRS and the other reporting systems and we have found the resource helpful in formulating research questions. There are, however, serious limitations on the usefulness of ASRS data for organizations. Because of confidentiality and protective agreements, organizations (and even aircraft types) involved in incidents are not available. While the data may identify generic trends and conditions in the system, they do not provide organizations with information on their own problems. Another limitation stems from the voluntary nature of the system. Because there is no formal mandate requiring submission of forms (although the immunity provision is a powerful inducement), the data provide no information on the base rates of particular problems in the aviation system.

Proactive Strategies for Diagnostic Data

We believe that the most useful data on an organization's practices can be gained by adopting a proactive stance, which can be achieved through a variety of techniques. As we indicated in Chapter 1, our investigations use multiple methodologies, but primarily surveys and systematic observation of behavior in operational and training environments. To a lesser extent, we rely on case study methods to investigate particular events, such as accidents, in depth. In previous chapters, we described how we use surveys, particularly the Flight Management Attitudes Questionnaire, as the largest source of data. We illustrated the case study approach in our description of the investigation of the Avianca crash in New York (see Chapter 3, Box 3.7).

Surveys Survey research allows the investigator to collect data from many respondents at relatively low cost. By using large samples (in

5   Useful information on the ASRS is available on the Internet at: http://olias.arc.nasa.gov/asrs.

many cases the surveys have involved everyone in a specific occupation, for example pilots or flight attendants, in an organization), we
can be more confident that responses are representative of the population in question. Survey research is often criticized by experimentalists
as relying on self-reports which may be subject to a variety of biases.
On the other hand, as in the case of culture, we are primarily interested in attitudes and values, which must necessarily be elicited from
self-reports. The way that different methodologies can combine to
confirm findings is illustrated with two theoretically interesting findings that first appeared in our survey data. Hofstede's dimension of
power distance as a value characteristic of Latin American and Asian
cultures was strongly supported in our data. As described in Chapter
3, we wrote an item directly related to the flightdeck, stating that
juniors should not question the decisions and actions of the captain to
make the concept relevant to respondents. This item, and the scale
associated with it, showed highly significant differences as a function
of national culture. We were able to validate the implications in our
case study of the Avianca crash. Even when their lives were in the
balance, the junior crew members did not directly bring their concerns
to the attention of the captain and they accepted, without question, a
routing from Air Traffic Control that left them without fuel some miles
from the airport (Helmreich, 1994).

Also, as we described in Chapter 3, we discovered through surveys that there was great variability in the acceptance of automation.
We found highly significant national differences in attitudes about
whether automation should be disconnected instead of reprogrammed
and perceptions of company expectations for its use. Attitudes toward technology are of both theoretical and practical significance
because they may predict how automation will be used in safety-
critical situations. Hence it was important to confirm that behavioral
relations with automation, the 'electronic crew member,' are indeed
problematic. We supplemented our survey data with direct observation of automation use by expert observers riding in the cockpit
during normal flight operations and found that there is indeed wide
variability in its use even within organizations in the USA (Helmreich
et al., 1996).

Surveys also provide important diagnostic information about operations, as we saw in Chapter 4. They provide inexpensive
information about the relevance of training, the level of teamwork
and cooperation amongst various employee groups, problem areas
or bottlenecks in daily operations and other areas of dissatisfaction.
The survey can also probe the safety culture: for example, do personnel know the proper channels for reporting safety concerns and are
they confident that the organization will act on expressed concerns?
Finally, the survey can identify areas of dissent or confusion, as we

found in the diversity of beliefs amongst pilots from the same organization about the appropriate use of automated systems (for example, Sherman *et al.*, 1997).

Systematic observations as data The ability to capture real-world behavior reliably provides the investigator with a powerful tool for understanding group processes. The approach we employ is in the tradition of Bales (1950) and has been used with other groups such as aquanauts (Radloff & Helmreich, 1968). Although group interactions are highly complex, there is a major advantage in the study of interpersonal acts: they are overt and observable. While we can only infer or elicit by questions what happens inside someone's head, the process of interaction is available, subject to the investigator's ability to record, code and interpret reliably.[6]

There are several hazards and methodological challenges in conducting observational research. One is the probability that the *process* of observation distorts behavior in a sort of psychological Heisenberg effect.[7] Our method of dealing with this very important issue has been to establish a relationship of trust with those observed. We promise each crew observed that everything seen is confidential and will only be used as part of a de-identified, aggregate database. Reinforcing this is a commitment from both management and unions to support the effort and to respect the sanctity of the data. One criticism of this approach is that crews observed will be on their best behavior and the picture of operations will be too rosy. While the extent to which observation influences behavior is ultimately unknowable, we have reason to believe that we do see representative behavior (see Box 5.5). Supporting this view is the fact that we observe a number of instances where crews violate Federal or company regulations and procedures (for example, failing to complete checklists or engaging in non-operational conversation during periods designated as 'sterile').[8]

6 We are not arguing that the unobservable motivations behind interpersonal interaction are not important. Rather we are saying that public interactions provide a useful picture of decision making and how teams function.
7 Nobel Laureate Werner Heisenberg gave his name to the fact that observing a phenomenon may alter it.
8 Perhaps the most egregious example of a crew's violation of regulations involved one of our observers who discovered that she and the captain of the flight were both graduates of the US Air Force Academy. The captain decided that it would be 'cool' if she flew the airplane – a major violation, giving control to a non-employee with no experience in that type of civilian aircraft.

Box 5.5   Best behavior

The following description of crew behavior at a major airline was written by one of our expert observers. If this crew was on its best behavior in front of the observer, it is scary to think what it may be like when they are not being observed.

The captain finally arrived in the cockpit 10 minutes prior to push-back. He appeared more cheerful than the previous day. The first officer and relief pilot were quite busy preparing the aircraft for departure. The captain set his flight bag down and, instead of preparing for departure, he presented a collection of four inch by four inch cartoon stickers, carefully peeled off the backing and applied three of them to blank areas on his instrument panel. He then asked the other crew members if they liked them. The first officer did not pay attention at first as he was busy on the radio. The captain persisted until the first officer finally talked to him about the stickers. The captain then handed the first officer three stickers and asked him to select one for his instrument panel. The first officer looked at me and then at the relief pilot in disbelief. He told the captain it was hard to choose, they were all so nice. The first officer then asked the relief to help him choose. After the choice was made this seemed to please the captain and he helped the first officer peel the backing off so as not to wrinkle the cartoon. The relief officer then commented that he had seen these stickers on other aircraft and wondered where they came from. The captain responded, 'Yes, somebody keeps removing them. Can you believe it? They look so much better than that dull gray instrument panel.'

A second problem is ensuring the reliability of observations. We have approached this by defining the behaviors to be measured in highly specific terms. For data collection we use expert observers (who are pilots or psychologists, or both). Our strategy is to use members of our research group as the core observers. This group is augmented by experts from the organization (usually pilots from the human factors, flight standards or training areas). Formal training is conducted using videotaped exemplars of the behaviors to be rated. After viewing examples, trainees assign ratings and subsequent discussion resolves discrepancies. Because observers who are not members of our research group cannot cross organizational boundaries to collect data in other organizations, we assess consistency by using the project observers as the standard and computing agreement between them and those nested in organizations. The results show high levels of agreement, indicating that observed differences between organizations are real and not an artifact of rater predilections.

Our observational instrument, the Line/LOS Checklist (LLC), is now in its fifth iteration (Helmreich *et al.*, 1997). The LLC is shown in Appendix C (pp. 261–264). As described earlier, the LLC defines observable actions that have been implicated in accidents and incidents.[9] To rate these behaviors, we have settled on a four-point rating schema that is anchored at one end by 'unsatisfactory', which is defined as behavior or performance that would fail formal evaluation, and at the other end by 'outstanding', defined as behavior clearly above the organization's expectations. The majority of behaviors receive a rating of '3', which is defined as meeting regulatory expectations. The final rating is '2', which is defined as 'minimum expectations' and represents substandard, but not failing, behavior. Initially, we asked raters to summarize observations across an entire flight. However, as we began to collect data we discovered that many crews showed large differences in *within-flight* behaviors. These differences are of interest because they could reflect a number of phenomena, from fatigue to complacency to escalating chains of errors. Accordingly, we moved to a more detailed coding schema that elicits ratings for each of four phases of flight (pre-departure, take-off and climb, cruise, and approach and landing). Two additional ratings are collected at a global level – overall technical proficiency and overall crew effectiveness. These are intended as summary evaluations.

The specific acts (behavioral markers) fall into four broad categories: team management and communications, situation awareness and decision making, automation management and technical proficiency. In the team management section, the behavioral markers include briefings, with separate assessment of technical and team-building components, monitoring of others, asking questions regarding actions and decisions, and leadership. Under situation awareness, markers include preparation for contingencies, prioritization of tasks, distribution of workload and conflict resolution. Automation management includes the establishment and use of guidelines for the employment of automation, the level of use of the automation (that is, whether the crew loses situation awareness when reprogramming the computer during high workload periods) and the extent to which entries in the flight management computer are verbalized and acknowledged. A set of markers deals with technical proficiency. These markers include altitude and terrain awareness,

---

9 The name Line/LOS refers to the situations in which observations can be collected. Line, of course, refers to normal flight operations. LOS is the industry acronym for Line Operational Simulation, referring to full mission simulations in which crew interactions are an integral part.

checklist compliance and the observation of sterile cockpit rules (avoiding social conversation during low altitude or ground operations).

In addition, extensive demographic information is collected, along with information on the crew's experience with one another and time on duty. The nature and extent of abnormal circumstances such as mechanical malfunctions and operational complexity, including high traffic, difficult terrain and weather, are also classified.

An unavoidable barrier to collection of systematic observational data is cost. Observations are necessarily made in real time and, if the interest is performance over long periods of time, such as transoceanic flight across multiple time zones, the observer is committed for an extended period to add one record to the data.

Systematic observations as line audits   We have worked with a number of major and regional US airlines to develop a *line audit* methodology to assess practices during regular flights (Helmreich *et al.*, 1996; Hines, 1998).[10] The line audit represents organizational use of systematic observation for self-diagnosis. This is, of course, the same systematic observational methodology that we use to evaluate group behavior as a basic research endeavor. To complete the medical analogy, the line audit is similar to a patient's annual physical examination. It represents measurement of all aspects of the system to determine areas of health and areas of potential risk.

The defining element of the line audit approach is its non-jeopardy nature. Although useful information is gained from formal crew evaluations (check rides), it is a given that crews being subjected to evaluation that can result in loss of qualification attempt to fly 'by the book'. Data collected under these circumstances may not be representative of everyday flight practices. The line audit, on the other hand, can provide a valid snapshot of normal operations. When the audit is endorsed by both management and union leadership, crews welcome systematic observation as a non-threatening and constructive assessment of flight operations.

The line audit also yields other important information. The strategy that we have employed uses a rating system that identifies exemplary as well as substandard behaviors. Knowing areas of strength as well as weakness gives an organization the opportunity to reinforce positive behavior and to direct most efforts toward areas in need of remediation. Training is most effective when it reinforces positive behavior, rather than simply sanctions negative acts.

---

10 Our focus to date has been on cockpit behavior, but the methodology, specifically the behavioral checklist, can be adopted for use with other employee groups, to gain a wider understanding of the organization's practices.

Focus Groups Organizations can also use structured group sessions (focus groups) to elicit information about employee concerns and suggestions. Such sessions also serve the important function of giving employees a sense of participation in the organization and in guiding its actions.

Incident reporting revisited Although we first mentioned it as a reactive strategy, incident reporting can be considered a proactive strategy, if handled appropriately. What organizations need is accurate data on events *in their own operations* and the ability to explore incidents more thoroughly if this is warranted. This requires a system that protects the individual while providing a complete record of events for analysis and action. Recently, the previously mentioned Air Safety Action Partnership (ASAP: FAA, 1997) has been developed as a cooperative endeavor in the USA between the FAA, airlines that voluntarily enroll and pilots' unions. ASAP gives immunity (with certain limitations) to crews reporting problems to the organization, including their own errors. The information received is carefully and rapidly reviewed by a joint team and action plans are developed to address issues uncovered. In addition, those reporting information to the system receive feedback on what remedial action has been taken to improve system safety. Although it has not been in existence long and only a limited number of airlines are participating to date, reactions to ASAP by all participants are highly favorable and a larger than expected number of reports are being received. An experimental data form to capture human factors aspects of incidents is shown at the end of Appendix C. To be successful, an effective incident reporting system must be placed in a context that supports and encourages full participation by pilots and others. The design of the reporting system is also critical. Reporting mechanisms must elicit enough information to allow analysis of the multiple factors that almost inevitably contribute to error. To that end, some education in the use of the system may be warranted. In the same vein, the ability to elicit additional data from reporters without threat can allow amplification and more complete analysis. (See Jones, in press, for further discussion of the proactive use of incident data in the air traffic system.)

Flight data recorder information Flight data recorder information from normal flights can also be a valuable diagnostic tool in determining patterns of deviation from acceptable flight parameters (although the expense may prohibit its use in many airlines). For example, the data can demonstrate that, at some airports, a number of pilots make unstabilized approaches. However, there are limitations on such data. The Digital Flight Data Recorder (DFDR) readout does provide information on the frequency of aircraft performance that is outside acceptable parameters and the locations where they occur, but these data cannot yield information on the human behaviors that were precursors of the event.[11] In the particular example, though, further investigation may show that Air Traffic Control is responsible. Ideally, the DFDR data track potential systemic problems, and pilot reports provide the context within which to diagnose the problems more fully.

Research Findings from Systematic Observations with the LLC

The database of systematic observations collected with the collaboration of a number of airlines has served as a resource for basic research as well as a diagnostic tool for organizations. In this section we discuss some of the findings from these data that are of both theoretical and applied interest. Because of financial and logistic limitations, our observational database is limited to US airlines, but it does include both domestic and international operations.

Does CRM Change Behavior?

One of the critical questions asked in the mid-1980s was whether or not CRM training has a positive effect on crew behavior and, by inference, on safety. The need for data showing behavioral impact corresponded with our research interest in the dynamics of team interaction. From this confluence grew our initial research using systematic observation. The head of flight operations at one major airline noted that CRM training was very positively received (in course evaluations) and produced significant, positive attitude change. However, he wanted to verify that the training was also reaching into the cockpit. Accordingly, we formed a research alliance to measure crew performance. Using an early version of the Line/LOS Checklist, we collected baseline performance data before the inauguration of CRM training and then, annually, for three additional years. As a result, we were able to develop a longitudinal database in which performance trends could be measured (Helmreich & Foushee, 1993). The data represent the performance of more than 2500 crews across the four-year period. The average ratings on a five-point scale for nine behaviors are shown for each year in Figure 5.6.[12] As the figure

---

11 Examples of events that trigger DFDR analysis include failure to fly stabilized approaches, engine overspeed and excessive rate of descent.
12 As noted earlier, these data were collected with the earlier version of the LLC which used a five-point rating scale.

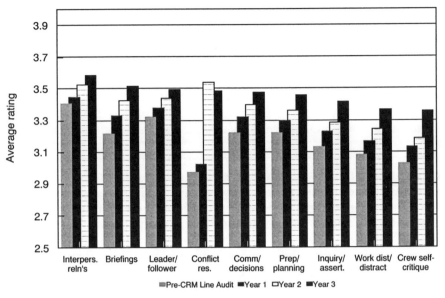

Scale: 1 = poor, 5 = excellent

Key: Interpers. reln's = Interpersonal Relations; Conflict Res. = Conflict Resolution; Prep/Planning = Preparation and Planning; Inquiry/Assert. = Inquiry/Assertion; Work dist/Distract = Workload distributed/Distractions avoided.

Figure 5.6   Crew performance before and after CRM training

indicates, there was a general improvement in organizational performance across time, but changes were incremental rather than dramatic. Additional validation of the impact of training can be seen in ratings of conflict resolution which show a dramatic increase between year 1 and year 2 of CRM training. The increase corresponds with the inclusion of this topic in annual training for year 1. Alone of the behaviors, conflict resolution shows a drop between year 2 and year 3. This could be either a regression to the mean effect or an indication that, without continuing reinforcement, old habits may re-emerge.

The results, in conjunction with participant evaluations of CRM training and attitude change, all measured in the same organization, provide strong support for the view that CRM programs do have a positive impact on crew practices in daily operations.

One might ask why such indirect measures are employed to validate CRM training. The reason is that the most obvious indicators, accident and incident rates, have fatal flaws (no pun intended). The overall accident rate (.037 fatal accident of per 100 000 departures) has far too low a base rate to be sensitive to changes in training practice in a reasonable time frame. Incidents are inconsistently reported and cannot provide an accurate measure of risk rate for particular threats (Helmreich *et al.*, 1990). The only workable strategy is to compile data using multiple methods and sources and use the results as triangulation to validate the impact of the program.

Between and within Organization Variability in Crew Performance

Between 1995 and 1997 we have collected data on the performance of crews in five major airlines in the USA, using our revised version of the LLC. The database now has more than 3200 flight segments from the five organizations. These observations were conducted as research for us and as line audits for the participating airlines. Using the methodology we have described, they served the dual purposes of providing us with data on team dynamics and performance and giving each organization a picture of its own operations and referents in the form of data from other organizations. William Hines of our research group has used this database to explore a number of theoretical issues in his doctoral dissertation. The examples in this chapter are drawn from his dissertation (Hines, 1998).

Commercial aviation in the USA and other developed countries is heavily regulated, with a strong emphasis on common standards in training and performance. Airline managers report high levels of standardization in their organizations with pride. In reality, we find that there is considerable variability among airlines, both in indirect indicators of culture that we have discussed and in performance observed during line audits. Figure 5.7 shows the differing patterns of ratings of overall crew performance across the five airlines. The differences are statistically significant and the range of substandard overall ratings (ratings of 1 and 2) across airlines is between 11 per cent and 19 per cent, which reflects distinct patterns of performance. More encouraging findings were associated with ratings of outstanding overall performance. These ranged from 10 per cent to 23 per cent. A number of reasons can be offered for the differences between organizations, ranging from resources available for training and maintenance to company expectations regarding performance. The reasons, however, are all related to the organizational and safety cultures of the organizations. These organizational differences are also paralleled in attitudinal differences as measured in responses to the FMAQ survey. The inexorable conclusion is that there are large cultural differences that play out not only in attitudes and values, but also in normal operations. These findings illustrate the need for organizations to strive to improve and standardize crew practices in normal operations and clearly have implications for the safety of operations.

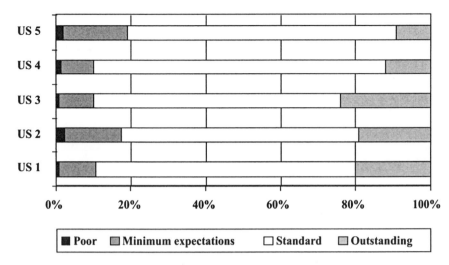

Figure 5.7   Distribution of overall crew effectiveness ratings in five major US airlines

There was also substantial variability in the number of below-standard ratings received by crews. We examined this by looking at ratings made during the approach phase of flight, which is where more than 70 per cent of accidents occur. Because automation was originally promoted as a deterrent to error and a means of enhancing flight safety, we computed the percentages separately for crews flying standard and advanced-technology aircraft. Figure 5.8 shows the percentages in each aircraft type across more than 3000 flights. As the data indicate, there were no significant performance differences between standard and advanced technology aircraft. This is important because it illustrates again that automation is not a panacea for human frailties (Rochlin, 1997; Wiener, 1993). While the task of flying and flight management is changed by automation, change does not necessarily equate to improvement.

About 70 per cent of crews received no below-standard ratings during approach, while approximately 12 per cent were rated as below standard on one marker. Around 5 per cent of crews were rated down on four or more markers. Given the number of flight operations conducted daily, this suggests that there are performance issues that need much more attention to maintain or enhance safety.

In our first investigations of crew attitudes at a major airline we were surprised to find highly significant differences in attitudes about how crews should conduct flights between aircraft fleets and crew bases. In practice, each aircraft fleet and each crew base tends to have a chief pilot who is responsible for flight operations, discipline and

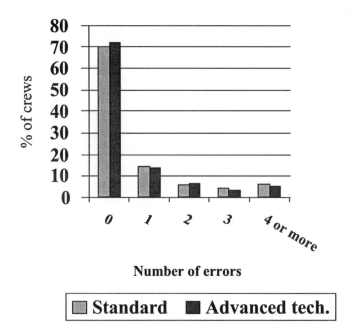

Figure 5.8   **Percentage of crews of standard and advanced technology aircraft receiving zero to four or more below-standard ratings out of 10 markers rated during approach and landing**

line evaluations. These chief pilots usually appoint those with congruent views to positions of authority, such as line check airman (senior pilots who evaluate pilot performance during line operations). These role models and decision leaders can strongly influence normative attitudes and behaviors.

Perhaps more surprising was the magnitude of behavioral differences between fleets. One might expect differences between the operation of wide-body aircraft flown in international service and smaller, narrow-body planes used for short-haul operations. However, we found that many of the largest differences were between similar aircraft flown in similar operations. Figure 5.9 shows the differing ratings of specific behaviors contrasting two narrow-body aircraft fleets in the same major airline. For this example, we picked the fleets with the most positive and most negative performance ratings. We present results in the form of a hi-lo chart. In this chart style, a rating of 3 falls on the axis with a value of 0. What is shown above the axis is the percentage of crews who were rated as outstanding (4) and below the axis is the percentage of crews who were rated below standard (1 or 2) on the particular behavioral marker.

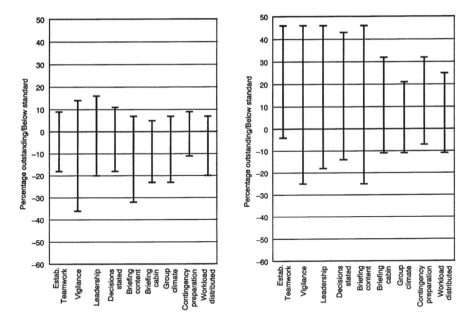

Figure 5.9 Differences in behavior between two narrow-body fleets within one airline

Starting with team formation in the pre-flight period, crews from the superior fleet showed higher percentages of outstanding performance and less substandard performance on most markers. These included vigilance, leadership, stating decisions clearly, including technical issues in briefing, briefing the cabin crew and making them a part of the team, maintaining a positive group climate, planning for possible contingencies in flight and distributing workload. The existence of such striking differences between components within organizations illustrates how subcultures can arise even in industries and organizations committed to following standard practices (recall the description of the Pan Am operation in Berlin in Chapter 4).

Chief pilots and check airmen whose operational beliefs and practices run counter to corporate and regulatory policies can easily undo the messages conveyed by the training department and management. We found, for example, that even in organizations that had established a corporate philosophy of automation use, line pilots persisted in operating counter to company policy. We have encountered check airmen who tell line pilots, 'Disregard what they tell you in the schoolhouse [training center].' Anecdotally, the check airmen in fleets with higher percentages of substandard behavior have been reported to be less enthusiastic about CRM precepts and less likely to stress CRM in evaluations. These behavioral findings support our discussion of the nature and extent of organizational subcultures in Chapter 4.

What Characterizes Effective Crews

One of the research goals in the study of crew behavior has been to specify the behaviors that contribute to effective performance. With the aggregate database of more than 3200 flights, we can test to see if there are predictors of overall crew effectiveness that are consistent across all organizations. Using multiple regression, Hines (1998) isolated a set of predictors of crew effectiveness that related to overall effectiveness judgments across all organizations and aircraft types from the aggregated data. Two of the most important predictors were establishing a team concept through initial briefings and providing guidance through including the cabin crew in the planning phase. Finding these to be significant predictors replicated the work of Robert Ginnette (1987) who, in an important observational study of airline crews, found that the establishment of team concepts and a combined plan of action *prior* to departure influenced performance throughout multi-day trips. The leadership established by the captain was another significant predictor. Leadership was also reflected in the marker on decision making which also contributed significantly as expressed by making sure that all decisions are understood and acknowledged. The final overall predictor was vigilance – maintaining close watch on current and developing situations, even during the most boring periods at cruise altitude. It is reassuring to note that these are all behaviors which form part of the core of CRM training.

The Effects of Operational Complexity on Performance

We were particularly interested in the effect of operational complexity on crew performance. Flying is an activity which can range from mundane, on days with perfect weather, a perfect airplane, little traffic and flat terrain, to extremely challenging, when any or all of the previous conditions change. For example, a maximally complex and challenging flight would be one into mountainous terrain in instrument meteorological conditions, in an aircraft with mechanical abnormalities. Each observer rated the complexity of flight on a four-point scale ranging from very low to very high. For purposes of analysis, we contrasted high-complexity flights (13 per cent of the sample) with those rated as very low (55 per cent of the sample). The results shown in Figure 5.10 reveal an interesting pattern of behaviors which is illustrated by two markers, 'appropriate distribution of work-load' and 'decisions clearly stated and acknowledged'. The variability of performance was significantly greater under challenging condi-

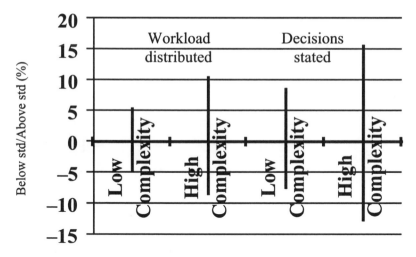

Figure 5.10 **Differential performance of crews under conditions of low and high operational complexity**

tions: a higher percentage of flights were rated as both outstanding and as below standard. The implication is that some crews rose to the challenge with enhanced performance while others showed performance deficits. Since challenge can be equated to risk, there is both good news and bad news in these findings. Developing techniques to enhance the performance of substandard crews in demanding situations will be an important challenge for organizations.

Automation Use and Operational Complexity

As we have shown in Chapter 3, there are wide differences between and within cultures in attitudes regarding automation. Several of the organizations where we have collected observational data have adopted policies giving crews discretion regarding the use of automation and encouraging them to establish clear guidelines for pilot flying and pilot not flying (PF–PNF) duties regarding programming and automation use. We found that, even in organizations where this philosophy of automation use was part of training, there was substantial variability in practices and that variability increased under conditions of operational complexity. Figure 5.11 shows the percentage of below-standard and outstanding ratings on two markers, establishing guidelines for PF–PNF duties and allowing sufficient time for programming automation before critical periods of flight. Data come from more than 1500 flights in advanced-technology air-

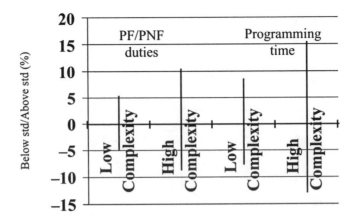

Figure 5.11   Differential ratings of automation use under conditions of low and high operational complexity

craft. As the figure indicates, behavior in high complexity environments shows the same pattern of increased variability seen on other markers.

Captains' Roles and Operational Complexity

One of the intriguing findings reported in the National Transportation Safety Board Safety Study (NTSB, 1994) was that captains were flying in 71 per cent of the accidents. In airline operations, captains and first officers normally alternate pilot flying and pilot not-flying duties on each flight segment. Thus the expected distribution of captain and first officer flying would be 50 per cent–50 per cent in both accidents and uneventful flights. In the more than 3200 flights in our line audit database, the distribution is almost exactly that (50 per cent–50 per cent). The significantly elevated percentage of accident flights where captains were flying suggests that they may be more likely to take physical control of the aircraft in abnormal or emergency situations or that mishaps are more likely to occur when the captain is in physical control – two quite different hypotheses. The data raise the possibility (quite threatening to the 'white scarf' image of the captain as the superman in the cockpit) that allowing the captain to fly in abnormal situations may be a counterproductive strategy. We have argued from a theoretical perspective that the best practice in emergencies should be to have the captain delegate flying duties to the first officer and devote his cognitive energy to *managing the situation*. Several organizations, including Japan Airlines, have adopted this strategy as part of their emergency operating procedures.

We explored this issue in our observational database. First, we used the same split of the data into low- and high-complexity flights (Hines, 1998). There were no differences in overall crew effectiveness or ratings of leadership as a function of pilot flying when the operational complexity was low. However, under complex conditions, crews with the first officer flying received significantly higher ratings on both overall crew effectiveness and leadership than those where the captain was in physical control. Differential ratings of crew effectiveness under high complexity are shown in Figure 5.12.

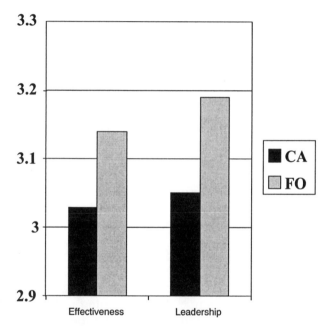

Note: The range of ratings is from 0 to 4; differences are significant at better than $p < 0.01$.

Figure 5.12   Ratings of overall crew effectiveness and leadership with captain and first officer flying under conditions of high operational complexity

It is reasonable to hypothesize that captains who must fly and manage, including making strategic decisions under highly complex and stressful situations, may experience cognitive overload. Especially given the narrowing of attention which occurs under high stress, it is likely that attempting to perform both flying and managerial duties may result in performance impairment. These data not only provide an interesting replication of the safety study in flights that ended happily, but also have strong implications for organizational practices. It may be advisable for organizations to provide more guidelines for division of flying and managerial duties under off-normal conditions.

The research findings from systematic observation show that, despite the high variability in the aviation system, there are regularities in behavior and problematic areas. These point to issues which must be addressed to enhance safety. In the next chapter we become more specific in describing actions, including training and diagnosis, that organizations can take to increase safety and, incidentally, efficiency in their operations. First, however, we demonstrate how the issues of culture, error and error management intersect in the operating room and show parallels between the flightdeck and the OR.

Cultures, Error and Error Management in Medicine

We have stressed the parallels between the cockpit and the operating room and have shown in Chapter 1 that very similar input–process–output models of team performance can be developed. We also demonstrated in Chapter 2 that doctors and pilots have strong professional cultures that can both enhance and reduce safety. The OR and the cockpit are embedded in organizational cultures that are replete with subcultures based on professional allegiance and organizational factors.

There are also some notable differences between the two domains. While airline pilots operate machines that are usually modern and well integrated, the OR is a hodgepodge of differing equipment strung together by cables and tubing.[13] As we pointed out, the OR is often described as an ergonomic nightmare. Unlike the mission of moving people or cargo from one point to another, the focus of attention in the OR is a patient who needs some form of corrective surgery and whose condition is variable and often unpredictable. We also pointed out that the OR is a psychologically more complex environment than the cockpit, requiring close coordination between members of different professional disciplines and subcultures: surgeons, anesthesiologists, nurses and technicians. At times there may be more than a dozen people in the OR during certain operations. With poor acoustics, audible alarms and the frequent playing of music, it is a noisy setting that can be distracting.

---

13 The idea of the 'Glass OR' with a fully integrated suite of monitors and controls may develop. It is unlikely that increased automation will produce a dramatic reduction in human error.

As part of their professional cultures, both doctors and pilots have a strong concern for the well-being and safety of those in their charge – patients and passengers. This concern obviously includes the avoidance of errors that might lead to catastrophic outcomes. In the case of physicians, it is reflected in the phrase *primum non nocere* (first do no harm) which is embodied in the Hippocratic oath.

Differing Attention to Error in Aviation and Medicine

Despite the commonalities, when we turn to the race to reduce and manage error, aviation appears to be far ahead. A number of explanatory hypotheses can be offered for the difference and no single explanation is likely to be satisfactory. In aviation, errors that result in crashes are highly visible and widely publicized. Public and media pressure to understand the root causes is enormous and, in most advanced countries, government agencies with vast resources undertake investigations that last until causal factors are uncovered.[14] The investigative process can also be problematic. In many air disasters, investigators look for a proximal cause (usually the pilots at the 'sharp end') and stop without examining the organizational and regulatory factors that may have contributed.[15] Once cause has been established, there are also strong pressures to blame and punish the responsible parties.[16] In many cases, particularly in the USA, this involves dismissal of those involved and massive litigation which can result in very high damage awards (including punitive damages where willful negligence is determined by the court).

We discussed earlier in the chapter the proliferation of confidential *incident* reporting systems in aviation. These allow the collection of more extensive information on a larger universe of events that might have proved catastrophic, but did not. In sum, relatively good, but not perfect, data on error are available in aviation and have led to the worldwide adoption of programs such as CRM. A final reason often cynically proposed for the greater concern with error management in aviation is that the pilots are usually the first at the scene of an accident and bear the consequences, while doctors who commit a lethal error can spend the same afternoon on the golf course.

14 The success of the US National Transportation Safety Board in determining probable causes of air crashes has been legendary. However, in recent years, the Board has been baffled by the inexplicable crashes of two B-737 aircraft and the explosion in flight of TWA flight 800, a B-747.
15 Recent investigations in the USA, Canada and Australia have cast a strong light on organizational issues. This is a most encouraging trend.
16 Dr John Lauber, formerly of the NTSB and now with Airbus Industrie, has pointed out an extreme example of 'blame and punish' in a case where the senior managers of a Chinese factory were executed for delivering a defective product.

The conditions surrounding medical error are complex and the lesser concern with public investigation and correction cannot be construed as a blanket indictment of the profession. Especially in the USA, a litigious culture has led to a proliferation of malpractice suits alleging medical error and the frequent award of massive amounts of punitive damage. Medical error can not only threaten doctors' licenses to practice, but can have the side-effect of creating enormous fees for malpractice insurance. Because medical errors occur one by one, there is far less visibility and public outcry when an error becomes known. Associated with lower visibility is an absence of government support for investigation. A final, less positive, factor is the tendency of professional cultures to protect their own, as we have noted in Chapter 2. In essence, one's peers are one's monitors. Medical societies, led by doctors, and hospitals are frequently reluctant to make instances of error public and to take action regarding those who err.

Although the situation is certainly less advanced than that in aviation, there are indications that things are improving and there are some empirical studies that help us understand the nature and frequency of medical error. One of the most influential investigations was the Harvard Medical Practice Study conducted by Lucian Leape and his colleagues (Brennan *et al.*, 1991; Leape *et al.*, 1991). In this massive study the hospital records of 25 000 patients were reviewed by experts for evidence of error. Not surprisingly, the largest source of error was in the administration of drugs (see also Belkin, 1997). In a more recent study of medication, 3.99 errors per 1000 administrations were found in a New York hospital (Lesar *et al.*, 1997).

In collaboration with Hans-Gerhard Schaefer, we looked for errors and problems in team coordination in the OR (Helmreich & Schaefer, 1994). As mentioned in Chapter 1, not only the dynamics but also the breakdowns are similar. We also found that many of the failures were at the intersection of the subcultures (that is, between surgeons and anesthesiologists). Table 5.1 lists errors that we observed during operations in a teaching hospital. As can be seen, they involve the familiar litany of communications problems, failure to follow SOPs, distractions and lack of vigilance. Most of the errors were trapped or mitigated before the patient suffered injury, but the level of risk in operations was clearly increased by these errors.

Table 5.2 lists breakdowns in team processes that we noted in the same hospital. One of the frequent problems was a failure to inform others of what one is doing. Many of the other weaknesses centered on leadership and the unwillingness of juniors to question the actions of seniors. In many instances, those with critical information remained silent. We also observed conflicts, frequently between surgeons and anesthesiologists, that were not constructively resolved (we provided an example of extreme conflict resolution in Chapter 1;

Table 5.1   Errors observed in operating rooms

Surgeon fails to inform anesthesiologist before administering drug with effect on blood pressure

Failure to complete checklist for anesthesia machine

Failure to react to blood oxygen alarms

Failure to monitor patient status

Resident reading manual fails to note patient emerging from anesthesia

Consultant distracted from decision on patient by problem in another OR

see also Box 5.6). We were disheartened by the fact that medical teams failed to profit from their experiences by debriefing after critical events. Finally, despite the fact that this was a teaching hospital, we saw very few instances of instruction and mentoring of junior team members.

Box 5.6   More conflict in the operating room

In Chapter 1 we gave an example of disagreements in the operating room that led to fisticuffs between the surgeon and the anesthesiologist. This is not simply an example of what has come to be called 'Road Rage' in the USA. The following is the verbatim headline and text of a news release in April 1996.

Surgeon Shoots During Operation
Anaesthetist Dead – Patient Faints

Rio de Janeiro. Reuters. A Brazilian surgeon shot a colleague, who was responsible for the anaesthesia of the patient, during abdominal surgery. While this was happening on Monday, the patient awoke from anaesthesia and, on seeing the bloodbath, fainted. The Resident who was present attempted to save the life of the anaesthetist, then ended the abdominal operation. The surgeon was long gone over the mountains.

There was disagreement regarding the surgery between the two doctors, members of a private clinic at Macae, near Rio de Janeiro, where the operation took place. During the dispute, the 60-year-old surgeon, Marcelino Pereira da Silva, took out a revolver and put three shots into the head of Elimson Ribeiro Elias, age 40. Search is on for the surgeon.

Table 5.2   Inadequate teamwork in the operating room

Failure to brief own and other team of plans for operation

Failure to speak up to inform team of work overload or patient problems

Failure to discuss alternatives and to advocate a course of action

Failure to establish leadership

Conflicts over course of action

Failure to debrief actions during operation

Failure to provide training for residents

Positive Developments: Acquiring Data

Incident-reporting systems   There have been a number of positive developments in medicine in recent years. Hospitals have become increasingly aware of the need for diagnostic data to maintain safety. The response has been the initiation of confidential incident-reporting systems that allow medical personnel to report safety problems and errors without jeopardy. As Leape (1994) points out, safety initiatives at the system level are taking advantage of the aviation experience. One of the most successful incident-reporting systems has been developed by anesthesiologists in Australia (Beckmann, Baldwin, Hart & Runciman, 1996; Beckmann, West, Groombridge, Baldwin, Hart, Clayton & Runciman, 1996). In an analysis of more than 2000 incident reports, the Australian group found that issues related to human interaction were causal in more than 70 per cent of the reports – a figure startlingly close to that for aviation mishaps (Williamson *et al.*, 1993). Efforts have also addressed errors made by physicians in general practice (Britt, *et al.*, 1997). Another program has been developed at the University of Basel/Kantonsspital in Switzerland under the direction of Sven Staender (Staender, 1997; Staender, *et al.*, 1997). The system, which is still under development, provides a global Website where medical personnel from around the world can share information on adverse events. Within the hospital, it is augmented by an intranet designed to capture incidents within the organization. Significantly, in summarizing the incidents in the database, Staender finds the same problems in communication that we had observed.

Donald Berwick of the Harvard Medical School has been a long-time advocate of continuous improvement in healthcare delivery (Berwick, 1989). As founder and CEO of the Institute of Healthcare Improvement, he has initiated a series of programs designed to help organizations collect diagnostic data and take proactive steps to increase safety and efficiency. One of the most recent initiatives was aimed at the reduction of medication errors in hospitals.

Quality assurance programs, including mortality and morbidity studies and audits, also yield important data that can be applied in the interests of safety, both through training and through organizational change (Davies, 1994; Helmreich & Davies, 1996).

Systematic observation   After we discovered that we could indeed observe the occurrence of error and the dynamics of team interaction in the OR, Hans-Gerhard Schaefer at Basel decided that it would be of value in medicine to be able to collect the same kind of systematic data that form the bases of line audits in aviation. He set out to adapt the Line/LOS Checklist, described earlier in this chapter, to the OR environment. In this he was joined by one of our students from the University of Texas at Austin, Bryan Sexton. The resulting Operating Room Checklist (ORCL) gave observers the opportunity to capture reliably team interactions during surgery (Helmreich, Schaefer & Sexton, 1995). After Schaefer's untimely death, Sexton continued to work with the human factors team to collect data during surgical procedures (Sexton *et al.*, 1997a). They found below standard communications in some phases of nearly 70 per cent of the operations observed. Many of these instances of flawed communication had the potential of adverse effects on the patient. There were also instances of conflict observed in 10 per cent of the operations monitored (Sexton, 1997). These results provided strong support for the concept of providing training in more effective communication and team coordination along the lines of CRM.

Surveys   Schaefer also concluded that the attitudes regarding teamwork, communications and leadership should be measured in all personnel working in the OR environment. Using the Flight Management Attitudes Questionnaire as the template, we developed the Operating Room Management Attitudes Questionnaire (ORMAQ: Helmreich & Schaefer, 1994). The ORMAQ also included the items reflecting personal invulnerability that were discussed in Chapter Two. The questionnaire has recently been revised by Bryan Sexton (Helmreich, Sexton & Merritt, 1997) and data have been collected in hospitals in the USA as well as Europe. Results show concerns with autocratic leadership and communication barriers between subcultures that are highly similar to those in aviation (Helmreich & Schaefer, 1994). We have also found that there is substantial variability in the organizational climate within (that is, between the various subcultures) and between organizations (Helmreich & Davies, 1996). One of the striking findings in response to open-ended questions about how to improve the job was a need for feedback on performance, which again supports the need for data on what happens in the OR.

Positive Developments: New Training

Simulation in anesthesiology   Anesthesiologists in the USA as well as Europe were among the first medical personnel to conclude that training approaches like CRM might be transferable from the cockpit to the OR. David Gaba of Stanford was one of the pioneers in the USA, through the development of what has come to be known as Anesthesia Crisis Resource Management (Gaba & DeAnda, 1988; Howard *et al.*, 1992). This program, and similar ones in the USA and Europe, have centered on the use of an anesthesia simulator, which consists of an instrumented, computer-controlled mannequin that can be used to simulate the anesthesia component of the OR (for descriptions of representative programs, see Chopra *et al.*, 1994; Christensen *et al.*, 1995; Good *et al.*, 1992; Kurrek & Fish, 1996).

While CRM training in aviation focuses on initial classroom training in relevant concepts, augmented by full mission simulations, the medical programs center on the simulator with limited didactic instruction (Davies & Helmreich, 1996; Helmreich & Davies, 1997). What is notable about these programs is that they focus only on one element of the OR environment, the anesthesia team. In some programs, actors are hired to play the role of surgeons. While the attempt to deal with interpersonal issues in the OR is commendable, one must conclude that failing to include the full team seriously degrades the value of the enterprise. It is not clear why the initiative has been with anesthesiologists and what barriers have kept surgeons away from the training.[17]

Full operating room simulation: the TOMS program in Basel   Again drawing from aviation experience and his observations, Hans-Gerhard Schaefer concluded that the most effective training should involve all OR personnel conducting meaningful work. He enlisted the support of the heads of surgery and anesthesia to develop an integrated program that became known as Team Oriented Medical Simulation (Helmreich, 1997; Helmreich & Davies, 1997; Schaefer *et al.*, 1995).[18] The program in Basel involves a fully equipped operating room built around a computer-controlled mannequin (appropriately named Wilhelm Tell). Wilhelm Tell can be anesthetized, and breathes, coughs and responds to the introduction of drugs, with vital signs portrayed on standard monitors. Unlike other anesthetic simulators, however, the 'patient' can undergo laparoscopic, abdominal surgery (using a pig liver embedded in the laparoscopic simulator). The pig liver is connected to the (artificial) circulatory system which is controlled by a pump.

Wilhelm Tell is scheduled on the hospital's daily calendar and the simulator is listed as another operating room. Staff are scheduled for the simulator as for a regular operation. On the scheduled day, they report to a conference room where they participate in a briefing regarding the goals and nature of the simulation. Then, in operating robes, they proceed to the simulator for the 'operation'. The facilitator of the simulation is located with the computer in a control room. There are multiple video cameras and microphones and the entire operation is videotaped. During the operation itself, various crises may be introduced – a hemorrhage, collapsed lung or cardiac arrest – that increase the need for joint decision making. At the completion of the simulation, a complete debriefing includes review and discussion of the videotaped behaviors during the surgery.

17   Certainly, there are greater difficulties in surgical than anesthetic simulation. One is also tempted to suggest that the NIH (not invented here) syndrome may have kept surgeons away.

18   Dr Daniel Scheidegger, Professor and Chair of Anaesthesiology, and Dr Felix Harder, Professor and Chair of Surgery, provided the essential organizational support. Financial aid from the Swiss National Science Foundation also aided the project. Other key personnel involved in the program were or are Dr Dieter Betzendoerfer, Dr Stephan Marsch, Dr Thomas Kocher, Dr Cristoph Harms and Dr Roger Zobrist.

Participant evaluations of the simulation are highly favorable (Sexton *et al.*, 1997b). The one weakness of the program, which it shared with the purely anesthetic simulations, was the failure to provide an initial awareness program which clarified the nature and extent of human performance limitations and the concepts of error management. The team at Basel is developing a comprehensive course that will supplement simulation training and the group is further coordinating human factors training with incident reporting.

Future prospects   It seems likely that error management will find a permanent place in medicine and may extend to all units where interdisciplinary teamwork is critical, such as the emergency room and intensive care units. However, the barriers associated with litigation and the tendency to protect one's professional peers will not disappear overnight. Some of the pressure for better management of error is likely to come from the movement toward managed healthcare and the insurers who must pay the cost of error. No matter what the impediments, at the organizational level the *value* of error management cannot be denied. In the next chapter we discuss some of the strategies that organizations can use to implement programs.

6 Implementing Error Management: Trust, Data and Interventions

We must try to trust one another. (Jomo Kenyatta, Statement, as first president of the Republic of Kenya, 1964)

We are all controlled by the world in which we live, and part of that world has been and will be constructed by men. The question is this: are we to be controlled by accidents, by tyrants, or by ourselves in effective cultural design? (B.F. Skinner, *Cumulative Record*, 1972)

The elimination of accidents and errors is an admirable goal, but it is also an unrealistic and unachievable goal. Accidents will always occur, although rarely, when there is a concatenation of infrequent circumstances in complex systems. In Reason's (1990, 1997) terms, when the gaps in system defenses align (latent failures), unpredictable catastrophes will happen. The elimination of human error is also an impossibility. Nature will continue to impose limits on human performance and imperfectible humans will continue to err. Chapter 5 introduced the concept of error management as a cultural universal which could shape organizational behavior in high-risk, sociotechnical industries. In this chapter, we discuss the implementation of error management (EM).

Safety Cultures are Built on Trust

As stated in Chapter 4, it is the organizational culture that shapes employees' perceptions of the relative importance placed on safety within the organization. A safety culture involves observable behaviors *and* underlying values, beliefs and assumptions. Employees in a safety culture are more than just a group of individuals enacting a set of safety guidelines. They are guided in their behavior by an organization-wide commitment to safety which is premised on

175

trust and the shared understanding that every member upholds safety norms and supports other members to that end. A safety culture is also proactive: it encourages and rewards vigilance and inquiry from all its members (Meshkati, 1994). Its goal is to mend the system rather than killing the messenger. (Box 6.1 describes the disastrous consequences of an organization's failure to be proactive.)

Box 6.1   Working on the railroad: reactive error management

The takeover and merger of the Southern Pacific Railroad with the Union Pacific Railroad is a classic example of things gone awry in complex organizations. Following the merger, many of the managers from Southern Pacific as well as many train crews took buy-outs for early retirement at a time when it was necessary to merge two complicated organizations and route structures.

Within a few months of the merger, the system began to unravel. Long delays in shipments became common and a shortage of managers familiar with the old operation led to many operational problems. A lack of crews resulted in much overtime and fatigue. The worst outcome was a series of accidents, some fatal, involving human error. In one three-month period, nine people were killed in three accidents.

One of the non-fatal accidents shows serious management problems. Union Pacific had refused for seven years to relocate a fuel cut-off switch located by the knee of the engineer. All other US railroads had moved the switch because it could be inadvertently nudged by the engineer, cutting off fuel to the engines. In the accident in question, the engineer accidentally hit the switch with his knee as the train was going down a steep grade. The brakes were insufficient to slow the train and it ran away until the coupler broke and 68 grain cars left the track, causing $4.4 million in damage. Union Pacific fired both the engineer and the conductor. The National Transportation Safety Board, however, found the crew blameless and censured management.

The organizational responses to the series of accidents included the appointment of a vice-president of safety and risk management reporting to the president, initiation of a fatigue management program and the endorsement of a 'blame-free workplace'.

Although these actions are appropriate and meritorious, they represent reactive responses to a clearly disastrous condition. It seems clear that a lack of data on system operations and a failure to diagnose operational needs to manage the more complex, merged situation created many of the problems. It is also unfortunately true that management has lost the trust both of front-line employees and of customers. Acceptance of the 'blame-free workplace' is made much more difficult by acts such as the firing of the crew involved in the accident described above. The organization must also face many embarrassing and potentially costly lawsuits from customers whose shipments have gone astray. In Texas alone, the railroad commission estimated that customers have lost between 300 and 400 million dollars in one year because of delayed or lost shipments.

Many of the strategies to unite and strengthen an organizational culture can also be applied to a safety culture. As expected, Senior Management plays a critical role in fostering a safety culture. If employees observe Management condoning or indirectly promoting something unsafe, they lose faith in the system and withdraw from active participation in the safety process. Similarly, a 'blame and punish' Management philosophy will send safety concerns underground. Thus the first task for Management is to gain and keep the trust of employees.

Management can place visible emphasis on safety with the establishment of a safety office that has authority, resources and credibility. The head of safety should report directly to the organization's Chief Executive Officer to ensure that safety concerns are addressed at the highest level.[1] The safety officer, in concert with the CEO, should have the authority to take immediate action to eliminate threats to safety. This can extend to grounding aircraft or suspending some types of operations.

The incumbent in the safety position needs credibility with both workers and management. Operational experience and experience in safety are obviously desirable, but the most important attribute is the employee's confidence that he or she has the authority, commitment and ability to address safety issues. The safety office should also have sufficient, qualified personnel to maintain a living database of safety-related information, to investigate and analyze incidents and potential threats, and to publish and distribute safety bulletins, posters, special alerts and so on.

The purview of the safety office extends beyond flight operations to encompass the infrastructure. This includes maintenance, ground operations and other support activities. The safety office needs to establish strong collaborative relationships with the training group, the flight standards group, and the managers of all operational units.

1   When the safety officer reports to lower-level managers with operational responsibilities, several problems can arise. One is defensiveness regarding one's own areas of responsibility; a second is dealing with safety problems that cross lines of responsibility.

In response to regulatory directives, the safety office may need to initiate actions in collaboration with other departments of the organization. Responses may include special training, safety bulletins and directing check airmen to look for particular practices on the line. On other occasions, check airmen may detect slippage in performance and alert the safety office to a growing problem.

In a true safety culture, communication is open and devoid of finger pointing or cover-ups. Organizational reality can be something quite different. Organizational politics and 'empire building' can hinder serious collaboration. Senior Management may want a safety officer in name only, and may deliberately appoint a safety officer who is perceived to be ineffectual. The organization can then lay claim to the position without being concerned that any real change will be effected. Safety costs money and has to compete with other organizational demands for resources in any profit-driven business. A safety office which can measure safety interventions and recommendations in terms of performance savings will have more chance of getting needed resources.

Managers, chief pilots, check and training captains, station managers and pursers are all role models for safety. These people must also 'walk the walk' of safety. They are responsible for knowing, enforcing and reinforcing safety procedures, which means they must be available and accessible to line personnel. They must listen to those who report safety concerns, they must act on those concerns and they must ensure that the organizational response is timely and information is relayed back to the employees. Likewise, new-hires should learn the correct safety procedures and standards through observation of these role models. A formalized mentoring system would allow a senior person to explain and exemplify the safety culture to the newcomer.

As part of promoting and encouraging a winning team in these safety-oriented organizations, success should always be defined in terms of safety records as well as productivity and financial records.[2] Guidelines for reporting error and safety concerns should be published and posted, publicly and repeatedly, as visual reminders of safety standards. Finally, operational response to catastrophic error conveys a message about the organization's safety culture. The response can be swift and open, focusing on what went wrong, or it can be defensive and secretive, looking only for a suitable scapegoat. The classic response, 'Who can we blame?', may be human nature, but it does little to improve the system's long-term defenses.

---

2   These safety records may only be reported internally, so as not to alarm the general public; nonetheless the employees need to know that error and safety are being tracked in the system.

The Unrocked Boat

Ironically, one of the threats to a safety culture can be safety itself. Organizations that have established and maintained a strong safety record risk becoming complacent and lowering their defenses. We know that errors occur in the most safety-conscious organizations and that the difference between safety and disaster is often luck. James Reason (1997) speaks of the dangers of the 'unrocked boat':[3]

> There is plentiful evidence to show that a lengthy period without bad accidents can lead to the steady erosion of protection, as productive demands gain the upper hand in this already unequal relationship. It is easy to forget to be afraid of things that rarely happen, particularly in the face of productive imperatives like growth, profit and market share. As a result, investment in more effective protection falls off and the care and maintenance necessary to preserve the integrity of existing defences declines. Not only that, productive growth is regarded as commercially essential in most organizations. Simply increasing production without the corresponding provision of new or extended defences will also erode the available safety margins. The consequence of both processes – neglecting existing defences and failing to provide new ones – is a much increased risk of a catastrophic and sometimes terminal accident. (p. 6)

Safety Cultures are Built on Data

In order to manage error proactively within an organization, Senior Management must be able to locate the causes of error. Thus at the base of any effective safety culture is data. Management needs to ask, 'Where are we making our errors? And what can we do to minimize their occurrence and impact?' Only the employees know where the errors are occurring, and in many cases they also have the solutions. Herein lies the fundamental connection between error management and safety cultures. An organization needs data about the type and sources of error in order to improve effectively (and efficiently) the system's defenses against error. Without the complete trust of the employees, the necessary information will not be forthcoming. Trust is built through shared values, integrity of leadership and common practices. Therefore an organization must introduce an error-tolerant safety philosophy in order to build trust, so that employees will report error and error-inducing situations, thereby allowing Management to be proactive and error-responsive, improving the

3   Reason attributes the phrase to Constance Perin, who used it in a discussion of safety at British Rail.

organization's defenses and the probability of safe organizational outcomes. Such a system allows Management to assess accurately its safety thresholds and weaknesses and provides a logic by which resources can be allocated in proportion to the safety improvements they offer.

Data can come from a variety of sources, each of which provides a partial picture of the system, and organizations will be best served by employing all of them. Using surveys to ask members of the organization to share their perceptions of safety-related issues provides data on a number of topics. In some instances, the problem has been identified as 'lack of timely feedback from Management', in other cases it has been employee ignorance of the safety reporting procedures, and, in others, training has been identified as failing to meet the needs of line personnel. The best surveys are designed in conjunction with members of the organization who are aware of controversial issues. For surveys to be useful, they must protect the anonymity of respondents, often by using a third party to administer and analyze them. (The issue again is trust.)

The line audits discussed in Chapter 5 provide the most comprehensive picture of normal system operations. It is our feeling that audit data yield a much more accurate picture of practices than performance during formal evaluation. One of the additional benefits of line audit data is the information collected on superior performance. Unlike the reactive data collection associated with accidents and incidents, this information focuses on successful individual and crew strategies and can be fed back to the training department and line personnel. Training by positive example is more instructive than training by case studies of what went wrong in accidents.

A revision of our behavior coding system is being developed to provide another sort of safety information – the management of error. In this version, which is designed to support error management, off-normal situations (for example, severe weather or mechanical failure) are identified, and crew behaviors in coping with the situation are evaluated, specifically to identify instances of error avoidance, error trapping and error mitigation. Summarizing the number and types of errors and their resolution provides other indicators of system performance. Tracking these data across time will tell an organization not only where errors are occurring, but also whether interventions have been successful in reducing the occurrence and impact of those errors.

Reporting programs such as the Aviation Safety Action Program (ASAP) at American Airlines form the backbone of safety cultures and aid in the implementation of error management by providing concrete examples of errors and how they were handled. To make ASAP data optimally useful, methods need to be developed to link them with information gleaned from surveys and audits. Digital flight data recorders also add to the information pool, as we noted in Chapter 5.

The Importance of Continuing Evaluation

Effective safety cultures rely on continuously updated information. Not only must the status of operations and opinions be monitored, data analysts should look for trends in a variety of indicators. For example, we were able to show that acceptance of CRM concepts had slipped in several organizations by examining attitude scores across time. Similarly, from line audit data we were able to validate improvements in performance over time following the initiation of CRM and the implementation of recurrent training in it. The data from the line audit, when given to the training department, guided the choice of curriculum topics for the following year. Similarly, from interview data collected during the line audit, one organization found problems in the dispatch of international flights and was able to correct them expeditiously.

In summary, safety cultures require a proactive error management philosophy which engenders trust and generates data. Box 6.2 tells the story of an organization which failed to sustain a safety culture. In common with Union Pacific (Box 6.1), this organization was also the product of a recent merger.

Box 6.2   Air Ontario flight 1363

On 10 March 1989, Air Ontario flight 1363 crashed immediately after take-off from Dryden, Ontario, en route to Winnipeg, Ontario. Both pilots, one of the two flight attendants and 21 passengers perished in the accident. The proximal cause of the accident was rapidly determined to be the fact that the flight took off with ice on the wings.[4] Both the Flight Data Recorder and the Cockpit Voice Recorder were destroyed in the fire that followed the crash. The open question was why a highly experienced crew committed such a basic error. The Canadian Parliament appointed a Commission of Inquiry, chaired by Justice Virgil Moshansky of the Supreme Court. The Commission launched an investigation that ultimately looked at all aspects of the Canadian aviation system, including the organizational culture of Air Ontario (Moshansky, 1992). One of us (RLH) served as a consultant to the Commission and investigated organizational and crew factors in the accident (Helmreich,

---

4   Ice contamination on the lifting surfaces of an aircraft interferes with airflow and loss of lift, causing a plane to stall.

1992). Just as there were contributing organizational factors in the Avianca accident, there were also crew and regulatory factors involved in Air Ontario. However, for the sake of discussion, we will describe only the organizational issues. (See also Maurino *et al.*, 1995.)

Air Ontario was the result of the merger of two regional airlines with distinctly different cultures, one operating in the relatively benign climate of Southern Ontario, the other more of a bush operation in the North. Following the merger, there was a bitter strike that left residual feelings of ill-will among pilot groups. The organizational climate was clearly negative.

The chief pilot was the brother of one of the primary owners of the airline. He had acquired the derogatory nickname, 'The Iceman', because of several instances of taking off with contaminated wings. He was also noted for pressuring pilots to fly aircraft with maintenance defects.

Air Ontario did not commit needed resources for the maintenance of the newly acquired jet aircraft and the crash airplane was dispatched with a number of maintenance problems. Flight operations had not developed and distributed approved flight manuals for the pilots of the Fokker – crews simply flew with the manuals of the airline which provided them with contract training.

Compounding organizational problems, Air Canada had just purchased an interest in Air Ontario, but did not provide its feeder carrier with the same level of training and resources, such as a CRM program.

Several dangerous normative practices had developed among pilots. One was a so-called '80 knot' check when taking off in icing conditions. During the take-off roll, each pilot would look out the window at 80 knots to see if snow had blown off.[5] The second practice was to write up maintenance snags (defects) on cocktail napkins from the cabin instead of the aircraft log, thus avoiding possible grounding of the airplane.

Overall, the safety culture at Air Ontario was near non-existent. Flight 1363 was improperly dispatched into worsening weather with few lines of defense against error and environmental challenge.

Error Management v. Risk Management

Before we turn to the next section, on interventions, we want to clarify the distinction between error management and risk manage-

---

5   While risky, this practice had not resulted in an accident in propeller-driven aircraft such as the Convair 580. It was not adequate on a swept-wing jet, especially when clear ice had formed under snow.

ment and their respective approaches to safety. The primary focus of risk assessment (and risk management) has been on minimizing loss, of finding out 'how safe is safe enough' by determining the odds (likelihood) and payoffs (cost–benefit analyses) of various outcomes in financial terms (Perrow, 1984). The process of risk management, as described in *Rupp's Insurance Glossary* (NILS, 1996) has the following steps: identify and analyze loss exposure, measure loss exposure, select technique or combination of techniques to handle each exposure, implement the technique, monitor the decisions made and make appropriate changes. The goal of risk management is to minimize loss. The goal of error management, on the other hand, is to *improve* the odds of safe outcomes. Error management has a more positive and proactive stance than the reactive (and ghoulish) stance of risk management. Also systematic data collected for error management could provide risk analysts with more accurate estimates of the likelihood of events than the current system which relies solely on the incidence of past events.[6]

Safety Cultures are Strengthened with Well-designed Interventions

The best interventions are based on data collected locally at the organizational level, using any or all of the methods mentioned previously, and are designed by company insiders with the help of the research community and professional consultants. Company insiders are the people who know the history, the personnel, the strengths and the perceived problems of the company. In other words, the insiders know the culture of the organization in a way that researchers, consultants and outsiders can never know. The insiders provide unique information about their organization, and it is the insiders who will know whether a new training program or intervention is likely to gain acceptance amongst the employees.

The research community can assist company insiders in the design of organizational interventions in several ways. First, there is human factors research in the fields of engineering, psychology and physiology. The best research in these fields helps define and understand the limits of human performance. This research can be applied to the development and evaluation of various countermeasures for error management. With minor modifications, research findings can be directly incorporated into training curricula, providing the necessary scientific basis for recommended actions. Researchers also develop

6 Accidents and incidents are very rare events – they are unreliable as statistical indicators of trends.

and modify the data collection instruments (such as surveys, behavioral checklists and incident-reporting forms) which help an organization to self-diagnose. Researchers may also train individuals in the use of these diagnostic forms.

The fundamental obligation of the research community is to keep the industry informed of its work and to make the research as accessible as possible. The Internet is proving to be a very effective means of disseminating research ideas and results. With the proliferation of electronic bulletin boards and websites, the Internet has also become a powerful means of collaboration and sharing of experiences for many researchers and practitioners. We would like to thank all those webmasters who keep the information current and available for all of us.

A good consultant can be invaluable to company insiders. With an outsider's objective perspective, and with experience gleaned from other organizations, the consultant can focus the insiders' attention on relevant issues by asking the questions that need to be addressed. Consultants can also help insiders avoid reinventing the wheel by offering past experiences and current solutions. It is the consultant's role to educate the organizational client to a level of self-sufficiency in diagnosis and intervention. In order to do their job well, consultants must also have ties to the research community to ensure they are kept abreast of important developments in the field,[7] and they must be sufficiently flexible to accommodate and incorporate each client's unique agenda. Box 6.3 relates one consultant's story of the need for flexibility while working in China.

Box 6.3   The 'Mercedes star': face and favor in China

During my stay in China, we often sat together in the evenings with other expats in the hotel bar, holding endless shop-talks about how to cope successfully with the Chinese environment. Every few days a new delegation arrived from another part of the world and there would be more stories.

A marketing manager from an internationally renowned car supplier told me a story which I remember because we had some similar experiences in our project. He was in China to build up a reliable network of local distributors for spare parts. One day he had an appointment with the general manager of a new private company. The meeting developed very positively. All the details about capacity, delivery system, custom issues and payment could

---

7   Some of the training disasters that we hear of are directly attributable to a consultant not being well informed about current trends and research findings in the field.

be resolved to his full satisfaction. Everything seemed to be settled and ready for an agreement. Relieved, he stood up to shake hands with his partners, when the Chinese manager said, 'By the way, could I ask you for a little favor? When you return to your country, could you please provide us with 150 of these little trademarks for those famous German cars: the three-pointed silver star inside a metal rim?' How do you respond to such a request in a country where saying 'No' is strictly avoided?!

In our project we had to face a Mercedes star occurrence when the flexibility of our project plan was tested. Having prepared a detailed research design for a five-week data collection phase in China, we were asked a few days after arrival by the local administrators whether we could complete the same thing in a third of the time since the necessary staff members were not available afterwards. Our mistake was that we assumed our research plan had been thoroughly discussed and settled in advance. So, friends, you had better watch out for the 'Mercedes star' – flexibility is the key to successful negotiations. (Juergen Hoermann, aviation psychologist, DLR, the German Aerospace Center)

With appropriate assistance from the research community and well-informed, flexible consultants, company insiders can determine what forms of data collection are feasible and how to diagnose the data for system vulnerabilities. Such an analysis will direct the design of resource-effective interventions. With continuing data collection, the insiders will also be able to evaluate the long-term effectiveness of different interventions. Underlying all this activity is the philosophy and rationale of error management as exemplified in the five precepts: human error is inevitable, there are limits on human performance, when limits are exceeded the likelihood of error increases, safety is a universal value and high-risk organizations must develop and maintain safety cultures. With this general model in mind, we turn to some specific examples of culture-sensitive interventions.

Culture-sensitive Training: CRM and National Culture

Unlike other forms of aviation training which focus on human–machine interactions, CRM training involves human-to-human interaction, and it is in these interpersonal interactions that culture is transmitted. As Chapter 3 has demonstrated, national culture influences how we talk to others, how we delegate and accept orders from others, how decisions are made, how risks are evaluated and how technology is utilized.

Trainees resonate to, and are more accepting of, training material that is culturally congruent, therefore training will always be more successful if it falls within the 'culture comfort zone' of the trainees. For example, in Anglo airlines CRM issues have been resolved by, among other things, assertiveness training for junior officers. This has been a relatively successful strategy in these airlines, because they all come from individualistic, low power distance cultures. The cultural norm of egalitarianism promotes direct communication and appropriate challenge, because it perceives the power relationship between captain and first officer as temporary and situationally specific. In contrast, assertiveness training for junior officers in Korea would be inappropriate at the present time, because it negates the rules of formality and 'face' which dictate communication in their cockpits. In other words, assertiveness as a CRM practice is outside the culture comfort zone of the Korean pilots, and such training would not transfer to the line. Box 6.4 is the candid tale of failed training, told by the consultant who conducted it.

Box 6.4   A CRM failure, a cultural victory

By the Spring of 1990, I was having pretty good success with CRM training at a variety of large US commercial carriers. The second-generation CRM programs were well accepted, although there were always a few who just didn't get it. There were occasional problems at CRM seminars that were attended by pilots from other countries, but this was dealt with by the statement that 'The airplane doesn't know and cares even less what culture is sitting in the cockpit – it only responds to the commands that it is given. And, besides, CRM is culture-free – the concepts and skills apply to all cultures across the board.'

I was engaged to deliver a series of traditional CRM seminars to pilots at a new airline in the Orient. This brand-new airline was starting out with long-range B767s and B747-400s, which were to be piloted by expatriate captains and local first and second officers. Compounding the start-up difficulties, the first officers were all ex-military pilots, the second officers were new-hire, ab initio trained pilots without either commercial or military experience, and Senior Management was a mix of European and Asian individuals.

I arrived at the airline with my course material and my American-made videotapes that recreated a series of CRM-based accidents at United, Delta, KLM, Air France and Northwest Airlines. To help me with the training, an older, retired Chinese captain, who had been a general in the Air Force, was assigned to help with translation and logistical support. The seminars all started well, with the

American captains doing most of the talking, and with the Asian participants listening intently and respectfully. We made it through the briefings activity although it was hard to get the first and second officers to ask questions after being briefed by the American, Australian and English captains. They would listen, nod their heads, and that was the end of it.

When we got to the assertion activity, my standard model on how to make an assertive challenging statement was presented and then the various seminar teams were given a case study accident to analyze. They were asked to come up with a properly assertive statement that would have called the captain's attention to the problem at hand or to the mistake that had been made. If done correctly, this act of assertive behavior would break the error chain and save the day.

During the team discussions, I noticed my designated assistant visiting each table and engaging the younger first and second officers in a very spirited discussion. When I asked what he was doing, the response was that the retired captain was informing and reminding the participants that there were absolutely no circumstances when a first officer should challenge or disagree with the captain. The rest of the day proceeded without much interaction, but with increasing withdrawal and negative body language from the Asian participants.

The next morning consisted of a training block involving resolving interpersonal conflict which ended up creating some unintended conflict of its own. The seminar participants were asked to discuss an interpersonal conflict that they had experienced in the cockpit, whether the situation was confronted, and how it was or was not resolved. This was an activity that seemed to work fine in the United States, in Ireland and in Australia, but this time I was greeted with silence. Finally, following more lecturing from me, a Chinese first officer stood up and stated in a very forthright manner, 'For two days you have been talking about how this training was needed in America. For two days you have shown us airline accidents that have occurred in the United States but have not happened here. You are trying to get us to do things like they do in America. It seems to me that Chinese culture has worked very well for the last 2000 years and we see absolutely no reason to change now.'

It was at that point that the light bulb came on and I realized that one size training does not fit all. Trying to deliver Western-style CRM training to an incompatible national culture was not as simple as we had ethnocentrically assumed. (Bill Taggart, training consultant)

To be better prepared for training in another national culture, a consultant should study the research literature on that national culture: the values, communication styles, methods of conflict resolution, decision making, managerial orientation and organizational behavior. A reading of the literature will help focus the consultant's thoughts on what to expect (that is, what might be different); however, these expectations will need to be modified and supplemented by insider information. National culture is channeled and modified by the organizational culture, this information can be provided by the company insiders.

Even when the consultant is from the same national culture, care is needed to avoid unintentional insult. As the outside 'expert', the consultant must take extra care to convey the message that the company insiders are the ones who know the problems and will ultimately solve them (see Box 6.5).

Box 6.5   Consulting or insulting?

I was hired by a South American airline to create a customized CRM course for its pilots. My objective was to observe cockpit as well as cabin crew members, so I would have a feeling for the way they operate. Even though I am a national of this particular country, I have lived in the USA for several years, so I did not want to assume anything: I needed to see how crew members at this particular airline interacted with each other.

One of my observation flights was a two-segment trip. The first leg was scheduled for 20 minutes, with no passenger service. The second leg would be one hour and 35 minutes, with dinner being served to a full-load aircraft. The Captain had been advised of my presence and agreed to help me as much as possible. I met the crew in the crew lounge, observed the briefing from the Captain and, on our way to the aircraft, I confirmed with him the schedules for that trip. Noticing the short flight time of the first leg I told the Captain that it would be a good idea to observe the pilots on this very busy 20-minute flight, and on the long second leg I could go back to observe the busy flight for the flight attendants. He concurred and said little about it. Both segments were uneventful.

Back in the States, a month later, I received a phone call from the Director of Operations inquiring about the 'problem' I had on the flight that night. He informed me that the Captain felt offended by my presence and that he almost disembarked me from the plane. The reason for his attitude was related to the fact that I had not asked his 'permission' on which seat to take – that I simply 'told' him where I would sit.

Eight months later, I was training this very same Captain to become one of this airline's CRM facilitators and had the opportunity to apologize for my 'misbehavior'. In his defense, he told me that not even the company's President tells him which seat he is going to take, but always asks the Captain's permission.

In a related vein, I also discovered that there were some people who wanted to destroy the course from the beginning, without giving it an opportunity to succeed. The director of training informed me that some pilots were upset because they had not been invited to be facilitators. As a consultant, it can be all too easy to unintentionally offend. (Antonio Schuck, aviation training consultant)

In sum, to develop interventions that are not culturally calibrated (based on local data and conditions) is to invite an expensive failure. Such an ill-considered approach is akin to prescribing medicine for a patient, based on another patient's diagnosis.

Culture-sensitive Training: National Culture and Professional Culture

In Chapter 3 we noted that a majority of the respondents agreed that a truly professional crew member could leave personal problems behind when flying. The average level of agreement across the 22 countries for this item was 67 per cent, and, with the exception of two countries, agreement in every country was more than 50 per cent, the highest endorsement being 97 per cent agreement amongst the Filipino pilots (see Figure 3.4). This item highlighted the fact that most pilots believe that the professional standard – the standard to aspire to – is one of invulnerability to stress. We also noted that the more pilots endorsed the professional standard as being invulnerable, the more their own scores reflected unrealistic attitudes.

The mechanisms needed to moderate the professional pilot culture toward greater acceptance of performance limits will vary as a function of national culture. Pilots from individualist countries are more likely to define professional norms by reference to their own personal standards, whereas pilots from collectivist or high UA countries are more likely to define their personal standard by reference to the group norm. (Cross-cultural research indicates that individualists' behavior is more closely linked to personal attitudes, while collectivists' behavior is more closely linked to group norms; see Triandis, 1994). For example, when faced with the apparent inconsistency that personal problems can impair performance, but that a professional can supposedly ignore personal problems, the individualist pilot may reason, 'Personal problems affect *me*, and *I* am a professional, therefore professionals must be affected by personal problems.' When faced with the same inconsistency, the collectivist pilot may reason, 'True professionals rise above their problems. *I am a member of this group*, therefore I cannot shame my group – I must not allow personal problems to affect me.'

To moderate attitudes in individualist countries, emphasis on individual awareness and responsibility is recommended. Pilots can be asked to consider their personal reactions to stress under different conditions, in an effort to normalize stress at a personal level. If more pilots in these countries acknowledge their personal stress, the professional standard will also normalize toward more realistic error management. Indeed, the individualist tendency to makes one's own rules can work to the betterment of general safety (see Box 6.6).

Box 6.6   The individual and error management

One particular Qantas Captain became known for carrying greater fuel reserves than any of the other pilots. It was the commander's prerogative to do so and this was never in question, but eventually the Head of Safety's inquisitiveness got the better of him. Asking the pilot why he carried 20 000 lb. extra fuel on every flight, he was told, 'because I can't fit any more in the tanks'. (Graham Braithwaite, aviation researcher)

The same approach cannot be used in collectivist or high UA countries. Encouraging pilots in these countries to consider their personal reactions to stress may only serve to heighten their sense of shame at not meeting the group's professional standard. A broader approach aimed at changing the group norms is necessary to give individuals 'permission' to modify their attitudes. Senior Management in these national cultures need to shape their safety cultures according to new norms of behavior, emphasizing error tolerance and error management. Efforts should be directed toward defining a company-wide group norm which states that 'human error is inevitable, so true professionals must be vigilant in their efforts to recognize and mitigate the limitations of human performance'. The organization plays a major role in shaping attitudes, particularly in collectivist and high PD countries, and employees will turn to their Management for guidance on standards.

Culture-sensitive Training: Error Management for Other Occupations

Just as training designed in one country has been exported to other countries without concern for local conditions, training designed for one occupation has been transferred to other occupations without due consideration of the culture and the context.

In 1998, CRM training will become mandatory for flight attendants and dispatchers in the USA. In the rush to comply with these new regulations, many airlines have already begun to implement CRM training for these groups. For the most part, this has been achieved by modifying the pilots' CRM courseware. Most of this training has been thinly conceived and is largely inadequate. For example, many airlines are focusing their CRM training for flight attendants on cockpit–cabin interactions. Certainly, there are barriers to communication between the cockpit and the cabin based on social, physical and professional differences (Chute & Wiener, 1996) and these barriers have been implicated in accidents. For example, in the Air Ontario crash, the flight attendant could see ice on the wings and was advised similarly by passengers, yet she still did not relay these concerns to the cockpit. Box 6.7 explores some of the underlying reasons for the communication barriers between cockpit and cabin.

Box 6.7   Cockpit–cabin communications

We surveyed pilots and flight attendants in one Anglo airline and found that pilots believed more strongly than flight attendants that the captain should encourage questions from the crew, and more pilots said they would speak up if they perceived a problem. On the other hand, cabin crew members did not think they should question the captain, they were less likely to question senior crew members' decisions and they said subordinates were sometimes afraid to disagree.

When asked what style of leadership they preferred, three-quarters of the pilots said they preferred a leader who consulted them before making decisions. In contrast, only one-third of flight attendants said they preferred a consultative leader, while 50 per cent said they preferred a directive (or, in some cases, autocratic) leader who made decisions promptly but explained them to the crew.

To what can we attribute these differential preferences for command and communication? First and foremost, there is power distance. Pilots, though not directly the flight attendants' bosses, are nonetheless perceived to be of a higher status within the company, hence the power distance between cockpit and cabin is generally perceived to be higher than between captain and co-pilot. Second, there is greater social distance or unease between cockpit and cabin. The social awkwardness is often compounded by gender and age differences (both of which can also influence power distance), occupational separation within the company and a physical barrier (the cockpit door). Third, there is an enormous difference in competencies with regard to knowledge of the aircraft. Simply as a function of their job, pilots have a much more sophisticated understanding of avionics and basic aircraft maintenance than do flight attendants.

Any one of these elements (power distance, social unease, difference in competencies) is enough to explain flight attendant reticence in the typical cockpit–cabin interaction. When we combine all three elements, it becomes painfully clear that to approach the captain about a possible aircraft malfunction is a very face-threatening activity for the cabin crew. The risk of embarrassing oneself is much higher if one speaks than if one stays silent. Under these circumstances, it is not surprising that flight attendants are less assertive, more afraid to disagree and less likely to challenge senior crew member decisions. Knowing that there are others on the plane equally or better qualified to diagnose safety problems, junior cabin crew members can rely on this diffusion of responsibility to give them greater solace and sanction for their silence.

Recognizing that a communication barrier exists, cabin CRM training has focused on briefings and how to communicate a concern to the cockpit. Some airlines are giving their flight attendants extra training in aircraft terminology to encourage and enable them to express their concerns accurately. This type of training is highly recommended and has received favorable ratings from pilots and flight attendants. Nonetheless, something is missing from this training. Because CRM training originated with pilots and was transferred without thought to the underlying rationale of CRM as an error management strategy, cabin CRM training has tended to focus on cabin interactions with the cockpit. But what about the majority of a flight attendant's job that has nothing to do with the cockpit? Flight attendants interact with other flight attendants, with passengers and with ground personnel. One of the industry's current concerns is the apparent rise in unruly passenger behavior. Flight attendants need training in how to manage these situations effectively, as the incidence of flight attendant abuse is increasing. Apart from the safety concerns (an unruly passenger can be unpredictable and volatile, endangering other passengers as well as the crew), the airline's reputation is at stake (a poorly managed episode encourages passengers to fly with other carriers).

In order to design a meaningful course for flight attendants, data on error and incidents should be collected *from flight attendants* and analyzed; the results would highlight the human factors issues that need to be addressed. Training to date has been conceived from a pilot perspective. While we strongly endorse the need for joint cockpit–cabin training, we want to emphasize that there are other human factors concerns in the cabin environment. We need to understand the context (physical working environment and task flow) and occupational culture (flight attendants are probably motivated differently from pilots) of flight attendants in order to design successful interventions. Applying pilot-style CRM to flight attendants or other occupations without due concern for the sources of error that arise in the particular occupational context is premature and limited, and is likely to overlook important issues.

Implementing Effective Error Management: A Case Study

In Chapter 4 we described how Continental Airlines moved from being a pariah among the major US airlines to winning awards for the quality of its service. Dedication to pleasing passengers in the cabin was accompanied by a commitment to making sure that flight operations were equally effective. The Senior Management of flight operations at Continental decided that the best strategy for optimizing flight operations would be to follow our guidelines for diagnosing the operation using systematic observations in a line audit and to survey all of the pilots in the airline. It was ironic that the day before we had a meeting scheduled to plan the audit and survey, a DC-9 landed with its gear up at Houston. It was immediately discovered that the wheels-up landing (in which no one was injured) was the result of human error: the crew failed to turn on hydraulic systems that enabled the lowering of the landing gear and the plane landed with the gear retracted. This is a situation that in most organizations would have resulted in strong defensive acts and the implementation of a 'blame and punish' reaction. In contrast, Continental's reaction was positive and proactive and can serve as a model for any high-risk industry. A very candid training module based on the accident was developed and delivered to all pilots.

The audit and survey were conducted as planned. When we completed analysis of the data, a meeting that included all the key players in the organization was scheduled. The results were presented and accepted non-defensively. To make sure that all operational concerns raised by the data were addressed, the second part of the day was devoted to a planning session to assign responsibility for addressing issues.

One of the outgrowths of the audit was the development of a new error management CRM course. This full-day course is being given to all pilots and serves as a replacement for the initial or awareness phase of training. In addition, a special course for instructors and evaluators was developed to provide training in evaluating and reinforcing error management. Other safety initiatives augment the survey/line audit program. Digital flight data recorder information is being collected and analyses will be integrated with other data sources. A non-jeopardy reporting system (ASAP) is also being developed and efforts are under way to integrate the information with audit data. Our research group is working to develop a checklist to help pilots making reports classify their actions systematically. A copy of the form is shown in Appendix C.

Continental also surveyed all of its flight attendants to help in designing a new CRM and safety course for in-flight personnel.

Do Error Management and CRM Generalize to Other Environments?

We have shown that CRM training has significant, positive effects on crew performance and have proposed error management as a universal rationale acceptable in all cultures. To date, several US airlines have restructured their training to center on error management. However, there are not yet data to validate the impact of this approach. In the USA, Southwest Airlines and Continental Airlines are developing CRM training for their flight attendants based on error management.

Given the similarities in risk and group dynamics, it would seem that this approach would work well with operating room teams. Several medical organizations have expressed interest in adopting this type of training, but there are not yet any data on participant reactions. Box 6.8 describes one physician's experience with uncovering medical error and reconciling approaches to human factors issues in aviation and medicine.

Box 6.8   Medical mishaps

Coroners (at least in name) date back to the time of King Alfred (871–910). Initially, the primary role of the coroner was to protect the financial interest of the Crown in criminal proceedings. By the second half of the thirteenth century, duties of the coroner included the holding of inquests on dead bodies, particularly when the death was sudden and unexpected. Since then, coronial investigations have evolved to the point where they may list the 'cause' and circumstances, although they may not name the 'guilty'. But much more may be possible because of an inquest being held in

Winnipeg, Manitoba and an air crash that occurred in 1990 in Dryden, Ontario.

In October 1995, an inquest was convened under the auspices of Associate Chief Judge Murray Sinclair. He was asked to preside over an investigation into the deaths of 12 infants and children who had undergone operations for congenital heart defects. All procedures had been carried out by one newly qualified surgeon at the Winnipeg Children's Hospital between February and December 1994. The 12 deaths represented a mortality rate of 33 per cent, a rate that was considered too high, and the pediatric cardiac surgical programme was therefore shut down in January 1995.

I had heard of the Pediatric Cardiac Surgery Inquest (PCSI) and hoped to become involved. In May 1996, I was asked by Don Slough, one of the Counsel for the Crown, to provide a systems perspective for the inquest. Over the next few days I thought about what I could offer to this already large investigation. I had been trained as an anesthetist and had set out an academic career, with my research oriented toward cardiac physiology and pharmacology. (At the same time I was also working as an anesthetist 2.5 days each week, as well as taking calls in the Operating Room and Labour & Delivery Suites.) But in 1983, my medical school, where I had returned as an Assistant Professor, had its first 10-year reunion. Several alumni were asked to speak. After pondering about what topic the audience – of fellow alumni, students, faculty, family members and even politicians – might find of interest, I hit on the idea of addressing the topic of 'Anesthesia in 1983: how safe is it?' I reasoned that safety was the one topic which would interest all members of the audience. The talk went well and, over the next few years, my interest in the topic deepened, and I gave up my other research.

In 1988, I was asked to review three deaths which had occurred in British Columbia, all during dental implant surgery. Nine months later we were able to present a report showing that the deaths were not related to the three different anesthetics given by three different anesthetists using two different anesthetic machines in two different offices. Instead, we showed that they were due to a massive air embolus that occurred when the oral surgeon had used tap water mixed with air to irrigate down through a hollow drill. The air was absorbed into the blood vessels of the lower jaw and carried via the jugular veins into the heart where, when sufficient quantity had been absorbed, an air lock developed and the patients arrested and died. Thus the deaths were not anesthetic deaths (as they had been labeled by the initial district coronial investigations and the pathologists) but surgical deaths, with a major contribution from the way in which the dental equipment was used. That investigation also emphasized to me the import-ance of other factors in these deaths, such as the role of regulatory agencies – not just the personnel involved.

Shortly after we had finished the investigation, I attended a meeting in Ballarat, Australia, where a number of anesthetists pre-sented ways of handling crises in the operating room. The meeting started with two representatives from the field of aviation, Dr Rob Lee (at that time, Assistant Director of the Bureau of Air Safety Investigation) and one of his staff, Larry Sheehan, who presented protocols for aviation crises. During one of the breaks, Rob Lee and I talked about the analogy between aviation and anesthesia – something which he had thought about for several years and on which he had spoken. I had also thought that the analogy was a fruitful one. The upshot was a visit to the Bureau and a chance to collaborate with Rob.

One of the first topics we tackled was a systematic method of investigating anesthetic accidents. We produced an outline and workbook and then started to take an in-depth look at the analogy between the two systems.

At about the same time, I decided to leave the operating room and concentrate on my research and also on the investigation of deaths in the operating room. Not too long after, Rob Lee arrived in Calgary to lecture at a meeting which I had organized on critical incidents in anesthesia. He had just encountered James Reason's (1990) work on system error. We saw its value as a framework for the logical investigation of all types of catastrophes, not just those in large-scale industrial complexes. We had just had an anesthetic-related death in the hospital and the anesthetist involved, Dr Chris Eagle, and I used the Reason model to investigate both the active and latent failures. The resulting paper was the first application of the Reason model to a medical problem.

Following the publication of that paper, I continued to investi-gate cases involving either mortality or morbidity. I also started to visit the Australian Bureau of Air Safety Investigation (BASI) as a visiting professor, where my understanding of aviation deepened. I also tried to give something back to aviation, if only in the form of providing my view of the similarities between aviation and anesthesia. I thought that I could, in effect, 'hold up a mirror' so that the aviation community could have a different perspective of themselves. On one of my visits to BASI I was invited to speak at the Australian Aviation Psychology meeting on the analogy be-tween the two systems. At this meeting I first met Bob Helmreich and began what has become an extensive collaboration.

In addition to the investigative work, I also continued to see patients in an anesthetic consultation clinic. Most of these patients were booked to have an operation and were seeing an anesthetist in the preparatory, preoperative phase. Some patients, however, were seen because of real or perceived problems with previous anesthetics. In addition, I joined the simulator team at the University of Basel as a quality assurance consultant (see Chapter 5). The operating room simulator in Basel was dedicated in November 1994, at about the same time that the tenth of the Winnipeg patients to die was undergoing cardiac surgery.

In all, 12 patients officially became the subjects of the inquest, although the Judge, in his statement as to who would have standing in the inquest, said that he would be interested in examining and looking at the deaths of other children who were in the care of the Pediatric Cardiac Surgical Unit. He also indicated that he would be prepared to hear evidence about other children who did not die. It is this degree of concern for both the living and the dead that is one of the hallmarks of this most unusual inquest. But above all there is the systems approach which this inquest has taken since Judge Sinclair's opening statements that the intent of the inquiry was not only to look at the circumstances of each of the children, but also to examine the way the unit operated, the way it was managed and administered, the way the hospital managed and supervised those who were involved, and as well the relationship between the hospital and the Government of Manitoba. And this is where I came in.

I received an enormous package containing all the files of the 12 victims, as well as other supporting documents and reports at the same time that Bob Helmreich arrived to speak at the inaugural meeting of the Calgary Medical Legal Society. Bob's introduction was by the Honourable Justice Virgil P. Moshansky, who had chaired the Commission of Inquiry into the Air Ontario crash at Dryden, Ontario, which Bob served as human factors consultant (Helmreich, 1992; Moshansky, 1992: see Box 6.2). Reading all five volumes of the Dryden Inquiry report and Bob's report, I was struck by strong similarities between factors identified in Dryden and those I could see in Winnipeg.

I then spent the summer of 1996 developing a model which would encompass all the interrelating factors, from the patients, the personnel, the environment/equipment, the organization and the regulatory agencies. The model was an amalgamation of three existing models, the Quality Assurance model of Donabedian (1968), the active and latent failure model of Reason (1990) and the interrelated human factors model of Helmreich & Foushee (1993: see Chapter 1), with additions, translations and re-interpretations. In September I presented the model to the inquest team, along with my view of the analogy to Dryden, and observed three days of inquest hearings.

By December 1997, the inquest had heard from about half the expected witnesses. Over 30 000 pages of transcripts had been produced, as well as countless reports by expert witnesses. I have been impressed with how well the Judge and all the legal counsel (of whom there are nearly 20) have learned the intricacies of pediatric cardiac medicine and surgery – another example of cross-profession transfer. I also remain convinced of the similarity between Winnipeg and Dryden, which exists on two levels. On the first level, there are the case-by-case details. The inquest has heard that the surgeon was just out of training and was the only trained pediatric cardiac surgeon in the province, let alone in the city. He therefore had no one with similar knowledge with whom he could discuss cases, either before, during or after surgery. In addition, he had completed much of his training in the USA before he came to the much smaller programme in Winnipeg. Compounding the lack of experience as a consultant surgeon, cultural translocation and unfamiliar environment was what seemed to be the surgeon's inability to ask questions about local protocols. For example, if the previous surgeon wanted to perform a procedure in the Intensive Care Unit (ICU) that was normally performed in the OR, he would book the OR and have all the personnel (anesthetist, nurses, heart–lung machine perfusionists) and equipment transported to the ICU. The new surgeon did not ask how he was to carry out procedures in the ICU but, then again, no one told him (until he tried to do a case and had the nurses running back and forth to the OR looking for equipment).

It was found that the anesthetists suddenly sent a memo in the surgeon's third month in Winnipeg stating that they would no longer provide anesthetic care for his open-heart patients. But the inquest has also heard how the anesthetists did not communicate this to the surgeon, who found out from a third party. Nurses complained to senior nurses and doctors about problems that they perceived, but then testified that no one seemed to listen or that they were told that their opinions did not count because they were nurses. The operations were carried out in the Children's Hospital in a small OR where day-to-day difficulties were encountered with control of room temperature (an important factor in the care of small children) and with noise from the air-handling system (which had ramifications for communication). The Children's Hospital was a physically separate building from the adult hospital, the Health Sciences Centre (HSC). The addition of a complex reporting structure from the Children's Hospital to the HSC did not completely address the isolation of the Pediatric Cardiac Surgical Unit. The previous surgeon had left, in part, because of lack of funding and inadequate assistance.

But on a second level, the inquest in Manitoba has the potential to do for medicine what Dryden did for aviation. And I say medicine and not just pediatric cardiac surgery because the lessons that can be learned from the inquest have relevance to every type of medical and surgical practice. Programs and practices should be set up, from the beginning, with a knowledge of the patient population to be served, with the right personnel (selected, trained, competent and sufficient in number), with the right environment and equipment, with an organizational structure that supports the endeavors and in a regulatory environment that wishes to provide appropriate care for the health of the people it serves. From the outset there should be a system of quality assurance: regular monitoring and documenting of processes and outcomes, with links back to the structural and procedural elements of the program. There should also be a system of ad hoc review, which can be set in place if there is a sudden and unexpected problem with the process or the outcome of care. And all of this should be set in an organizational and regulatory culture which recognizes that human errors will occur but attempts proactively to manage them. If the inquest in Winnipeg can show how to do this, the deaths of passengers in Dryden and patients in Winnipeg will not have been in vain. (Dr Jan M. Davies, anesthesiologist)

Another question is whether error management can be adapted to other professions and domains that do not involve such visible risk. It is our belief that the approach can be much more widely employed. Boeing, the major US manufacturer of aircraft, hosted a seminar in 1996 to discuss whether the principles of CRM could be applied to high-performance management teams (Boeing, 1996). There was a general consensus among participants, who came from both academia and a range of professions and organizations, that the principles were generally applicable.

We receive frequent phone calls from organizations that feel they might benefit from CRM and error management strategies. Among those who have discussed related problems are software programming teams and bankers. We were struck by the comments of a banker who pointed out that his staff had committed an error in transferring funds that amounted to 100 million dollars. He argued that, although there were not physical consequences, the error was highly consequential. Reason (1997) also discusses the errors and failures in detection involved in the trading losses of Barings Bank and its subsequent failure.

At this point, we can only speculate on future applications. However, it is our feeling that, as long as humans work in teams in organizations, errors will occur and error management will be essential.

7 When Cultures Collide

Intercultural sensitivity is not natural. It is not part of our primate past, nor has it characterized most of human history. Cross-cultural contact usually has been accompanied by bloodshed, oppression, or genocide... We ask learners to transcend traditional ethnocentrism and to explore new relationships across cultural boundaries. This attempt at change must be approached with the greatest possible care. (Bennett, 1993, p.21)

The global village is fast becoming a reality. Commercial aviation is increasing rapidly and will continue to increase well into the next century. New companies are starting up and established companies are expanding, merging and forming global alliances with international partners. Increased travel throughout the world has increased the demand for experienced pilots, and a well-trained pilot can almost always find employment overseas should home markets be unreceptive. The net result of this rapid expansion in world commercial travel is that more and more pilots are flying with crews of different nationalities, with different levels of experience and different standards. We devote Chapter 7 to an investigation of the multicultural experience.

We know from Chapters 3 and 4 that pilot behavior is influenced not only by professional culture, but also national and organizational culture. So what happens when pilots fly with pilots from other national cultures? What happens when the cultural assumptions about performance and cockpit interactions can no longer be taken for granted? In this chapter, we explore some of the difficulties that expatriates and mixed-culture crews encounter. Our primary data come from surveys in several multicultural organizations. We asked respondents to answer open-ended questions regarding the positive and negative aspects of multicultural interactions (Merritt, 1995; Merritt & Ratwatte, in press). We also draw on data from Chapter 3, and on our own experiences working with members of multinational organizations. We finish the chapter with a discussion of cultural adaptation and acculturation, and training for intercultural effectiveness.

We have enlisted the aid of several friends to help us with this chapter. Captain Bumgarner, an American pilot who has flown for airlines in the Orient for more than five years, has contributed a very interesting piece on how Anglos can adapt to the Asian environment; Captain Radzi of Malaysian Airlines describes how his airline decided to deal with cultural issues when they first started to recruit expatriate pilots; and Captain Ratwatte, originally from Sri Lanka and now working for Emirates Airlines, describes the benefits and advantages that he has discovered working in multicultural crews. We are sure the reader will find their first-hand experiences very enlightening.

Multicultural Misunderstandings: What did he say? What is he doing? And why doesn't he just do it my way?

Language

Language is probably the most fundamental source of problems in cross-national work groups. It may seem trite, but you cannot communicate effectively if you cannot speak the language. English is the official language of commercial aviation, and it creates four distinct interaction possibilities within the cockpit, and between the cockpit and support groups such as Air Traffic Control (ATC). Linguistically, there is English with English, English with non-English support (for example, Anglos flying in Asia), non-English with English support (for example, the Avianca flight from South America flying into New York) and both non-English (for example, most parts of Europe). Box 7.1 provides three examples of linguistic confusion with varying consequences: Anglo pilots talking with non-English ATC, a non-English pilot adjusting to English, and English speakers with heavy accents.

Box 7.1   Language difficulties

1   A Flying Tigers 747 cargo flight was preparing for landing in Kuala Lumpur, Malaysia, in 1989. The following clearances and acknowledgements were made:
ATC: '...descend to two seven zero zero (2700).'
Pilot: 'Roger – Cleared to twenty seven hundred – we're out of forty-five.'
ATC: '...descend two [to?] four zero zero – cleared for NDB approach 33.'

Pilot: 'OK – four zero zero.'

Intended clearance was 2400 feet, but what the pilots read back was 400 feet. The controller did not catch the readback error, perhaps because he was not a native English speaker, and the aircraft crashed into a mountain peak at 481 feet.

2 (Learning to fly in a foreign land.) Phraseology was very hard to handle. I still remember an instructor talking about 'displaced thresholds' on a runway, and 'don't land on the chevrons'. The only chevrons I knew were gas (petrol) stations, and I was really puzzled by this remark for a long time. Probably why I'm so into standard operating procedures now. (Captain Surendra Ratwatte, Emirates Airlines)

3 (Diabolical dialects.) With the introduction of transponders to aviation, the terms Mode A, Mode C and Mode S arrived with an interesting communicational problem. On approach to Melbourne, one particularly strong-accented Australian was heard to call 'Mayday'. The ATC tower was gripped with excitement as they tried to ascertain the cause of the emergency. Several more calls later from a remarkably calm-sounding crew led to the discovery that he was saying 'Mode A' not 'Mayday' and so the practice of calling 'Mode Alpha' was born. (Graham Braithwaite, British safety researcher working in Australia)

There is more than ample opportunity for misunderstandings and false assumptions when all crew and support are native-speakers of English, but what of the other situations? The Aviation Safety Reporting System (ASRS) is a non-jeopardy system in the USA that provides limited immunity to pilots who report events that might result in a possible violation or a threat to safety. Orasanu *et al.* (in press) summarize ASRS data from US crews flying in other countries between 1986 and 1992 showing that language barriers were the most frequently cited problems, with phraseology, ATC speech rate and lack of party-line information[1] accounting for another large set Orasanu *et al.* (in press) also extracted 100 ASRS reports using the key words 'culture' and 'communications problems' and found that language/accents and dual language switching (for example, Air Traffic Control speaking English to foreign pilots and the local language to local pilots) accounted for approximately half of the problems reported. Some pilots have told us that, in certain parts of the world, non-standard requests are often met with eerie silence from ATC.

1 Pilots often listen to ATC communications with other pilots to help them maintain full situation awareness. When some of those communications are in the local language, pilots lose valuable information.

Unable to understand, the local controllers 'go quiet', leaving the crew to fend for themselves.

When non-English crews interact with English-speaking support staff,[2] the situation can be fatal, as in the case of the Avianca crew who were unable to convey the seriousness of their fuel situation in a way that alerted the New York ATC to their dilemma. Some Chinese airlines have addressed the language problem by adding another crew member, a translator, to handle ATC communications on international flights. While this short-term solution may be effective in standard operations, emergency or non-normal conditions could be very risky. Not only does the crew lose potentially valuable time in translations, but the translators are not actually pilots, which means they may be unable to accurately convey issues of concern.

In a related area, we conducted a pilot survey at a Taiwanese airline which had begun employing expatriate Anglo captains. When asked to list the most frustrating things about working with pilots from another culture, the following concerns (translated into English) were voiced by Chinese pilots who work with expatriate captains.

- Because communication is difficult, it is easy to misunderstand each other in emergency situations.
- In an emergency situation crew coordination becomes slower owing to the communication.
- Under an emergency, there is big trouble for communication.
- The most frustrating thing is if there is an emergency situation. Communication will be a big problem.
- There is no problem under normal situations, but the communication speed would be a problem under emergency.

The responses from the expatriate Anglo captains echoed this concern. They reported that it requires greater effort and concentration to ensure that no confusion exists and that the time spent ensuring understanding can be at the expense of aircraft monitoring and swift action in an emergency. Countering the barriers imposed by language, many respondents reported that they do engage in more cross-checking for understanding, and that they use Standard Operating Procedures (SOPs) as countermeasures against misunderstanding.

Taking another perspective on the 'non-English with English support' scenario, some non-native speakers of English have commented that English speakers do not speak distinctly. We met a Pakistani

2   In many cases the aircraft computers and warning systems are also in English. For example, the Ground Proximity Warning System alerts crews when they are too close to terrain by sounding a 'pull up, pull up' warning. In one chilling accident report, the last words on the cockpit voice recorder were one Chinese pilot saying to his co-pilot in Chinese, 'what does "pull up" mean?'

pilot once who spoke with a perfect 'BBC English' accent. Referring to the heavy American accents he encounters at New York Air Traffic Control, he said, 'Forget about us foreign pilots, how about getting those guys in the Tower to speak English?'

The final group, non-English with non-English, encounter different problems. Orasanu *et al.* (in press) also extracted reports with the key phrase 'communication problems' from the International Air Transport Association database which collects reports from non-US pilots in the USA and elsewhere. Most reports dealt with false assumptions or confusion over call signs, while only a few reports dealt with language/accent problems or language switching as mentioned in the ASRS reports. The authors speculate that the differences between the two data sets may reflect greater attention to clear communication or a different level of adaptation to linguistic diversity on the part of non-US pilots who fly in more multicultural environments. With both parties speaking in their second or third language, there is the tendency to speak 'simple English simply', that is, to speak succinctly, precisely and without embellishment.

In sum, there is a huge difference between the normative mandate that English be the language of the cockpit and the reality of varying levels of verbal expression and understanding among non-native speakers of English. From his own experiences as an Anglo researcher in a German-speaking hospital, one of our colleagues, Bryan Sexton, has identified what he calls the 'Nod-n-Grin' response. Embarrassed that they have missed the intent of a statement the first time, and rather than pursue something which they may still not understand (more embarrassment), people may nod and feign understanding as a way to save face. Such misunderstandings and non-clarifications can be dangerous when full and shared awareness of a situation is needed.

The simple reality is that a very high level of linguistic proficiency is needed before one can communicate effectively at the level that a time-critical, non-standard or emergency situation may dictate. Some solutions to this difficult problem are offered in the recommendations section at the end of the chapter.

Command Differences

In Chapter 3, we found strong cross-cultural differences in command expectations and preferences amongst pilots of 22 countries. For example, agreement with the item 'Junior crew members should only question the actions of the captain when the safety of flight is threatened' ranged from as little as 9 per cent in one country with egalitarian, low power distance values, to 71 per cent in the country with the most hierarchical orientation. Given that these differences exist, it is not difficult to imagine the confusion that some mixed-culture crews must experience. Putting an overly assertive, egalitarian-minded first officer with a hierarchically minded captain who expects deference could be very disruptive, just as the overly friendly and informal captain can unnerve the high power distance junior officer.

Consider these comments taken from a survey of pilots working for a multinational airline in the Middle East. Their frustrations included the following.

- Cultures where the captain is treated as a god and he himself treats others with modest disdain. This creates friction with crew members from other cultures.
- When customs dictate that there is only one captain and he is not to be questioned; occasionally non-standard procedures are required and there is marked inability to think independently and overreliance on the captain.
- When there is a cultural reluctance to advise a more senior person of an observed mistake.

These comments, primarily from Anglo-Western pilots who favor low power distance and open discussion in the cockpit, indicate sources of friction with other nationalities. Interestingly, comments from some European and Asian pilots point to the ethnocentric assumptions of some Anglo-Western pilots regarding their own 'superior' flying skills. As one pilot commented, 'It is sad that pilots of most every other nationality are ready to acknowledge the need to modify their behavior in multicultural crews, but some Anglos are not.' Such an uncompromising attitude is clearly antithetical to teamwork and can be a source of real animosity. Captain Bumgarner addresses command issues in more detail later in this chapter. As the stories in Box 7.2 show, body language and local customs can also conspire to confuse command expectations.

Box 7.2   Body language

1   The Indian expatriate co-pilot shook his head in agreement after the captain gave him a lengthy airways briefing. Thinking that the co-pilot did not understand the briefing, the captain began again. Again the co-pilot shook his head. This went on for the third time. Finally, the captain asked, 'Which part do you not understand?' The co-pilot replied 'I understood it the first time, captain.' 'Then why did you shake your head?' 'To show you that I understand and agree with what you plan to do.' 'You should have nodded when you agree, not shake your head.' For the co-

pilot, the shaking of the head from side to side without moving the position of the nose indicated understanding and agreement. If one disagrees then the head shaking involves the nose going from side to side as well.

2　There was once a Brazilian captain of Italian descent. Having no Auxiliary Power Unit (APU) he made a sign, the flat of the palm hitting the closed fist of the other to the ground engineer. As they made the turn for the bay, the captain saw the engineer rooted to the ground. The captain again gave the sign. Still no response. As the airplane got nearer, the action got more vigorous. This time the engineer stood there, legs slightly apart and hands on the hips. When the airplane came to a stop, the engineer plugged in the headset and said, 'You do that again and I'll bash you up!' Taken by surprise, the captain asked, 'What is happening here, what did I do?' Only then did he realize that it was a bad sign that he was showing to the engineer. (Captain Azmi Radzi, Malaysia Airlines)

Rules, Procedures and Automation

Chapter 3 also highlighted strong cross-cultural differences in the preference for rules and procedures, and preference and reliance on automation. For example, agreement with the item, 'Written procedures are required for all in-flight situations' ranged from 16 per cent to 84 per cent across the 22 countries. These differences suggest that managers of multicultural organizations may find it difficult to gain equal acceptance of company procedures. In the cockpit, a pilot who has been trained to operate the automation 'by the book' can become frustrated with a co-pilot who prefers to disengage the automation and exercise some personal control in piloting. Those who adhere strictly to rules see others as indulgent and undisciplined; those who exercise personal discretion see others as rule-bound and inflexible.

In our experience with multicultural airlines, we have noticed a trend toward more rules and procedures. Even pilots who would normally resist such levels of proceduralization tend to embrace SOPs as a way to avoid confusion and false assumptions in the multicultural cockpit. Similarly, company-issued automation philosophies and policies clarify the expectations for behavior in the cockpit. With pilots coming from different countries and diverse training backgrounds, these companies have learned to explicate many expectations which might otherwise be taken for granted in monocultural airlines.

Other Differences

Other issues that can create tension among multicultural groups include religion, politics, economics, humor, history and, yes, racism (see Box 7.3).

Box 7.3   One pilot's experience

I applied to the airline as a bit of a joke, because I was very upset at the way the airline back home (in Southern Asia) was being mismanaged by government-appointed flunkies. When I got the job, I couldn't refuse. My country was in turmoil, with night curfews in the city, people being abducted and killed, bodies left on the streets, stuff you can't imagine if you haven't been in the middle of it.

I was surprised to find that, although this was a new airline, it was astoundingly racist. The airline was in its infancy and was being run by an Irishman. The British were trying to oust him and take over. Two of us had been hired by the Irishman, for whom it was a political ploy. I was told by a British manager that I didn't have the experience needed and all kinds of other rubbish. I later found out that I was actually more experienced than most of the other new hires, who were all white of course! Almost quit, but was too proud and stubborn to do that; it would merely have confirmed the prejudices anyway.

A couple of American captains were very supportive, as was the small Asian contingent. The company was full of little cliques who tried to swell their membership through recruitment; very childish stuff. This situation went on for a while, until an ex-British Airways guy was brought in, who sorted stuff out.

In retrospect, the whole experience has been very good for me. The Irishman has since been relegated to well-paid purgatory. Professionally, it has been very demanding, and I think I'm a better pilot for having come here. To give them their due credit, once a pilot has proved to have the required professional capabilities, the British leave him or her alone. The only problem I've had since then was a Pom but that was after a couple of years in command. We discussed the matter and the rest of the flight went off well, though cockpit temperatures were a little on the low side. (Captain from South Asia, now working for a multicultural airline)

Pilots in our surveys have expressed concern that, because they do not know the training background and experience level of their co-pilots, they cannot predict their behavior with any certainty. They have also commented that relationships on duty with individuals of other nationalities are not as relaxed as with members of one's own, because of customs conflict, and that long flights can be oppressive because of language barriers and different senses of humor. Social separation post-flight, based on rank or cultural group, also makes it difficult to establish a team spirit or group identity. A study of civilian aircraft concluded that safe cockpits are characterized by open communication, good fellowship and helpfulness (Redding & Ogilvie, 1984). Multinational crews can be compromised in both regards: language barriers and cultural differences may inhibit the open communication and team fellowship needed for safe flying.

Other, more idiosyncratic differences which we observed in our global database may also provide opportunities for misunderstanding. For example, Brazilian pilots ranked advancement to high-level jobs as their most important work value, while Taiwanese pilots ranked it second to last in a list of 17 work values. Methods of pilot motivation that stir Brazilians are likely to have little impact on the Taiwanese. Korean pilots report greater shame when they make a mistake in front of other crew members.[3] A management policy to encourage individuals to share their mistakes publicly as a safety policy is unlikely to gain instant acceptance in this culture.

Filipino pilots view their airline as being like a large family, and favor a more benign, paternalistic command style (this applies to the cockpit as well as Management). In contrast, most Anglo-Western pilots prefer a much more open command style and would not react favorably even to the best-intentioned paternalistic control.

Anglo pilots (from Australia, British Hong Kong, Ireland, New Zealand and the USA) were united in ranking sufficient time away from the job for personal or family life as their number one work value. This insistence on personal time could be construed by others as a lack of commitment to the company. It also raises the very interesting issue of how much time one should dedicate to the job and the company as opposed to personal time. The answer to this question is culturally determined; a review of vacation time and standard hours in work contracts across nations will reveal the different cultural emphases on work and leisure.

In sum, cultural differences, variations in aviation experience and background, and linguistic difficulties can create uncertainty and hesitation in the cockpit, which can be hazardous in time-pressure situations. If not managed appropriately, initial uncertainty can esca-

---

3   An extreme example of shame culture in action is seen in the behavior of a Korean flight crew who chose to remain in the cockpit of their burning B-747 rather than face the shame of responsibility for injury and damage.

late into frustration, resentment and even paranoia, thereby creating an even more serious safety threat.

With these concerns in mind, are multicultural cockpits inherently a safety threat? Captain Ratwatte, a pilot flying for Emirates, a multicultural airline in the Middle East, says 'no' and presents a convincing case for the many advantages of multicultural cockpits (Box 7.4).

Box 7.4   The advantages of a multicultural cockpit

When working as an expatriate, every day is spent in a foreign culture. It becomes necessary to use the principles of CRM all the time, not just to pass a check-ride. For many of us, CRM becomes a useful tool in coping with life in a strange land. What works in the cockpit seems to also work in Flight Operations, other departments of the company and, in fact, almost anywhere we have to deal with people on a daily basis. It starts to become routine, for the unspoken assumptions and agreements that one makes so effortlessly in one's own culture are no longer an option. Every statement has to be considered carefully: there are employees from over 70 nationalities within my company and it is all too easy to offend.

The varied mix of people we fly with, and the fact that English is a second language for many of them, makes it vital that the thought process be articulated very clearly. Clear, concise verbalization of intent and requirements must take place and be undertaken 'by the book'. This leads to a high degree of Standard Operating Procedures (SOPs) being used, as it is otherwise all too easy to get confused. Our pilots are forced to cross-check constantly in order to confirm that what was discussed is what is being done. After a while this becomes natural, a definite plus for safety.

We have pilots who have flown to just about every major airport in the world, including those in the former USSR and mainland China. Some of their insights and experiences are promulgated through company publications or policies. Even more of it is shared in the conversations that take place in the cockpit during those long night flights. This valuable exchange of knowledge cannot be quantified, nor can it be easily formalized. The likelihood of such a barter taking place, however, is much more likely in a multicultural airline due to the paucity of neutral topics, and also the variety of experiences between the pilots. 'Local knowledge' is invaluable and is much easier to unearth in a company that recruits from all over the world.

Regardless of the country of origin, any international flight, by its very definition, is a multicultural experience. A crew well versed in dealing with many cultures and accents within the cockpit is better positioned to cope with a variety of such inputs from outside. Anyone who has heard an American pilot trying to cope with rapid-fire instructions from Paris ATC in *franglais* will know what I'm talking about. Quite often another pilot will intercede and translate the instructions, much to the relief of everyone else.

These, then, are the strengths of flying in a multicultural environment. Communication, both within and without the flight deck, tends to be clearer and more standardized. Pilots tend to be more adaptable to different accents and methods of doing things. There is a greater reservoir of experience to draw from, and a wider dissemination of this knowledge due to aviation being sometimes the only common interest. CRM becomes the linchpin that holds all this together, rather than just a passing fad. (Captain Surendra Ratwatte, Emirates Airlines)

Captain Ratwatte acknowledges that cultural differences can initially be a problem, but he argues that cultural awareness, flexibility and a 'best practices' approach can introduce safeguards into the system which enhance efficiency as well as safety in the multicultural cockpit. In other words, culture can be a problem in the cockpit, but only if its influence goes unacknowledged. As a result, a well-managed multicultural cockpit is as safe as any other well-managed cockpit, although some of the safety concerns may differ.

In our work with multicultural airlines, we have noticed that the same qualities that make a good monocultural pilot also make a good multicultural pilot. The best pilots are not only technically competent, but they are also aware and respectful of their fellow crew members, they show a healthy respect for SOPs and other organizational policies, they utilize CRM strategies as a means of managing various cockpit activities, they are dedicated to safe and professional practice, and they will go the extra distance to ensure that a high level of safety is maintained. In contrast, a pilot who performs poorly in his own country, perhaps a 'boomeranger' with poor acceptance of CRM concepts, is likely to perform even more poorly or more rigidly as an expatriate pilot in a foreign environment.

Is it enough for an expatriate pilot to be a good pilot? Are there other qualities or skills which are needed to ensure a smooth transition and adaptation to a new job in a foreign country? In the next section, we discuss the research on cultural adaptation and acculturation, to be followed by Captain Bumgarner's entertaining and thought-provoking comments on adapting to the Asian way.

Cultural Adaptation and Acculturation

As more companies globalize, sending personnel overseas for short-and long-term assignments and recruiting experienced personnel from outside their country, the issue of successful cultural adaptation has taken on a new financial significance. It is estimated that US firms alone lose $2 billion a year in direct costs because of personnel returning from overseas assignments prematurely (Nauman, 1992). Early return rates are highest for assignments in developing countries and poor adaptation of the spouse and family is often cited as the main reason for early return (Stephens & Black, 1991). Failure rates, as measured by early returns, are about 15–40 per cent for American business personnel and, of those who stay, less than 50 per cent perform adequately (Copeland & Griggs, 1985). One study of international development workers found that only 20 per cent were considered highly effective in their jobs (Kealey, 1990). Another study concluded that, although most international workers were considered technically competent, they lacked the cross-cultural skills needed for fully effective performance (Gertsen, 1990). The message from these statistics is clear: ignoring culture can be a costly mistake, a considerable drain on resources and a serious threat to the long-term success of an international venture.

If we define intercultural effectiveness as being as effective in the host culture as in one's home culture, then technical competence alone is not sufficient to ensure success. Effectiveness also involves personal and family adjustment (being happy and satisfied with life and conditions in the host country) and successful intercultural interaction (being socially involved with nationals and demonstrating interest in and knowledge of the host culture). Interestingly, there is evidence to show that those who are the least effective in relationships with host nationals and demonstrate little insight into the culture are also the ones who claim no difficulties and tend to minimize the importance of cross-cultural dimensions (Bochner, 1981).[4]

Effective recruitment and personnel selection for intercultural work activity addresses not only technical competence but also skills and attributes such as openness, flexibility, patience, maturity, stability, self-confidence, perseverance, problem-solving, tolerance, professional commitment and initiative (Kealey, 1996). These qualities will ensure that technical competence is demonstrated in a culturally appropriate manner, so ensuring maximum transfer and exchange of skills. It will also reduce the likelihood of personnel terminating their over-

---

4   It is difficult to read this sentence and not draw a parallel to CRM. Those pilots who have traditionally shown the poorest understanding of CRM are also the ones who tend to minimize the importance of CRM skills.

seas assignments prematurely and maximize a company's return on its training investment.

Intercultural training can also facilitate adjustment to a new culture and improve the quality (and, in some cases, duration) of overseas performance (see Gudykunst *et al.*, 1996, for an extended discussion of this topic). Participants in intercultural training would ideally include all workers posted or recruited overseas, and their families. Facilitators for the training would include an experienced (that is, culturally adjusted) expatriate and a host national.

Cultural self-awareness is the first step to accepting and adapting to other cultures and ultimately becoming as effective in the host culture as in one's own culture. To that end, 'intercultural trainees' need to have some theory of culture from which they can interpret new interactions and new customs. Without an underlying rationale for the new behaviors, trainees cannot generalize to other 'foreign' behaviors, and cannot begin to make sense of their new environment. Trainees will gain the greatest insights by learning a theory of culture which encompasses not one, but many cultures. The true benefit of this general culture approach is not that trainees become anthropologists, but rather that they develop insights into their own culture and its idiosyncrasies by constantly comparing it with others. In Box 7.5, Captain Radzi describes the Malaysia Airline's proactive approach to the introduction and integration of expatriate pilots.

Box 7.5   The multi, multicultural Malaysian experience

Malaysia is a multiracial, multicultural and multireligious country. Her 20 million population consists of people from three major races, the Malays, the Chinese and the Indians, and scores of other races all living in a fairly small country. The interactions between the communities is very high. One of our national pastimes can include eating. This is where we interact most often. For example, we may have a Malay breakfast, an Indian curry lunch and a Chinese dinner. You could say we make a meal out of every meal.

In such a society there is a greater need for interdependence. I don't think any one race could exist without the others. In any case it might be very boring. Isn't variety the spice of life? And who knows spices better than we Asians?

Yes, we have had our differences. So far, God willing, we have managed to resolve them quite amicably. When Malaysia Airlines expanded very quickly in the late 1980s we had a sudden influx of expatriates into our system, the majority of whom came from Australia and New Zealand. Population-wise we were looking at about 400 pilots or just under 40 per cent. Such a large population brought about some unique problems, mainly the assimilation of these expatriates into the host country: a culture shock if you like, not only for the expatriates but also for the locals.

Malaysia is primarily a collective society with a high power distance. The expatriates generally have a high individualism and a very low power distance. Brought together, we have a team whose members are quite opposite to each other from a cultural standpoint. This may cause difficulties in the workplace, and indeed it has. There were minor 'skirmishes' that happened in the cockpit. We could do one of two things: pretend that this does not happen and let the expatriates fend for themselves, or address it squarely. We decided to do the latter.

We had an induction course for all the expatriates that came into Malaysia Airlines in the late 1980s. The emphasis of the course was to explain the various idiosyncrasies that we Malaysians have, to help the expatriates understand the cultures in the Malaysian workplace. (At about the same time, we were also embarking on our own CRM program.) The induction course proved to be very successful so we decided to make culture the basis of our CRM course.

The CRM development team consists of pilots and flight engineers from all the nationalities, both locals and expatriates. Examples of cross-cultural situations based on real-life experiences were discussed in an open manner and related back to Hofstede's dimensions of national culture. The primary objective was to make the cockpit a safer place to work in. Looking back, the time spent during development was sometimes frustrating, sometimes discouraging, but never dull. Indeed, there were some very hilarious moments. When viewed from a non-threatening, but focused angle, we had a good laugh at ourselves. The 'skirmishes' became valuable learning experiences. (Captain Azmi Radzi, Malaysia Airlines)

One of the authors was fortunate to visit and observe a Malaysia Airlines CRM seminar and was very impressed with the facilitators' handling of cultural issues. An Indian and a New Zealander, they guided the class of pilots, cadets and flight attendants through an explanation of Hofstede's dimensions of national culture with ease and good humor. They encouraged the class to imagine the extremes of each dimension, and to discuss the strengths and weaknesses of different combinations: a high power distance captain with a low power distance first officer, a collectivist captain with an individualist first officer, and so on. Having tried repeatedly at mealtimes and breaks to elicit some comments from the unfailingly polite Malays about the new expatriates and their behavior, and having failed to hear one negative comment, it was perversely rewarding to hear the whole class agree that the worst possible combination in the cockpit would be two individualists, that is, two Westerners. (Who would take orders and who would conform?) It is a reminder to us all that our cultural values will always produce some cultural biases about what we believe to be the best behavior – certain cultures are just more polite about it than others.

Having shown an airline's proactive stance toward cultural integration, and before we conclude with some recommendations for multicultural organizations, we turn now to an individual's story of how he adapted to a new cultural environment. Captain Robert R. Bumgarner's story is rather long, but we found it so interesting and informative that we have reproduced it here in its entirety. In his own words, here is Captain Bumgarner.

When the Golden Rule Doesn't Work

When I came to Asia five years ago to fly for a Taiwanese airline, I recall an expatriate veteran at the airline warning me that the most common phrase I would hear from my Taiwanese colleagues would be, 'But Captain, you just don't understand.' Looking back, he was right – and so were all the Taiwanese who uttered that phrase to me during the intervening years. I really did not understand.

Western pilots immigrating to an Asian airline environment will encounter a maze of confusing and sometimes contradictory cultural signals. Most national cultures offer a simple rule to guide human behavior in such unfamiliar circumstances. Christendom's Golden Rule, 'Do unto others as you would have them do unto you', is a good example. In Asia, the rule from Confucian teaching is stated negatively: 'What you do not like when done to yourself, do not do to others.' These deceptively similar notions can lead Westerners to believe the transition to Asian living will be simple: just treat other people the way you want to be treated and all will be well.

The problem with treating people from different cultures the way you like to be treated is that they frequently do not expect to be treated in that manner – and their idea of how they should treat you is unlikely to coincide with your expectations either. For example, a highly individualistic, low power-distance American coming to group-oriented, high power-distance Taiwan will want to make friends with his Taiwanese colleagues in the same way he did at home. He will eagerly introduce himself with a handshake and tell people to call him by his first name. He will not notice, of course, that in Asia the Western 'first name' is the 'last name', one way Asians tell you that the family or group is more important than the individual. It will also take a while to notice that few 'juniors' ever feel comfortable calling a 'senior' by a given name or nickname. But Captain ...

Shortly after I came to Taiwan, I made friends with a Taiwanese first officer who shared an interest in tennis. Over the years, we became close friends, so close in fact that I am now godfather to his son. To this day, despite the strongest remonstrations from me, he still calls me Captain and will not address me in any other manner. Such unqualified respect is flattering – and sometimes annoying – but also lies at the root of a major weakness of Asian first officers: they are very reluctant to challenge the Captain at times when they should. But Captain ...

The notion of fraternal submission permeates Asian culture. It is expected that elders and superiors should be respected and served. Application of this basic tenet extends into every corner of the culture, including the cockpit. It won't take long for a Westerner to learn that the pilot in command is expected to sit in the front of the crew bus and to exit the bus first. He will also notice that crew members will dutifully follow him in seniority order through the terminal and will seldom even walk abreast of him, much less pass him. The bad news is that this makes conversation difficult on the walk to the plane and can lead to serious problems if the Captain elects to take the stairs while other crew members scramble to maintain proper order on the escalator next to him. On the plus side, it eliminates the risk of the Captain being knocked down in a mad scramble for first choice of rooms at the layover hotel, a common problem with all-Western crews. But Captain ...

Respect for 'pecking order' is one of the first lessons that Westerners living in Asia must learn. In cases where the Westerner is senior, this is not too difficult – just smile a lot and humbly accept being treated like a god. But Westerners who find themselves in the role of junior, particularly when 'senior' is an Asian Captain, often start bumping into some serious mental blocks to acceptable performance and harmonious relationships. In such cases, the junior Captain is expected to initiate contact with the senior Captain and to express in some subtle way his subordinate position. Taiwanese pilots commonly address respected seniors with the term *jiao guan*, meaning instructor or senior officer. The senior knows his role and will sometimes avoid any contact with subordinates until properly approached by them. This coldly distant behavior still surprises me when I operate as part of a multiple-captain crew and find that I sometimes have to chase the other Captain through Dispatch to introduce myself or say hello. But Captain ...

Similarly confusing situations confront Westerners in their dealings with airline staff. Westerners are very accomplishment-oriented:

more correctly, individual accomplishment-oriented. They generally enjoy responsibility and are very comfortable going directly to responsible people in the companies for which they work to express their disagreement with policies they view as unworkable, inefficient or ineffective. Unfortunately, this practice collides with a basic tenet of Asian management which translates roughly, 'If you don't have the position, don't question the policy.' But Captain ...

Westerners often must learn the hard way that business policy in Asian companies is the product of much discussion and has been 'chopped'[5] by many managers. This approach to policy making spreads risk and assures support for policies once implemented. To an Asian manager, criticism of company policy by Westerners is often shocking and can be indicative of disrespect for the group or, worse yet, a threat to the manager's position. Westerners are often surprised by the ruthless retaliation with which such criticisms are met. But Captain ...

Differences in the interpretation and administration of contracts is another likely venue for cultural discontinuity. Westerners are accustomed to working under defined contractual conditions with specified pay and benefits – and they expect to be rewarded or acknowledged for exceptional performance. They also have clearly defined notions about integrity, honesty and fairness when it comes to contract administration and workplace relationships. But these Western notions spring from a focus on individual rights and simply do not translate well in an Asian context where the rights of the group are superior to the rights of the individual. Westerners will discover that Asian managers tend to do what's best for the group when they encounter unexpected or altered circumstances and feel quite comfortable setting aside the interests of an individual in any case of conflict. But Captain ...

Buffeted by such broad cultural differences, the unprepared Westerner is often propelled into a state of withdrawal and cultural defensiveness, causing him to make the host culture bad and wrong. Human beings always find it more comfortable to make the other guy wrong than to go through a struggle with their own values and belief systems. But this is exactly the action needed if one hopes to fit into a strange and different culture. In the words of Confucius, 'When an archer misses the center of the target, he turns around and looks for the reason in himself.'

The most successful expats I have met – ones who have lived and worked in several different countries – approach the task of learning

---

5   A chop is the elegant Asian equivalent of a signature stamp. Individuals have their name idiograph carved on a piece of stone, quartz, jade or wood, and use it with a red ink pad. Managers indicate they have read and approved a document by leaving their chop (signature).

about a new culture with a light attitude: they treat the process as a voyage of discovery, as an adventure. 'The adventure continues' is one of their common responses to new and challenging situations. And they chuckle every time they hear someone say, 'But Captain, you just don't understand.'

When in Rome ...

With an open-minded attitude and spirit of adventure firmly in place, the next question to be considered by a transplanted Westerner is, 'How can I learn to fit in?' An old adage often attributed to St Augustine, suggests: 'When in Rome, do as the Romans do.' Basically, this piece of Western wisdom tells the foreigner to conform his or her actions to those of the locals. I hope by now the reader is beginning to get the idea that this formula may work when one is transitioning from one Western culture to another Western culture, but that, as is the case with the Golden Rule, it may not work so well when the transition is from a Western to an Eastern culture.

In the West, attitudes and intentions are obvious. In Asia, they are far more subtle, sometimes so subtle as not to be noticed be Westerners. A recent Korean Civil Aviation Bureau (CAB) study of relationships between Korean pilots and expatriate pilots revealed some interesting viewpoints that are probably shared by pilot groups at most multicultural airlines in Asia. Responding to questions about the causes of cockpit problems, 65 per cent of the expatriate captains pointed to 'language' as the primary factor; only 15 per cent of the Korean captains identified 'language' as a major issue while the rest of them felt 'a different way of thinking' (47 per cent) or 'different customs' (36 per cent) caused most problems in the cockpit. Interestingly, none of the expats thought 'customs' was a problem.

A scholar once observed that 'Somebody discovered water, but it probably was not the fish who swim in it.' This notion applies equally to the cultures we humans swim in. Cultural programming is developed over many years – indeed, over a lifetime – and is so complex, yet so subtle, that it is very hard for any of us to identify all of the elements and expected behaviors that comprise it. For the expat, 'language' is an easy response, a cop out, if you will, to a very complex issue.

Asian thinking is different from Western thinking. Asian customs are different from Western customs. And, of course, Asian language is vastly different from Western languages. In many cases, it is simply impossible – or inappropriate – to translate familiar English language words into an Asian language. There are so many cultural differences that the notion of acting native-like or becoming bicultural is unworkable for most expats. Because of these broad cultural differences, the Taiwanese know that few Westerners will ever understand their customs and traditions. They don't expect you to act like a Taiwanese, but they do expect you to respect them and to be courteous to them. The situation can be likened to visiting the home of a distant relative you've never met. You are not familiar with their traditions, what time they eat, what they wear to dinner, how they entertain themselves after dinner, what time they go to bed and when they get up in the morning. When you find yourself in such situations, you go out of your way to ask for guidance, to express your willingness to conform and not offend, you pitch in and try to help them with chores around the house, and you don't try to push your own beliefs and traditions on your hosts.

'When in Rome ...' is really an impractical approach for Westerners transitioning to Asian living. I believe a more workable approach is to act like a guest, realizing that you are different and not equal, and that you must work to learn the traditions of your hosts. This approach can be described as, *'When in Rome, act as the Roman's guest.'* If you act like a considerate guest, you will be well-received and find Asian living a pleasant experience. Eventually, you may even learn how to do things in a humorous way that will ingratiate you to your hosts so that they will begin to appreciate and enjoy your company.

Tips to Smooth Your Transition

Treat it like an adventure   Imagine you are on an excursion to a strange, foreign land as you approach your transition to Asian living – you really are. If you are clear that you are a guest and that you really don't know much about Asian culture and Asian thinking, you will have the attitude of a student, a 'beginner's mind'. You will seek to learn as much as you can about your host's culture and will come to enjoy the experience as you would any other interesting learning opportunity. And you will not be upset when you encounter the strange and unfamiliar. Remember, you only get upset when something happens that you do not expect or when your intentions are thwarted.

Be polite and respectful at all times   Learn to resist your natural tendency to be individualistic. You have two ears and one mouth: try to listen at least twice as much as you talk. And always ask yourself whether what you are about to say is courteous and considerate before you say it; that is, engage brain before putting mouth into gear!

You should also be aware of a few traditional ways of behaving which are common to most of Asia. First, always address a colleague, superior or subordinate, by their surname and 'mister' or 'miss' until they ask you to do otherwise. Second, you should offer your business card, held with two hands, when meeting someone in a business situation for the first time; you will notice that Asians carefully study the other person's card for a few seconds before putting it away.[6] Third, Asians hold older persons in high regard. Displaying extra courtesy and visible acknowledgment of the presence of an older person will reflect well on you.

Enroll them in helping you   It has been my experience that one of the most effective ways to approach new relationships in Asia is with an admission that you don't know a lot about the culture, but that you really do want to learn. I consciously try to enroll my Asian friends and colleagues in my education and invite them to share responsibility for my success.

Similarly, if you expect your Asian first officer to speak up when you make a mistake, you must first make him comfortable doing so; then you must make sure he understands that you consider it his duty to do so. I usually close a cockpit briefing with a few comments on CRM and include a statement that my feelings will not be hurt if they question what I do or speak up when they do not understand what I've said or done. Doing the right thing is more important than who's right!

A little Mandarin goes a long way   You can often break the ice with an Asian colleague, business associate or taxi driver if you make an effort to learn at least a few words of the local language. Hello (*ni hao*), how are you? (*ni hao ma*), good morning (*dzau*), good evening (*wan an*), please (*ching*), thank you (*xie xie ni*, pronounced 'sye sye'), excuse me (*dui bu qi*), you're welcome (*bu keqi*), it doesn't matter/it's okay (*mei guanxi*), it's not a problem (*mei wenti*), are a few standards. Captains who learn standard PA announcements in the local language become legends in their own time.

Don't ask why, ask what   A famous American advertising slogan goes, 'Why ask why?' A Westerner transitioning to Asian culture would do well to adopt this slogan in regard to many of the unusual situations they encounter in Asia. Asians simply are not taught to question the reasons for everything as are most Westerners and you will find that they almost never ask questions during training sessions. Indeed, one of the most challenging tasks for a Westerner who conducts training in Asia is to gain any measure of class participation.

6   In some companies, the phone number can reveal a person's status. The closer the last four digits are to zero, the more important the person is.

Responses to your 'why' questions can only be evaluated in terms of norms from your own culture. Most of the answers you receive will either be difficult to understand or nonsensical to you. A more useful question is 'what' (*shenme*). This question will enable you to discover what your Asian interlocutor wants or needs. It's much easier to fulfill needs than to figure out why they're needed.

Be helpful but humble   You will usually find many opportunities to be of help at most Asian airlines. However, in making an offer to help, you should also know that Asians are generally wary of apparent ambition. The wisdom goes, 'The superior man does what is proper to the station in which he is – he does not desire to go beyond this.' So, when you offer to help 'improve' things, you walk a fine line between being of assistance and being intrusive. The best way to approach making suggestions for change is to ask your immediate superior if he or she wants any suggestions before you offer them. If the response is affirmative, ask about form: should it be verbal or presented in writing and, if so, to whom should it be addressed? You must be very careful about face issues when you start writing critical letters, particularly when those criticisms go to someone senior to the responsible person! You should also realize that most policy changes result from lots of discussion that incorporates personal concerns and consideration of alternatives before any formal meetings are held. Policies rarely change because one person writes a letter.

Develop a 'thick face'   An ancient piece of Chinese wisdom states, 'When you conceal your will from others, that is Thick.' From this basic idea comes the notion of 'thick face'. It literally means to hide what you feel, want or need from others, ostensibly so that they will be unprepared to thwart your intentions. Most Westerners tend to wear their feelings on their sleeves, there for all to see. In Asia, you would do well to control your emotions and not show them, hide your ambitions and not express them, and keep most of your opinions to yourself unless they are specifically requested – and then be very careful that you word them considerately and respectfully.

Do not confront those in authority   This goes at work, in social situations, or when dealing with government officials. It simply does no good to confront someone in a position of authority. They are likely to take your attitude as a personal insult and demonstrate to you quite clearly how little power you have in the situation. When you have what you think are legitimate and necessary concerns about a policy, procedure, rule or service being rendered to you, you must learn to couch your criticisms respectfully and tactfully. Obviously, sarcasm is out. Speak in a level tone of voice and express your concern as questions whenever possible: do not simply state that the policy or person you are addressing is wrong. You should learn to state issues in a manner that respects the person you are addressing or the persons who made the policy or rule in question. Phrases like, 'That's interesting, I haven't seen that before. However, I am a bit confused – I wonder if you could help me understand how...' or 'I'm sorry, I guess I don't understand. Captain (or some respected authority) told me that (blah blah blah). Would you prefer I do it this way?' Here, invoking the thinking of a respected third party removes you from direct criticism and leaves open the opportunity for the other person to control the result. A low-key approach will save a bit of face for the other person (and for you) and increase the likelihood of successful result.

Work on your guan xi   The word guan xi in Mandarin means relationships. Everything in Asia is driven by relationships. Work on them, at every level. The attitude, 'What can I do to help?' usually opens lots of doors to new relationships. Your Asian boss is the product of a culture based on respect and deference. You must treat him in this manner. There is also a mutuality to all Asian relationships: just as the subordinate must defer to the superior, the superior has obligations to the subordinate. If you approach your superior with the proper attitude, he is duty-bound to consider your concerns and to try to help you if it is within his power to do so. You will know when he cannot help with your problem because the conversation will turn to unrelated matters and drag on for a considerable period of time. Don't interrupt this process; it's your boss showing his concern for you.

Business is business, social is social   Make a concerted effort to separate business from pleasure, particularly when it comes to social events such as dinner or a night out with Asian friends. It is impossible to overemphasize the importance of food to most Asians. One of the most common Chinese greetings is, 'Have you eaten your fill?', replacing the Western 'Hi' or 'How are you?' Sharing food is how Asians demonstrate goodwill and camaraderie; eating is like a sort of festival or celebration. Eating rituals and traditions are also very symbolic for Asians. Everyone eats out of the same bowls to show common dependence on each other, round tables increase interaction, and people are expected to share what food they have with others in their group. The custom on sharing does not mean that a person should share when it is convenient, but that a person is expected to share at all times, even to the point of denying oneself. Go out of your way to bring extra food to a social gathering. You will be amazed at how bringing a few treats to important meetings can reduce criticism and facilitate good results.

A few tips when you're invited to dinner: (1) don't try to split the check with your host – it's an insult; (2) avoid controversial issues at the dinner table and try to find topics for discussion where agreement is likely; (3) it's okay to leave some dishes not fully eaten, but you should at least sample them all; (4) don't leave chopsticks sticking in a rice bowl – this is only done to honor a deceased or missing person; and (5) always be effusive in your praise for your host's generosity and taste in selecting such a fine feast.

Finally, with regard to dating: if you find the temptation irresistible, keep it private.

Recommendations and Conclusions

As the quotation at the beginning of this chapter suggests, the history of cross-cultural contact has been one of bloodshed and oppression; ethnocentrism is the norm and intercultural sensitivity the exception. But economic forces are moving us toward a more global working environment, forcing us to be better neighbors. As this chapter has shown, *culture can be a problem, but only if its influence goes unacknowledged.* To that end, we conclude the chapter with some recommendations for enhancing safety and efficiency in multicultural organizations.

We believe that there are several ways in which a multicultural organization can promote safety (and harmony). The first is to set clear organizational standards and policies that eliminate previous cultural assumptions and explicate all the organization's goals and procedures. More than monocultural organizations, multicultural companies must be explicit with their directives. Adopting a 'best practices' approach to standards and procedures allows all employees to focus on the important outcomes and helps avoid ethnocentric biases.

Training is the second tool for enhancing safety. When asked how the airline could maintain or improve its current safety record, the answer from pilots at one multicultural airline was, 'Train, train, train.' Simulator training in particular becomes a powerful (and safe) means of rehearsing the company standards and procedures. Multicultural organizations may need to allocate more resources to training to ensure that all employees, regardless of background, can perform to the company standard during normal *and* abnormal conditions, with sufficient remedial training offered as required.

Two other forms of non-technical training could also be considered. Intercultural awareness training could be provided to expatriates, their families *and* the host nationals. This training, before and after arrival in the new country, will facilitate quicker adaptation to the new environment, fewer early terminations, stronger cooperation (and less defensiveness) amongst employees and more effective long-term performance.

Language training may also be necessary. For example, English is the official language of aviation and its practice should be mandated: a company-supported language school is imperative for pilots and highly recommended for their families. Language training is not just for the non-native English speaker. Anglo pilots, who have been arbitrarily granted the linguistic advantage, should be given special training in how to communicate simply, slowly, and precisely with non-Anglo personnel as required.[7] All pilots should strive for open and unambiguous communication in the cockpit; one pilot's struggle to be precise in his second or third language should be matched by another pilot's willingness to listen closely and respond simply with a minimum of words. This training would also facilitate cockpit–ATC interactions in most parts of the world. There may be some technological fixes for the language problem, such as electronic translators, datalink or electronic transmission of text messages, but they may generate new problems as they solve others, and may be inadequate in abnormal situations.

The third area in which a multicultural organization can enhance its prospects is through recruitment. New employees should be selected not only for their technical competence but also for their potential to be interculturally effective. Research has identified certain attributes as good predictors of intercultural success; these include patience, maturity, stability, self-confidence, perseverance, problem solving, tolerance, professional commitment and initiative. A company that selects personnel by these criteria as well as technical competence stands to reduce turnover, improve employee cooperation, stabilize the working environment, increase productivity and save money.

In conclusion, perhaps there is no such thing as a truly monocultural organization. Drawing on information from the previous chapters, we argue that all organizations are a blend of national, regional, organizational and occupational subcultures. These influences can be ignored, to the detriment of the organization, or they can be studied, appreciated and integrated to form a strong, healthy and unique organization.

---

7   Contrary to popular misconception, speaking more loudly does not facilitate comprehension.

8 Cultural Psychology: a Synthesis

The three cultures, national, professional and organizational, have both positive and negative influences on the way individuals, teams and organizations function. As world commerce becomes more global and people more often work with others whose cultural values differ, the need to deal effectively with issues of national culture will be increasingly recognized. However, as we have shown, these three cultures intersect, with organizational culture having the most proximal impact on behavior at the 'sharp end'. While ignoring cultural issues in high-risk organizations increases the probability of accidents and incidents, cultural problems in all types of organizations may cause losses in efficiency and profits.[1] In contrast, dealing with cultures positively and proactively should improve the organization's climate and productivity, and facilitate the emergence of a safety culture.

As we stressed in Chapters 5 and 6, organizations have a critical need for data on their cultures and how they are manifested at the operational level. Without this information, it is impossible to address cultural issues appropriately. Data, of course, come in many forms. As researchers, we recognize the limitations of purely quantitative measures and the need to explore the deep structure of situations. In writing this book, we have tried to augment 'hard' data with the insiders' reports scattered through the text in boxes. Without the collaboration of those immersed in organizations, understanding will necessarily be incomplete.

Organizations not only need information, they need personnel who know how to obtain data, to interpret them and to implement appropriate interventions. As we pointed out in Chapter 6, trust is an essential element of effective organizational strategy. In this case, the

1   General Motors' experience in attempting to sell the Chevrolet Nova in Mexico is an oft-told cautionary tale. Sales were abysmal; perhaps no one in Detroit had figured out that *no va* in Spanish means 'It doesn't go.' Fortunately, the only damage was to the bottom line and managerial egos.

insider must have the trust of those at the highest level of the organization, who have the resources to make things happen.

While responsibility for interventions related to culture and safety
rests with Senior Management, the issue of who should deal with
data, analyses and recommendations is not simple. Many organizations do not have the resources (or the managerial support) to fill a
position that deals with research and intervention in culture and
error management. There is also the possibility that insiders may be
subjected to pressures to ignore problems in the interest of production. Even with adequate resources, there are simply not enough
people to go around who have expertise in research and in dealing
with the intersection of the three cultures. Part of the shortage, if we
can so characterize it, comes from relatively recent awareness of the
operational importance of culture. Part also comes from the way
universities have dealt with interdisciplinary training.

The Academy and Culture

Research into theoretical issues that are enacted in real-world settings (for example, the effects of national culture on automation use)
poses a problem for university researchers. To maintain academic
credibility, the dictum of 'publish or perish' must be observed. To
survive and to be a credible mentor, the academic must be able to
function in the academy and the 'real world.' This dual practitioner
must be able to conduct research that has the same rigor as that of
experimental psychology.[2] As we stressed in Chapter 1, we feel that
the distinction between basic and applied research is a pernicious
one. Research in the interest of the cultural issues we have considered has not only immediate practical value, but also the ability to
refine our theories of humans as social and working animals.

Culture, like contemporary human factors, is an inherently interdisciplinary topic that cuts across traditional academic/departmental
boundaries in universities. A full understanding of the roles of cultures necessarily includes elements of cognitive, industrial and
organizational, social and personality psychology, as well as management, sociology, anthropology and human factors.[3] There is not a

2   This probably poses a greater problem for those whose disciplinary home is a
    department of psychology where the norm in social psychology has been to
    conduct research on campus using student subjects. Nevertheless, it can also
    pose problems for those in business schools who are torn between campus
    responsibilities and field research.
3   By human factors, we are referring to the interpersonal aspects of the workplace.
    Ergonomics (the traditional 'knob and dial' human factors) is more closely
    allied with engineering, perception and physiology. Cognitive psychology cuts
    across both domains of human factors.

cadre of scientists whose expertise covers the breadth of these specialties. In the long range, what is probably essential is a re-examination of the training of behavioral scientists.

Academic training, like academic research, is subject to fads and fancies (Jones, 1985). The goal of multidisciplinary (or interdisciplinary) training is frequently espoused, sometimes practiced and usually abandoned. Many of the interdisciplinary programs that were proudly heralded after World War II faded away. However, it is possible that a resurgence of interdisciplinary education is now under way. Informally, we observe an increasing number of students who are embracing double majors, combining areas such as psychology and anthropology or management and psychology.

Box 8.1 Surviving an interdisciplinary education

I spent my undergraduate and graduate years at Yale University, an institution that was committed to interdisciplinary programs, albeit briefly. At the undergraduate level an interdisciplinary honors major called 'Culture and Behavior' offered those of us who opted for it the opportunity to complete a quadruple major with concentrations in psychology, sociology, anthropology and biology.[4] At the same time, the faculties of the social sciences were combined (along with psychiatry) in a building called the Institute of Human Relations.

I only dimly appreciated what an extraordinary education I was receiving. The interdisciplinary courses were team-taught, usually by senior faculty, and the interactions among leading scientists in the several disciplines were stimulating, if esoteric. Only many years later, when we began our explorations of culture, did I realize that I actually had received a preview of issues that still challenge the field. I also acquired, post hoc, a real appreciation of the wisdom of the maxim that it is a shame to waste education on the young.

By the time I returned from Navy service to begin graduate school, most of the interdisciplinary focus had evaporated. Indeed, I was warned by a faculty member that I should specialize as quickly as possible during my graduate training, if I wanted to get a job at a major university. Within a few years the departments had moved to isolated and individual buildings. It was a brief moment, but a shining one. (Robert Helmreich)

---

4   There were a number of other programs, many of which combined science and liberal arts (for example, physics and philosophy) and, in the graduate area, law and psychology.

Some of the factors that led to the demise of interdisciplinary programs reflect problems with the social sciences in general. Each of the constituent disciplines has its own jargon and methodologies, not necessarily respected (or understood) by the others. This differentiation does not facilitate cooperation at the faculty level and can be confusing to students. Similarly, multidisciplinary efforts have been less valued and rewarded by one's peers than efforts focused within a specialty. Perhaps the greatest barrier, at all levels – from student to professor – is presented by the perceived need to specialize at the earliest possible moment. Even undergraduates are susceptible to pressures to define a narrow set of interests to ensure admission to the most prestigious graduate program, while graduate students want to carve their own professional niche as rapidly as possible. The proliferation of ever more specialized journals reflects increasing narrowness within disciplines. Rather than integration, we seem to be facing Balkanization of the social sciences.

Is the situation hopeless? We think not. Necessity frequently dictates change. Growing recognition by the real world, and even by the academic community, of the importance of cultural issues may provide the needed impetus to rethink academic priorities.[5] The pressures seem to be building, not only from an applied perspective, but also from theoretical psychology. In social psychology, evidence is growing that many of the cherished findings (often seen as universals) are moderated by culture (Smith & Bond, 1993). Culture is also finding its way into college texts and into both undergraduate and graduate curricula.

Cross-cultural *psychology* is still not a fully mature discipline. As we have discussed in Chapter 3 and Appendix A, there are daunting methodological problems as well as the reality that cross-national studies are much more costly to conduct than home-based research with undergraduates. Nonetheless, as awareness of culture grows, researchers may develop new and creative ways to study cultural issues. For example, just as the Internet has become an invaluable mechanism of exchange for those working with CRM, it may also allow students at all levels, including undergraduates, to collaborate without vast resources.[6]

In graduate training, the study of culture may end up following several paths. On one, there may be an increase in the number of

5   In an investigation of issues involved in automated aircraft, the FAA Human Factors Team (FAA, 1997) singled out cultural issues as critical. Similarly, the National Transportation Safety Board, as we have noted, has increasingly addressed organizational culture as a contributory factor in accidents.
6   We realize that long-distance cross-cultural research poses the same problems that research without insider insights does in organizations. Nonetheless, the opportunities for learning and correction of inaccurate cultural stereotypes are great.

programs offering degrees in cross-cultural psychology as an academic specialty. This could lead to both positive and negative outcomes. On the positive side, with broader emphasis and more programs, the study of national culture would become more recognized as a needed specialty. On the negative side, a primary focus on national culture could obscure the important contributions of professional and organizational cultures intersecting with national culture.

Another outcome might be the establishment of culture as a *significant* component of established disciplines in the way that cross-cultural social psychology has emerged as a subspecialty of social psychology. Although not related directly to the workplace, cultural issues in developmental psychology may re-emerge as important and exciting topics.

Different disciplines have approached different cultures. Business schools, especially departments of management, are placing more stress on organizational culture both as a research topic and as a component of the curriculum (for example, Trice & Beyer, 1993). Research in psychology departments has not paid much heed to organizational and professional issues, leaving these to business colleagues. Similarly, empirical studies of the sequelae of national culture have tended to remain in psychology departments. What we feel is lacking is an attempt to bridge the disciplinary differences among the academic departments and to include the perspectives of anthropology and sociology. We recognize that a call for more areas of study and greater breadth is not in fashion today. Nevertheless, we feel that an exposure to multiple perspectives and methodologies would better prepare students to function in changing research and organizational domains. It is our strong belief that the training of graduate students should stress breadth, with the goal of producing scholars and practitioners who can function with equal facility in academia, in industry and in government. In this vein, both of us, if asked, would define ourselves as *cultural, rather than cross-cultural, psychologists*.

Box 8.2   From cowboys to croissants

I left the University of Texas Aerospace Crew Research Project in December 1997 after accepting a job with Jean Paries' Human Factors and Safety consulting group, Dedale, based in Paris, France. The opportunity was simply too good to refuse. As a cross-cultural researcher I wanted to immerse myself in a non-Anglo culture and discover first-hand the experience of culture shock and adaptation. I also wanted to transition from academia to industry, to observe the differences and shifting priorities, and I knew that Dedale had a good reputation and would offer me many challenges.

I turned to the literature on cultural adaptation and acculturation in preparation for the move and gained many helpful insights. I worked with a very patient French tutor for several months. I gathered information on Paris from the Internet. I internalized Captain Bumgarner's advice: 'When in Rome, act as the Roman's guest' as my creed. When the time came, I was as ready as I could be.

As I write this, I have been in Paris for only seven weeks. My French has not improved, but my English seems to be deteriorating nicely. I seem to be deconstructing one language in order to understand another. Each day brings frustration and anxiety, but then there are those small moments of joy when I think I may have understood something or even better may have been understood by others. I am beginning to think that this may be the biggest challenge of my life to date. I also think it may be the most interesting. (Ashleigh Merritt)

What Does the Organization Do Until the Doctor Comes?

We have noted the increasing emphasis on cultural issues in the workplace. Both national and organizational culture have strong implications for safety and profitability. At present there are many more issues than there are researchers who can address them, especially at the cross-national level. As an interim strategy, organizations can make every effort to ensure that culture (of whatever variety) is not overlooked in the process of diagnosing and treating organizational ills. The example of CRM is a good one. The best designed training programs can only achieve their potential impact if they are harmonized with the national, professional and organizational cultures. At this stage of knowledge there are clearly roles for outside researchers and consultants, as we discussed in Chapter 6. The organization may need to use several researchers or consultants to get the interdisciplinary skills needed.

We feel that most organizations, especially in safety-related domains, will feel the need for an in-house expert who can provide advice and coordinate culture-related activities. Without denying the need for doctoral level researchers, we suggest that the initiation of an MBA in Culture degree would be of great value. Holders of this degree would have familiarity with both theoretical and methodological issues surrounding culture. Such individuals could serve as organizational watchdogs and interface with consultants and researchers. Such a role would be consistent with the general research/action strategy we propose in the following section.

Evolutionary Action Research as a Collaborative Strategy

The continuing litany of the culture researcher is the dearth of subjects and resources needed to conduct meaningful research. As we have discussed, many cultural issues, especially ones involving organizations or professions, are not amenable to laboratory research in the traditional experimental design employing student subjects. Hence the researcher needs the cooperation of real organizations engaged in real activities to obtain meaningful results.

On the other hand, as we have stressed, organizations need valid diagnostic data to manage human error and enhance safety and system effectiveness. It is our belief that Kurt Lewin's (1946) model of action research discussed in Chapter 1 remains the optimal strategy for research, diagnosis and application. There is no reason why theoretical interests in culture or group dynamics cannot be advanced at the same time that organizations are receiving vital data to guide their management.

We add the term *evolutionary* to action research because the research process will necessarily change and mature as theory develops and data grow. Our cross-cultural experiences fit this model well. We started with a simple survey to begin to explore the attitudes underlying cockpit behavior. As we discovered the power of organizational and national culture, the research began to grow in scope and the areas assessed expanded. Similarly, we began to augment attitudinal data with systematic observations of crew behavior and these measures changed as data and theory accumulated. Our behavioral system is now in its fifth generation, with the addition of a new approach to classifying the *management* of human error.

Unlike simple hypothesis testing in the laboratory/experimental tradition, evolutionary action research seeks to isolate and validate relationships that cannot be derived from extant theories. In this approach, the challenge is to replicate, validate and cross-validate findings, since traditional experimental designs incorporating random assignment of subjects to conditions are inappropriate and unusable. Action research should not be limited to quantitative methods alone. Much of the richness of culture derives from qualitative material and case studies. While the latter have been harshly castigated by experimentalists, qualitative approaches in concert with quantitative data provide a far deeper understanding of phenomena than either alone. Quantitative measures specify the influence of culture, while qualitative data give insights into the deep structure.

Into the Future

We hope that our discussion of the three cultures has served to raise awareness of their importance in the workplace. Our greatest hope is that we may encourage organizations to make culture a meaningful part of their research, analysis and action, and that we have encouraged more scientists to join us in the pursuit of culture.

Appendix A: Methodological Issues in Cross-cultural Research

Culture is a variable that is beyond experimental control. (Van de Vijver & Leung, 1997, p.3)

Cross-cultural research has some unique methodological issues (Bond & Smith, 1996; Triandis, 1980; Van de Vijver & Leung, 1997). These issues focus on equivalence and bias and include culture-sensitive sampling of the data, awareness of item and culture-level response biases and decisions regarding the appropriate level of analysis and the number of analyses necessary to fully understand the data. In this appendix, we discuss the issues that were relevant to our study and provide solutions to the problems that we encountered.

Cross-cultural Sampling

Data collection in our study was opportunistic: any airline that agreed to participate in the study was welcome. (Developing contacts with researchers and practitioners in other parts of the world was an essential part of our work, and developing these friendships was also one of the most personally rewarding aspects of the work.) As part of our contract with these airlines, we agreed to analyze all the data that they sent to us, regardless of what our research needs might dictate. As a result, our final data set included airline groups of widely disparate sizes, from an Argentine sample of 39 to samples in the USA exceeding 2000 pilots. The challenge was to design a study which utilized as many of the data as possible, while simultaneously recognizing and not overshadowing the information provided by the smaller groups.

Defining Group Membership

The first task was to define and select the cultural groups. Hofstede (1980) has argued the need for 'narrow samples' in cross-cultural work, which is to say that one cannot compare the attitudes of nurses from Finland with those of construction workers in Brazil and hope to arrive at any definitive cultural conclusion. The more all other variables except cultural membership are kept constant, the more confident one can be that the resulting differences are due solely to culture. To that end, our narrow sample consisted of male, commercial airline pilots across different countries.[1] (Data from military pilots and female pilots were not used because of insufficient numbers across countries.)

Next, particular care was taken to derive culturally homogeneous samples. Putting multicultural airlines to one side for the moment, only airlines which were predominantly owned, managed and operated by members of the same national culture were used. That is, once the questionnaires were collected from an airline, a subset was selected for our study based on information in the demographic section: male pilots, captains, and first and second officers, whose present nationality and nationality at birth matched the nationality of the airline. These subsets were selected to maximize cultural strength and homogeneity within groups. (Expatriate pilot data were not used in the cross-cultural analyses because these pilots' attitudes may have been affected by working in another national environment, and therefore could not confidently be attributed to any one national culture.) We also considered command position in our early analyses, but found that differences between captains and first officers were insignificant when compared with the cross-cultural differences that we observed.

Equalizing Group Contributions

The pilot database included airline groups of widely disparate sizes. Larger groups could easily outweigh the influence of the smaller groups in the analyses if something was not done. The easiest technique was to constrain all sample sizes to the size of the smallest group. Random subsamples of 50 pilots were drawn from the larger cultural groups to match the smaller groups. When analyses were run on this reduced data set, we could be confident that all groups

1   The potential disadvantage of this approach is the emergent influence of one occupational culture, as we see in Chapter 3. Hofstede's dimension of Masculinity–Femininity was not replicated, in part owing to features of the professional pilot culture.

contributed equally to the results. The disadvantage of this approach was that many of the data which were collected were not used (and no researchers want to give up data that they have worked so hard to collect).

A second approach converted raw scores to proportions, in effect converting the data to percentages. In this way, the important information was the percentage of pilots in each group who endorsed a particular item, regardless of the original sample size. Chi-square analyses based on percentage scores can then be used; for example, we used this technique with the automation items in Chapter 3.

Another approach to sample differences was to use Hofstede's technique of country-level scores (Hofstede, 1980). For every questionnaire item, an airline score was calculated by taking the average of two scores: the average of the captains' scores for that item, and the average of the first and second officers' scores for the item. For those countries represented by more than one airline, the airline means for each item were then averaged to form the country mean. (Averaging within position before averaging for an airline, and averaging across airlines to derive a country score where appropriate, seemed the best approximation of Hofstede's method of weighting each occupational group equally within a country.) This approach used all the collected data, albeit in a very condensed form, and every country was assured an equal influence because every country contributed one data point per item to the country-level analyses. The disadvantage of Hofstede's approach, however, is its reliance on the mean as the single statistical parameter: intracultural variation is ignored with this approach.

A fourth approach was the most statistically sophisticated, but only suitable for some analyses. In order to use all the data, to maintain an equal contribution from each country and to retain information about within-culture variation, we created an aggregated correlation matrix. A correlation matrix of relevant items (work values or attitudes) was derived from all the captains' responses in each country, and another was derived from all the first and second officers' responses. Each country's matrices were then transformed to standard scores using the Fisher r to z transformation. All the matrices were then averaged to form one matrix, which was then converted back to correlations. This aggregated, averaged, correlation matrix was then used as the basis for the exploratory factor analyses.

We used all four techniques at different points in the data analyses, and were able to triangulate the results.

Construct and Method Bias

While considerable effort was made to ensure culture-sensitive sampling and analyses, it is important to acknowledge a construct bias (Van de Vijver & Poortinga, 1997). The items of the questionnaire were written by Anglo researchers (an American and an Australian) and, as such, the study is contaminated with a Western bias. While the item design was directed by our reading of the cross-cultural literature, nonetheless, the items reflect our outsiders' rather clumsy perspective of other cultures. For example, the items written to reflect command styles and interactions probably reflect Anglo norms to a greater extent than other countries, simply because we did not know how else to frame the questions. Consequently, when pilots of other cultures answer these items, we gain an understanding of how much they match or deviate from Anglo expectations of leadership, but we do not really develop a strong understanding of their unique leadership issues and norms. In a sense, we can find out how well the Anglo command style 'fits' other countries, but we do not know if intrinsic aspects of non-Anglo command styles have been overlooked. Ideally, a cross-cultural survey would contain items contributed by all cultural groups to be sure the domain of interest, such as leadership, is adequately covered without bias. Collaboration with indigenous researchers or subject matter experts can help clarify these issues.

Method bias was also an issue, in that familiarity with survey techniques varied across countries. For pilots in some countries, surveys were standard, anonymous, trustworthy forms of amassing pilot opinion. In other countries, there was a distrust of the process, a concern that anonymous responses could still be traced back to individual pilots. We always made a point of including in the cover letter a clear statement assuring the confidentiality and security of the data.

Inter- and Intracultural Analyses

Robinson (1950) and others (Bond, 1988; Leung, 1989; Leung & Bond, 1989) have demonstrated that correlations and associations observed in aggregated culture-level data might differ in magnitude or sign from those observed in individual-level data. In other words, as one shifts from intracultural analyses to intercultural analyses, the items which were useful measures within a culture may not discriminate successfully across cultures. As this fact is not intuitively obvious, let us consider which items would be most appropriate for intercultural scales, as opposed to intracultural scales.

In scale development, one is interested in a full range of scores across the population of interest, producing an unskewed distribution and high item variance (De Vellis, 1991). One is interested in discriminating among members of the group on the particular construct of interest and therefore is looking for items which maximally separate members of the group. When one looks at intercultural analyses, one is still interested in maximally separating members of the group, but this time 'members of the group' refers to cultures, not individuals within cultures.

To find items which would be suitable for intercultural analyses, one might begin with items within cultures which are highly skewed; the high level of endorsement amongst members of the culture indicates that an item reflects a commonly held belief or cultural norm (Triandis, Bontempo, Leung & Hui, 1990).[2] To discriminate maximally amongst cultures, the ideal item would show strong agreement in one culture (high negative skewness), strong disagreement in another culture (high positive skewness) and other cultures somewhere between the two. The result at the culture level is a full range of scores, high item variance and unskewed distribution. Consider then that the ideal item for cross-cultural comparisons would have small within-culture variance (to indicate a cultural norm) relative to its between-culture variance. In other words, the qualities that make an item unsuitable for intracultural analysis (minimal variance, skewed distribution) may render it highly suitable for intercultural analysis.

Items which are 'successful' at the intercultural level are difficult to locate in the data because of their unique statistical properties, and they can only be discovered by researchers who are immersed in the data at the intracultural as well as the intercultural level. There is no comprehensive analytic technique which can isolate these variables: only a detailed knowledge of the item distributions and correlations within and across cultural groups, combined with a strong theoretical perspective or interest, can guide selection of items for culture-level analyses.[3] Because we analyzed the data and prepared a report for every airline – in effect, a series of intracultural analyses over four years – we became very familiar with the idiosyncrasies and emerging patterns of the data. A complete cultural analysis should always include intracultural as well as intercultural analyses.

2 An item which is highly skewed in the same direction both within and across all cultural groups may be an indicator of a universal norm. This was the approach we used to establish pilot norms in the skewness analyses.
3 Developing scales at the cross-cultural level can be ultimately defeating because of these unique item properties. Cross-cultural scales tend to neutralize interesting emic (within–country) differences in the pursuit of scalar etic (between–country) equivalence.

Cultural Response Bias

Identifying the Problem

While the problem of response bias is not new to psychology, cross-cultural research encounters its own unique problem, the possibility that systematic variation in item response can be attributed to culture. For example, a less extreme response style, a tendency to overuse the mid-range of a scale, has been demonstrated with Japanese and Korean students and managers (Chun et al., 1974; Stening & Everett, 1984; Zax & Takahashi, 1967). This response style has been linked to the cultural norms of modesty and caution in these Asian cultures: to use the extremes would be to stand out, to bring attention to oneself. In contrast, some Romance cultures (from the Mediterranean and South America) appear to overuse the extremes of the scale to demonstrate sincerity; that is, if they agree, they agree 'strongly' (Hui & Triandis, 1989): to use the middle of the scale might make one appear guarded and not emotionally sincere.

While admonitions abound in the literature as to the existence of cultural response styles (Berry, 1980; Chun et al., 1974; Hofstede, 1980; Poortinga & Berry, 1989; Stening & Everett, 1984; Triandis, 1972), there is surprisingly little discussion and almost no agreement as to how to treat the problem. Essentially, the difficulty lies in separating true scores from bias. This is a common psychometric problem yet, despite some very sophisticated statistical techniques, the truth remains that true scores can only be estimated. Also, if response is confounded with culture, to what extent *should* culture be stripped from the response? Do Japanese subjects give neutral responses because they are undecided, or because they are modest or cautious? If the answer is the latter, then will they not also be modest or cautious in the behavior which is being tapped by the item?

We tested for cultural response sets in the pilot data using contingency tables. The original FMAQ contained 17 work values items, later reduced to 13. The response bias analyses were conducted after we collected data from 15 countries and we used the full set of 17 items. The items were based on an ascending five-point scale ranging from 'no importance' to 'utmost importance'. Six new variables were created for every individual for each group. The first variable was a count of the number of times that 'one' was given as a response to any of the 17 values items, the second was a count of the number of times that 'two' was given, and so on for the five response options. A sixth variable was computed to control for missing responses. These variables, which captured all possible responses and summed to 17 for every individual, were summed and averaged for each airline group. The result was a general response pattern – the overall tendency to assign ratings of '1' to '5' to *any* item, regardless of content – for each group. (For example, Figure A.2 shows the general response tendency is for 33 per cent of the Japanese pilots to give the most neutral response of 'three', compared with 25 per cent of Anglo pilots and 15 per cent of Brazilian pilots. The pattern is reversed for the extreme score of 'five': 40 per cent of Brazilian pilots gave this response, compared with 22 per cent of Anglo pilots and only 8 per cent of Japanese pilots. In other words, the Japanese pilots exhibited a preference for the mid-range of the scale, regardless of the item, while Brazilian pilots exhibited a preference for the extreme of the rating scale, just as the literature had predicted.)

A new matrix was created based on the count variables for each airline group in each of 15 countries. To control for unequal sample sizes, the count variables were transformed to convey proportions rather than actual Ns. This group-level data matrix was used to test for systematic relationships between culture and response bias. We used the chi-square statistic to analyze the full pattern of results, not simply differences in one category, and to pinpoint significant areas of discrepancy. Cramér's V coefficient (Cramér, 1946) was used to establish the effect size: it can be interpreted as analogous to the R^2 in multiple regression.

A set of chi-square analyses was conducted with different subsets of airline groups, starting with five US airlines, and progressing to more heterogeneous subsets to determine the extent of possible response set differences. Effect sizes ranged from a non-significant .02 for the five US airlines (that is, there were no significant differences amongst the pilots of the five US airlines in their general response patterns) to .04 for the five Anglo countries (USA, Australia, New Zealand, Ireland and British Hong Kong; Figure A.1 highlights the similarity of these patterns), .16 for five Asian countries (the Philippine pilots showed more of an extremity bias, while the Japanese and Korean pilots demonstrated a neutrality bias), and 0.31 for a comparison of Brazilian, Anglo and Japanese response styles (Figure A.2 highlights the dissimilarity of these patterns).

These results indicated the extent to which data transformations would be necessary for intercultural comparisons. Essentially, any analyses based solely on Anglo countries would not require data transformations, but all other analyses, whether they were Asia-based, or a mix of Anglo and non-Anglo countries, would benefit from data transformations which minimized conflicting response sets.

A series of chi-square analyses were also conducted on the attitudinal data to determine the extent of cultural response sets when the data were anchored with a neutral mid-point as opposed to an ascending scale as used for the values items. The data were converted to a three-point response-intensity scale (0 = 'neutral', 1 =

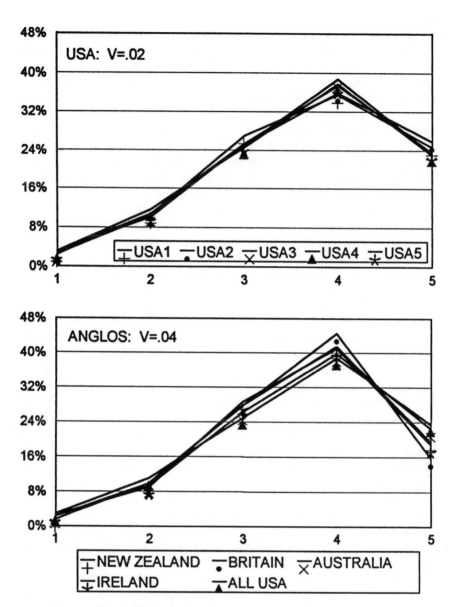

Figure A.1   Frequency distributions of 17 value items
(similarities) based on a five-point Likert scale, five
US airlines and four other Anglo airlines with
average USA distribution

'*slightly* agree or disagree', 3 = '*strongly* agree or disagree') which
could detect extremity and neutrality biases. Effect sizes for the

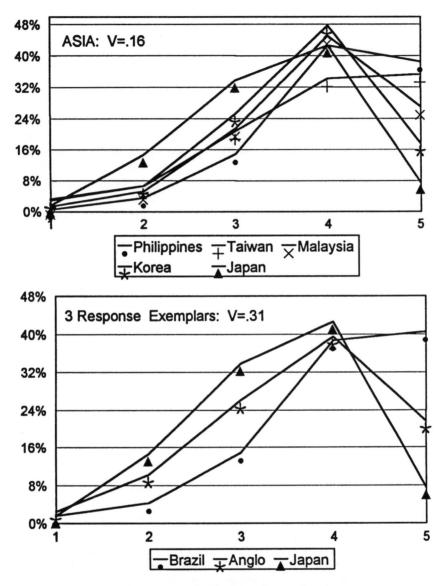

Figure A.2 Frequency distributions of 17 value items (dissimilarities) based on a five-point Likert scale, five Asian airlines and three response set exemplars

attitudinal items followed a similar, but less extreme, pattern than the values items. For example, the largest effect size for any attitudinal analysis was .14, compared with an effect size of .31 when tested across the same countries with the values items. Scales which incorporate a neutral mid-point are a more effective means of controlling cultural response bias than unidirectional scales.

Neutralizing Cultural Response Bias

All data transformations are inherently flawed: assumptions are made and some information about the raw scores is always lost. However, the above analyses show that the work values items could not be used in their raw score form in any intercultural analyses. Before deciding on an appropriate data transformation, we experimented with four variations, in two data sets, using factor analysis and ANOVAs. The four variations were raw scores, Schwartz's (1995) method (score = raw score –cultural group's mean score for the items + grand groups' mean for the items), a variation of Schwartz's method that made fewer assumptions about the data and did not confound level of analysis (score = raw score –*individual's* mean score for the items + grand groups' mean for the items) and Bond and Leung's method (Bond, 1988; Leung, 1989; Leung & Bond, 1989) which standardized the work values within every subject. We conducted analyses with an Anglo sample of data, where cultural response bias was not an issue, to understand how the transformations affected the data. We also ran the same analyses with a non-Anglo sample to see the extent of the differences when response bias was an issue.

The four techniques produced convergent results in the Anglo sample as expected, but solutions varied when response bias was present. Leung and Bond's (1989) method was adopted for this study because it made the fewest assumptions and the most straightforward transformations. When the work values items were standardized within every subject, information about ranking and distance between items was retained, while extreme response patterns were 'shrunk' and neutrality patterns were 'stretched'. Also this technique makes no assumption about response bias at the group or country level: it applies a standard transformation to all the data, such that, if cultural response biases do exist, they will be neutralized to some extent and, if they do not exist, the data have undergone a minimal, standardizing transformation. Schwartz's technique was also used in a section of Chapter 3 because Schwartz's transformed scores retain the meaning of the original scale and the reader can more easily interpret the differences.

Simple ranking also proved to be an effective, albeit simple, approach to cultural response sets. Converting each country's mean scores for the values items to ranks effectively removed any culture-level response bias. The advantage of rankings is that the numbers carry an innate meaning which transformed scores often lose. That is why we used ranks to describe much of the values data in Chapter 3.[4]

With the attitudinal data, we could not use Bond and Leung's double-standardization technique. The attitudinal scale divides the intent of the responses cleanly between 'agree', 'neutral' and 'disagree', and standardizing the data within subject would produce a floating mid-point which would seriously distort the data. Our simplest, most effective transformation was to collapse the 'slightly agree' and 'strongly agree' categories into one category, and similarly with the 'slightly disagree' and 'strongly disagree' categories. Using the percentage agreement or disagreement in a data set effectively neutralizes unequal sample sizes *and* extremity biases, and retains the essential meaning of the item responses. We used this technique to great effect with the automation items.

Two other data transformations were used with the attitudinal items in different analyses. When individual items were analyzed for group and command position differences, a covariate was added to the analysis. Each individual's raw score mean on the 17 work values items was used as a measure of individual response intensity, and this variable was used to partial out the influence of response sets. When the items were analyzed collectively, as in factor analysis, raw scores were converted to correlations within each group, which were then averaged (via the Fisher r to z transform) to form one correlation matrix for the analyses. In this way, cultural response sets were standardized, via correlations, within each group, before cross-cultural analyses began.

In sum, several different transformations were used to neutralize cultural response sets, and interpretations were made based on a convergence of results. The simpler transformations, ranks and percentage agreement, were used in Chapter 3 to facilitate the readers' understanding of the data. Cultural response sets may be troublesome methodologically, nonetheless, they are culturally informative in a general sense. For example, if the response patterns were reversed so that Japan and Korea showed extreme checking, and Brazil and the Philippines showed a neutrality bias, an explanation other than cultural congruity might be reasonable. However, the patterns are not reversed, and the response sets *do* seem to illuminate a feature of the culture.

---

4   The more we experimented with different statistical transformations, the more we found ourselves relying on simpler measures such as ranks and percentages to understand the data.

General Analytic Strategy

We acknowledge that more sophisticated analytic techniques exist for the study of group-level data (the adventurous reader is directed toward Van de Vijver and Leung, 1997). We also acknowledge that the Anglo bias of the questionnaire has restricted the scope of our interpretations. However, we believe that we have treated the data fairly, that is, we have investigated the data thoroughly at the intracultural and intercultural levels in order to locate and understand meaningful patterns, we looked for cultural similarities – not just differences – in our results, and our conclusions are conservatively drawn from multi-method probes of the data. Using several analytic strategies, we have built a detailed, richly layered and ultimately convergent understanding of the data.

Appendix B: Data

Table B.1 Rankings of the work value items within each country

Country[1]	A	B	C	D	E	F	G	H	I	J	K	L	M
					13 Work values [2]								
Argentina 38	6	3	2	7	13	9	5	11	8	1	4	10	12
Australia 484	7	4	2	3	11	10	8	5	12	1	6	9	13
Brazil 439	6	1	2	5	13	9	8	10	4	7	3	11	12
British HK 207	3	4	2	5	10	9	7	8	11	1	6	12	13
Denmark 140	4	8	6	3	9	12	7	6	10	1	2	11	13
Germany 215	5	6	1	4	10	11	8	7	9	2	3	12	13
Greek Cyprus 51	3	5	1	4	13	11	7	8	10	6	2	9	12
Ireland 271	6	7	2	4	9	10	8	3	12	1	5	11	13
Italy 476	5	12	7	3	8	9	13	4	10	1	2	6	11
Japan 50	6	8	2	3	13	11	7	5	10	1	4	9	12
Korea 123	2	13	1	4	12	5	6	10	11	8	3	7	9
Malaysia 427	3	5	1	7	13	10	6	8	9	4	2	11	12
Mexico 160	6	7	1	2	13	10	4	9	8	3	5	11	12
Morocco 51	6	7	1	2	13	9	8	12	5	4	3	10	11
New Zealand 379	4	5	2	3	11	9	7	8	12	1	6	10	13
Norway 139	6	7	2	5	9	13	8	3	11	1	4	10	12
Philippines 111	6	2	1	3	13	11	7	8	10	5	4	9	12
S. Africa 181	5	1	2	3	12	10	6	8	11	4	7	10	13
Sweden 156	3	7	6	2	9	10	8	4	13	1	5	11	12
Switzerland 173	5	7	3	1	10	9	8	6	12	2	4	11	13
Taiwan 319	7	12	1	4	13	10	9	11	8	2	5	3	6
USA 4449	8	7	1	3	12	10	5	6	9	2	4	11	13

Notes:
1 Countries are listed in alphabetical order. The number after each country refers to the number of pilots in the sample from that country.
2 Work values:
   A   Maintain good interpersonal relationships with fellow workers.
   B   Have an opportunity for advancement to higher-level jobs.
   C   Have security of employment.
   D   Live in area desirable to you and your family.
   E   Have a changing work routine, with new, unfamiliar tasks.
   F   Have a warm relationship with your direct superior.
   G   Have an opportunity for high earnings.
   H   Have challenging tasks to do, from which you get a personal sense of accomplishment.
   I   Know everything about the job, to have no surprises.
   J   Have sufficient time left for your personal or family life.
   K   Work with people who cooperate well with one another.
   L   Find the truth, the correct answer, the one solution.
   M   Observe strict time limits for work projects.

Table B.2   Item means and effect sizes for the attitudinal items

Item	Mean of the countries' means	Range of country mean scores	Effect size for differences	Number of countries in sample[a]
The CA should take charge/fly in emergency	3.02	2.03–4.58	0.26	22
Crew should not question CA unless emergency	2.43	1.62–3.81	0.17	22
F/O should never assume command	2.41	1.71–3.60	0.09	22
Flight success due to CA's technical skills	2.74	1.77–4.62	0.24	22
CA who encourage crew questions are weak leaders	1.28	1.07–1.97	0.07	22
Junior crew should not question the CA	1.44	1.17–1.98	0.09	22
I rely on superiors to tell me what to do in emergency	1.94	1.59–2.59	0.07	22
Subordinates afraid to disagree	2.99	2.26–3.78	0.14	22
[R] CA should encourage crew questions	4.28	3.69–4.81	0.06	22
Command scale (range: 0–100)	**30.5**	**18.53–45.72**	**0.37**	**22**
I am less effective when stressed/fatigued	4.12	3.5–4.4	0.05	22
Personal problems can adversely affect my performance	3.58	2.7–4.1	0.07	22
I am more likely to make judgment errors in emergency	3.09	1.9–4.4	0.18	22
[R] Fatigued, I still perform effectively	2.66	2.3–3.3	0.05	22
[R] Inexp/less capable crew do not adversely affect my performance	3.41	2.9–4.1	0.08	22
[R] My decision-making ability is just as good in an emergency	3.48	2.9–4.6	0.07	22
My stress (range: 0–100)	**55.20**	**36.1–65.7**	**0.09**	**22**
Alert others when overloaded	4.09	3.60–4.48	0.03	22
Should mention stress to others before/ during a flight	3.71	2.6–4.6	0.16	22
Should monitor each other for stress	4.59	4.1–4.9	0.07	22
Should be aware of others' problems	4.09	3.31–4.45	0.06	21
Should take personalities into account	4.21	3.60–4.60	0.07	19
Stress of others (range: 0–100)	**78.2**	**65.1–87.9**	**0.12**	**18**
[R] A truly professional crew member can leave personal problems behind when flying	3.70	2.9–4.8	0.17	22
Org.'s rules should not be broken, even when employee thinks so	3.09	2.57–3.99	0.06	22
Written procedures are necessary for all in-flight situations	3.02	2.05–4.36	0.24	22
Rules & order (range: 0–100)	**56.8**	**44.65–78.62**	**0.34**	**22**
Better to agree than voice a different opinion	1.56	1.21–2.27	0.09	22
If I perceive a problem, I will speak up	4.37	3.02–4.75	0.11	22
Debriefing is important	4.13	3.07–4.78	0.25	18
Pre-flight briefing is important	4.72	4.45–4.98	0.05	18
Pilot flying should verbalize plans & check for understanding	4.78	4.35–4.97	0.08	18
Communication & coordination as important as tech. skills	4.85	4.65–5.00	0.04	19

Notes:
[a]   The FMAQ was modified in 1996 after the dissertation analyses were completed. Items which were skewed or poorly worded were dropped from subsequent administrations of the form.
[R] = reverse scored items.

Table B.3   Automation items: percentage agreement across 18 countries

Country	Automation items[1]														
	1	2	3	4	5	6	7	8	9	10	11	12	13	14	15
USA	82	74	58	47	42	60	30	15	39	55	71	80	57	74	78
Australia	73	87	77	64	51	61	18	27	36	28	75	52	45	92	88
NZ	75	79	76	64	57	76	22	54	38	35	46	57	84	91	74
Ireland	36	55	50	68	69	63	7	10	51	60	87	79	34	88	81
S. Africa	70	83	87	50	51	77	30	38	37	55	70	72	27	88	80
Switzerland	67	62	42	56	77	80	0	15	46	78	64	90	62	93	69
Italy	68	71	81	—	49	72	45	21	24	84	73	83	71	—	76
Germany	67	61	68	42	61	66	9	20	29	47	78	75	75	82	70
Gk. Cyprus	98	93	96	36	36	29	34	58	24	40	56	64	78	96	78
Denmark	63	65	50	—	55	54	9	7	30	68	86	67	60	—	80
Norway	70	54	49	—	66	66	6	3	36	69	88	79	36	—	84
Sweden	70	65	52	—	55	66	12	12	41	73	81	74	50	—	84
Brazil	90	87	96	67	28	50	61	73	29	53	26	84	92	88	80
Mexico	94	90	89	48	29	59	74	66	28	68	32	72	83	95	89
Philippines	87	89	87	31	35	38	69	40	31	62	66	66	60	91	67
Malaysia	83	75	95	65	51	62	56	45	44	55	48	81	61	89	76
Taiwan	85	89	93	48	33	65	56	35	32	73	72	84	60	94	75
Korea	100	89	100	44	19	52	70	37	22	74	78	67	30	96	48

Notes:
1   Items:
   1   I prefer flying automated aircraft.
   2   Under abnormal conditions, I can rapidly access the information I need in the FMC.
   3   The effective crew member always uses the automation tools provided.
   4   When workload increases, it is better to avoid reprogramming the FMC.
   5   I am concerned that the use of automation will cause me to lose flying skills.
   6   It's easy to forget FMC operations that are not performed often.
   7   I look forward to more automation – the more the better.
   8   In order to maintain safety, pilots should avoid disengaging automated systems.
   9   There are modes and features of the FMC that I do not fully understand.
  10   Automated cockpits require more verbal communication between crew members.
  11   I regularly maintain flying proficiency by disengaging automation.
  12   Automated cockpits require more cross-checking of crew member actions.
  13   My company expects me to always use automation.
  14   I make sure the other pilot acknowledges programming changes I make in the FMC.
  15   I feel free to select the level of automation at any given time.
2   Items 4 and 14 were dropped from later administrations of the FMAQ; hence there are some missing data.

Table B.4 Country scores from Hofstede's original study, and pilot scores calculated using Hofstede's items and formulae

Country	IDV Hof.[a]	IDV Pilots[b]	PD Hof.	PD Pilots	MAS Hof.	MAS Pilots	UA Hof.	UA Pilots
Argentina	46	153	49	89	56	40	86	30
Australia	90	158	36	36	61	36	51	42
Brazil	38	126	69	125	49	41	76	56
British HK	89	154	35	59	66	36	35	37
Denmark	74	143	18	29	16	4	23	29
Germany	67	131	35	84	66	–14	65	41
Gk. Cyprus	35	127	60	63	57	26	112	51
Ireland	70	147	28	55	68	23	35	20
Italy	76	131	50	72	70	–29	75	42
Japan	46	152	54	62	95	18	92	41
Korea	18	114	60	105	39	–6	85	84
Malaysia	26	118	104	99	50	26	36	42
Mexico	30	139	81	100	69	42	82	28
Morocco	20	133	77	103	46	–7	54	66
New Zealand	79	155	22	41	58	40	49	29
Norway	69	149	31	17	8	–4	50	25
Philippines	32	133	94	100	64	45	44	40
S. Africa	65	152	49	44	63	61	49	26
Sweden	71	157	31	36	5	23	29	9
Switzerland	68	145	34	65	70	–25	58	20
Taiwan	17	137	58	90	45	–38	69	73
USA	91	152	40	52	62	29	46	47
Range	17–91	114–158	18–104	17–125	5–95	–38–61	23–112	9–85
Standard Dev.	25	13	23	29	21	27	23	18
Correlation	0.69**		0.77**		0.17		0.45*	

Notes:
[a] = Hofstede's country scores.
[b] = Pilots' scores calculated using Hofstede's items and formulae.
** $p < .01$, * $p < .05$.

Appendix C: Research Instruments

Flight Management Attitudes Questionnaire

As part of NASA/FAA sponsored research, we are collecting flight operations data from pilots and other flight personnel in a variety of cultural settings around the world. This questionnaire is part of a worldwide study aimed at understanding flight management attitudes in different countries. All data are strictly confidential and results will be presented only at the group level. No individual feedback will be given to management, so feel free to express your opinion. Your participation in the study is valued and appreciated.

Please answer by writing beside each item the letter from the scale below.

A	B	C	D	E
Disagree strongly	Disagree slightly	Neutral	Agree slightly	Agree strongly

___ 1. The captain should take physical control and fly the aircraft in emergency and non-standard situations.

___ 2. It makes no difference to me which company I fly for.

___ 3. Captains should encourage crew member questions during normal flight operations and in emergencies.

___ 4. Even when fatigued, I perform effectively during critical times in a flight.

___ 5. I work better when the operating procedures are flexible.

___ 6. Pilots should be aware of and sensitive to the personal problems of other crew members.

___ 7. The organization's rules should not be broken – even when the employee thinks it is in the organization's best interests.

___ 8. I expect to be consulted on matters that affect the performance of my duties.

___ 9. Senior staff deserve extra benefits and privileges.

___ 10. I let other crew members know when my workload is becoming (or about to become) excessive.

___ 11. Captains who encourage suggestions from crew members are weak leaders.

___ 12 My decision-making ability is as good in emergencies as in routine flying conditions.

___ 13. A debriefing and critique of procedures and decisions after each flight is an important part of developing and maintaining effective crew coordination.

___ 14. The pilot flying the aircraft should verbalize plans for procedures or maneuvers and should be sure that the information is understood and acknowledged by the other crew members.

___ 15. Junior crew members should not question the captain's or senior crew members' decisions.

___ 16. Passengers are never too demanding.

___ 17. It is better to agree with other crew members than to voice a different opinion.

___ 18. The pre-flight briefing is important for safety and for effective crew management.

___ 19. I am more likely to make judgment errors in an emergency.

___ 20. The captain's responsibilities include coordination between cockpit and cabin crew.

___ 21. Working for this organization is like being part of a large family.

___ 22. Crew members share responsibility for prioritizing activities in high workload situations.

___ 23. Successful flightdeck management is primarily a function of the captain's flying proficiency.

___ 24. If I perceive a problem with the flight, I will speak up, regardless of who might be affected.

___ 25. I am ashamed when I make a mistake in front of my other crew members.

A	B	C	D	E
Disagree strongly	Disagree slightly	Neutral	Agree slightly	Agree strongly

___ 26. In abnormal situations, I rely on my superiors to tell me what to do.

___ 27. Crew members should not question the decisions or actions of the captain except when they threaten the safety of the flight.

___ 28. I am the passengers' servant.

___ 29. I am less effective when stressed or fatigued.

___ 30. Leadership of the crew is expected to come solely from the captain.

___ 31. My performance is not adversely affected by working with an inexperienced or less capable crew member.

___ 32. To resolve conflicts, crew members should openly discuss their differences with each other.

___ 33. Crew members should monitor each other for signs of stress or fatigue.

___ 34. I become impatient with passengers who expect a lot.

___ 35. I am proud to work for this organization.

___ 36. A truly professional crew member can leave personal problems behind when flying.

___ 37. There are no circumstances (except total incapacitation) where the first officer should assume command of the aircraft.

___ 38. Written procedures are necessary for all in-flight situations.

___ 39. Crew members should feel obligated to mention their own psychological stress or physical problems to other flight crew personnel before or during a flight.

___ 40. Good communication and crew coordination are as important as technical proficiency for the safety of flight.

___ 41. During periods of low work activity, I would rather relax than keep busy with small tasks.

___ 42. Personal problems can adversely affect my performance.

___ 43. Effective crew coordination requires crew members to take into account the personalities of other crew members.

___ 44. Uncertain situations often require quick decision making.

___ 45. I like my job.

___ 46. How frequently, in your work environment, are subordinates afraid to express disagreement with their superiors?
A. Very frequently
B. Frequently
C. Sometimes
D. Seldom
E. Very seldom

___ 47. How often do you feel nervous or tense at work?
A. I always feel this way
B. Usually
C. Sometimes
D. Seldom
E. I never feel this way

Please read the following descriptions of four different leadership styles, and answer the questions that follow.

Style 1. Usually makes his/her decisions promptly and communicates them to his/her subordinates clearly and firmly. Expects them to carry out the decisions loyally and without raising difficulties.

Style 2. Usually makes his/her decisions promptly, but, before going ahead, tries to explain them fully to his/her subordinates. Gives them the reasons for the decisions and answers whatever questions they may have.

Style 3. Usually consults his/her subordinates before he/she reaches his/her decisions. Listens to their advice, considers it and then announces his/her decision. He/she then expects all to work loyally to implement it whether or not it is in accordance with the advice they gave.

Style 4. Usually calls a meeting of his/her subordinates when there is an important decision to be made. Puts the problem before the group and invites discussion. Accepts the majority viewpoint as the decision.

___ 48. Which one of the above styles of leadership would you *most prefer* to work under?
A. Style 1
B. Style 2
C. Style 3
D. Style 4

___ 49. In your organization, which one of the above styles do you find yourself most often working under?
A. Style 1
B. Style 2
C. Style 3
D. Style 4

Work Goals

Please answer the items below by writing beside each item a letter from the scale below.

A	B	C	D	E
Of very little or no importance	Of little importance	Of moderate importance	Very important	Of utmost importance

Please think of your *ideal* job – disregarding your present job. In choosing an *ideal* job, how important would it be to you to:

___ 50. Maintain good interpersonal relationships with fellow workers or crew members?
___ 51. Have an opportunity for advancement to higher-level jobs?
___ 52. Have security of employment?
___ 53. Work in an environment where the group's achievements are valued over your individual success?
___ 54. Live in an area desirable to you and your family?
___ 55. Have a changing work routine with new, unfamiliar tasks?
___ 56. Have the time to consider more than one solution to a problem?
___ 57. Have a warm relationship with your direct superior?
___ 58. Have considerable freedom to adopt your own approach to the job?
___ 59. Have an opportunity for high earnings?

A	B	C	D	E
Of very little or no importance	Of little importance	Of moderate importance	Very important	Of utmost importance

___ 60. Have challenging tasks to do, from which you get a personal sense of accomplishment?

___ 61. Know everything about the job, to have no surprises?

___ 62. Have sufficient time left for your personal or family life?

___ 63. Work with people who cooperate well with one another?

___ 64. Have a job or career that will bring you prestige and recognition from others?

___ 65. Find the truth, the correct answer, the one solution?

___ 66. Observe strict time limits for work projects?

Cockpit Automation

The following items deal with attitudes regarding flightdeck automation. For purposes of this survey, automated aircraft are defined as those with a programmable Flight Management Computer (FMC). If you are currently flying an automated aircraft, base you responses on experience in this airplane. *If you have not flown such an airplane, base your answers on your expectations regarding such aircraft.* Please answer by writing beside each item a letter from the scale below.

A	B	C	D	E
Disagree strongly	Disagree slightly	Neutral	Agree slightly	Agree strongly

___ 67. I prefer flying automated aircraft.

___ 68. Under abnormal conditions, I can rapidly access the information I need in the FMC.

___ 69. The effective crew member always uses the automation tools provided.

___ 70. When workload increases, it is better to avoid reprogramming the FMC.

___ 71. I am concerned that the use of automation will cause me to lose flying skills.

___ 72. It's easy to forget how to do FMC operations that are not performed often.

___ 73. I look forward to more automation – the more the better.

___ 74. In order to maintain safety, pilots should avoid disengaging automated systems.

___ 75. There are modes and features of the FMC that I do not fully understand.

___ 76. Automated cockpits require more verbal communication between crew members.

___ 77. I regularly maintain flying proficiency by disengaging automation.

___ 78. Automation leads to more efficient, safer operations.

___ 79. Automated cockpits require more cross-checking of crew member actions.

___ 80. My company expects me to always use automation.

___ 81. I make sure the other pilot acknowledges programming changes I make in the FMC.

___ 82. I feel free to select the level of automation at any given time.

A	B	C	D	E
Disagree strongly	Disagree slightly	Neutral	Agree slightly	Agree strongly

___ 83. Automated systems should be used at the crews' discretion.

___ 84. Flying highly automated aircraft alters the way crew members transfer information.

___ 85. I try to use automation as much as possible during flight operations.

___ 86. It is difficult to know what FMC operations the other crew member is performing.

Background Information

Gender (M or F) _____

How many years have you been with this organization? _____

How much experience do you have in this aircraft (hours)? _____

Total flight hours (approximate) _____

Crew Base _____

Fleet (Aircraft type and series) _____

Crew Position:

_____ Captain

_____ First Officer

_____ Second Officer

Status:

_____ Line Pilot

_____ Instructor

_____ Check Airman

_____ Management

_____ Other_____

How many years have you been employed within the aviation industry generally? _____

Nature of flying background (check one) Military_____ Civilian_____

What is your nationality? _____

What was your nationality at birth (if different from your present nationality?) _____

Thank you for your time

Operating Team Resource Management Survey

The success of the survey depends on your contribution, so it is important that you answer questions as honestly as you can. There are no right or wrong answers, and often the first answer that comes to mind is best. All data are strictly confidential and results will be presented only at the group level. No individual feedback will be given to management, so feel free to express your opinion. Your participation in the study is valued and appreciated.

Part I: Operating Room Management Attitudes

Please answer by writing beside each item the letter from the scale below.

A	B	C	D	E
Disagree strongly	Disagree slightly	Neutral	Agree slightly	Agree strongly

___ 1. The senior person, if available, should take over and make all decisions in life-threatening emergencies.

___ 2. The department provides adequate, timely information about events in the hospital which might affect my work.

___ 3. Senior staff should encourage questions from junior medical and nursing staff during operations if appropriate.

___ 4. Even when fatigued, I perform effectively during critical phases of operations.

___ 5. We should be aware of and sensitive to the personal problems of other OR team members.

___ 6. Senior staff deserve extra benefits and privileges.

___ 7. I do my best work when people leave me alone.

___ 8. I let other team members know when my workload is becoming (or about to become) excessive.

___ 9. It bothers me when others do not respect my professional capabilities.

___ 10. Doctors who encourage suggestions from OR team members are weak leaders.

___ 11. My decision-making ability is as good in emergencies as in routine situations.

___ 12. A regular debriefing of procedures and decisions after an OR session or shift is an important part of developing and maintaining effective crew coordination.

___ 13. Team members in charge should verbalize plans for procedures or actions and should be sure that the information is understood and acknowledged by the others.

___ 14. Junior OR team members should not question the decisions made by senior personnel.

___ 15. I try to be a person that others will enjoy working with.

___ 16. I am encouraged by my leaders and co-workers to report any incidents I may observe.

___ 17. The only people qualified to give me feedback are others of my own profession.

___ 18. It is better to agree with other OR team members than to voice a different opinion.

___ 19. The pre-session team briefing is important for safety and for effective team management.

___ 20. It is important that my competence be acknowledged by others.

___ 21. I am more likely to make errors or mistakes in tense or hostile situations.

___ 22. The doctor's responsibilities include coordination between his or her work team and other support areas.

___ 23. I value compliments about my work.

___ 24. Working for this hospital is like being part of a large family.

___ 25. OR team members share responsibility for prioritizing activities in high workload situations.

___ 26. As long as the work gets done, I don't care what others think of me.

___ 27. Successful OR management is primarily a function of the doctor's medical and technical proficiency.

___ 28. A good reputation in the OR is important to me.

___ 29. Errors are a sign of incompetence.

___ 30. Department leadership listens to staff and cares about our concerns.

___ 31. I enjoy working as part of a team.

___ 32. If I perceive a problem with the management of a patient, I will speak up, regardless of who might be affected.

___ 33. I am ashamed when I make a mistake in front of other team members.

___ 34. In critical situations, I rely on my superiors to tell me what to do.

___ 35. I value the goodwill of my fellow workers – I care that others see me as friendly and cooperative.

___ 36. I sometimes feel uncomfortable telling OR members from other disciplines that they need to take some action.

___ 37. Team members should not question the decisions or actions of senior staff except when they threaten the safety of the operation.

___ 38. I am less effective when stressed or fatigued.

___ 39. It is an insult to be forced to wait unnecessarily for other members of the OR team.

___ 40. Mistakes are handled appropriately in the hospital where I work.

___ 41. Leadership of the OR team should rest with the medical staff.

___ 42. My performance is not adversely affected by working with an inexperienced or less capable team member.

___ 43. To resolve conflicts, team members should openly discuss their differences with each other.

___ 44. Team members should monitor each other for signs of stress or fatigue.

___ 45. I become irritated when I have to work with inexperienced medical staff.

___ 46. I am proud to work for this hospital.

___ 47. All members of the OR team are qualified to give me feedback.

___ 48. A truly professional OR team member can leave personal problems behind when working in the OR.

___ 49. There are no circumstances where a junior team member should assume control of patient management.

___ 50. Team members should feel obligated to mention their own psychological stress or physical problems to other OR personnel before or during a shift or assignment.

___ 51. In the OR, I get the respect that a person of my profession deserves.

___ 52. Human error is inevitable.

___ 53. The concept of all OR personnel working as a team does not work in our hospital.

___ 54. Personal problems can adversely affect my performance.

___ 55. Effective OR team coordination requires members to take into account the personalities of other team members.

___ 56. I like my job.

___ 57. I always ask questions when I feel there is something I don't understand.

Part II: Leadership Styles

Please read the following descriptions of four different leadership styles, and answer the questions that follow. Consultants, please think of your Department Chair when answering the next two questions; Residents, please think of the Consultants; Nurses, please think of the Head Nurses.

Style A Leader usually makes decisions promptly and communicates them to subordinates clearly and firmly. Expects them to carry out the decisions loyally and without raising difficulties.

Style B Leader usually makes decisions promptly, but, before going ahead, tries to explain them fully to subordinates. Gives them the reasons for the decisions and answers whatever questions they may have.

Style C Leader usually consults with subordinates before reaching decisions. Listens to their advice, considers it, and then announces decision. Expects all to work loyally to implement it whether or not it is in accordance with the advice they gave.

Style D Leader usually calls a meeting of subordinates when there is an important decision to be made. Puts the problem before the group and invites discussion. Accepts the majority viewpoint as the decision.

___ 1. Which one of the above styles of leadership would you *most prefer* to work under?

___ 2. In your organization, which style do you find yourself most often working under?

Part III: Work Goals

Please answer the items below by writing beside each item a letter from the scale below.

A	B	C	D	E
Of very little or no importance	Of little importance	Of moderate importance	Very important	Of utmost importance

Please think of your ideal job – disregarding your present job. In choosing an ideal job, how important would it be to you to:

___ 1. Maintain good interpersonal relationships with all other OR personnel?
___ 2. Have an opportunity for advancement to higher-level jobs?
___ 3. Have security of employment?
___ 4. Work in an environment where the group's achievements are valued over your individual success?
___ 5. Live in an area desirable to you and your family?
___ 6. Have a changing work routine with new, unfamiliar tasks?
___ 7. Have the time to consider more than one solution to a problem?
___ 8. Have a warm relationship with your direct superior?
___ 9. Have considerable freedom to adopt your own approach to the job?
___ 10. Have an opportunity for high earnings?
___ 11. Have challenging tasks to do, from which you get a personal sense of accomplishment?
___ 12. Know everything about the job, to have no surprises?
___ 13. Have sufficient time left for your personal or family life?
___ 14. Work with people who cooperate well with one another?
___ 15. Have a job or career that will bring you prestige and recognition from others?

Part IV: Teamwork

Please answer by writing beside each item a letter from the corresponding scale.

A	B	C	D	E
Very low	Low	Adequate	High	Very high

Please describe your personal perception of the *quality of teamwork and cooperation/communication* you have experienced with:

___ 1. Surgical Consultants

___ 2. Surgical Residents

___ 3. Surgical Nurses

___ 4. Anesthesia Consultants

___ 5. Anesthesia Residents

___ 6. Anesthesia Nurses

___ 7. Orderlies

___ 8. Department Leadership

Comments

1. How can the effectiveness of OR teams be increased?

2. How can the job satisfaction of OR teams be increased?

Background information

Gender (M or F): _____

Nationality: _____   Nationality at birth (if different): _____

Position:

___ Anesthesia Resident   ___ Surgeon Resident   ___ Operating Room Nurse

___ Anesthesia Consultant   ___ Surgeon Consultant   ___ Nurse Anesthetist

___ Anesthesia Private   ___ Surgeon Private Practitioner ___ Orderly
       Practitioner

How much experience do you have in this specialty (years)? _____

Thank you for completing the questionnaire – your participation is appreciated

LINE/LOS CHECKLIST

Observer is to complete one form for each flight segment

Airline				Demographics		Capt.	1st Off	Engineer
Date (Mo. Yr.)	LOE			Domicile				
Observer ID	LOFT			Years of experience – all airlines				
Route	Scenario ID			Years in position – this A/C				
A/C Type & Series	Line Obs.							
Hrs Observed								

			Check One Box
If crew observed for more than one leg;	Leg No.	of	First leg flown together		More than one day flown together
Indicate Pilot flying:			First day flown together

CREW PERFORMANCE RATING BY PHASE OF FLIGHT

1	2	3	4
Poor – Observed performance is significantly below expectations. This includes instances where necessary behavior was not present, and examples of inappropriate behavior that was detrimental to mission effectiveness.	Minimum Expectations – Observed performance meets minimum requirements but there is ample room for improvement. This level of performance is less than desired for effective crew operations.	Standard – The demonstrated behavior promotes and maintains crew effectiveness. This is the level of performance that should be normally occurring in flight operations.	Outstanding – Performance represents exceptional skill in the application of specific behaviors, and serves as a model for teamwork – truly noteworthy and effective.

The following performance markers are specific behaviors that serve as indicators of how effectively resource management is being practiced. They are not intended to be exhaustive lists of behaviors that should be seen, but rather as exemplars of behaviors associated with more and less effective crew resource management. It is not expected that all behaviors will be seen for every phase of a specific flight. When performance is rated either as (4) or (1), please describe the causes for the *specific* rating in the COMMENTS section. Be concise. General comments are to be made at the end of this form.

Team Management & Crew Communications	Pre-depart	T/O & Climb	Cruise	Des/Appr Landing	COMMENTS
1. Team concept and environment for open communications established and/or maintained; e.g., crew members listen with patience, do not interrupt or 'talk over', do not rush through the briefing, make eye contact as appropriate.					
2. Briefings are operationally thorough, interesting, and address crew coordination and planning for potential problems. Expectations are set for how possible deviations from normal operations are to be handled; e.g., rejected T/O, engine failure after lift-off, go-around at destination.					
3. Cabin crew is included as part of team in briefings, as appropriate, and guidelines are established for coordination between flightdeck and cabin.					
	Passengers are briefed and updated as needed; i.e., delays, weather, etc.				
4. Group climate is appropriate to operational situation; e.g., presence of social conversation at appropriate times. Crew ensures that non-operational factors such as social interaction do not interfere with necessary tasks.					

Team Management & Crew Communications (cont.)

	Pre-depart	T/O & Climb	Cruise	Des/Appr Landing	COMMENTS
5. Crew members ask questions regarding crew actions and decisions; e.g., effective inquiry about uncertainty of clearance limits, clarification of confusing/unclear ATC instructions.					
6. Crew members speak up, and state their information with *appropriate* persistence, until there is some clear resolution and decision; e.g., effective advocacy & assertion: 'I'm uncomfortable with..., Let's...'.					
7. Operational decisions are clearly stated to other crew members and acknowledged, and include cabin crew and others when appropriate; e.g., good cross-talk between pilots, everyone 'on same page'.					
8. Captain coordinates flightdeck activities to establish proper balance between command authority and crew member participation, and acts decisively when the situation requires.					

Situational Awareness & Decision Making

	Pre-depart	T/O & Climb	Cruise	Des/Appr Landing	COMMENTS
9. Workload and task distribution is clearly communicated and acknowledged by crew members. Adequate time is provided for completion of tasks; e.g., establish well in advance who is flying the leg, establish responsibility for non-routine types of communications.					
10. Secondary operational tasks are prioritized so as to allow sufficient resources for dealing effectively with primary flight duties; e.g., dealing with passenger needs, crew meals, company communications.					
11. Crew members demonstrate high levels of vigilance in both high and low workload conditions; e.g., active monitoring, scanning, cross-checking, attending to radio calls, switch settings, altitude callouts, crossing restrictions.					
12. Crew prepares for expected or contingency situations including approaches, weather, etc.; e.g., stays 'ahead of curve'.					

Automation Management

	Pre-depart	T/O & Climb	Cruise	Des/Appr Landing	COMMENTS
13. Guidelines are established/followed for the operation of automated systems; i.e., when systems will be disabled, programming actions that must be verbalized and acknowledged.					
14. PF and PNF duties and responsibilities with regard to automated systems are established/followed; e.g., FMS entry and cross-checking.					
15. Crew members periodically review and verify the status of aircraft automated systems; e.g., optimum cruise level, correct profile for active runway.					
16. Crew members verbalize and acknowledge entries and changes to automated systems parameters.					
17. Crew plans for sufficient time prior to maneuvers for programming of Flight Management Computer.					
18. Automated systems are used at appropriate levels; i.e., when programming demands could reduce situational awareness and create work overloads, the level of automation is reduced or disengaged, or automation is effectively used to reduce workload.					

Special Situations

	Pre-depart	T/O & Climb	Cruise	Des/Appr Landing	COMMENTS
19.	Positive and negative performance feedback is given at appropriate times and is made a positive learning experience for the whole crew – feedback is specific, objective, based on observable behavior, and given constructively; e.g., critique of take-offs and/or landings.				
20.	Performance feedback is accepted objectively and non-defensively.				
21.	When conflicts arise, the crew remains focused on the problem or situation at hand. Crew members listen actively to ideas and opinions and admit mistakes when wrong, conflict issues are identified and resolved.				
22.	Crew members recognize fatigue and take specific steps to help maintain crew alertness; e.g., use of fatigue countermeasures such as social conversation, physical activity, caffeine management, walking through the cabin.				
23.	Crew actions avoid the creation of self-imposed workload and stress; e.g., avoiding late descents due to lack of situational awareness/planning.				
24.	Crew members recognize and report work overloads in self and others; e.g., stating, 'I'm getting loaded up here; can you take over…?'				
25.	When appropriate, crew members take the initiative and time to share operational knowledge and experience; i.e., new crew members, routing, airports, situations.				

Technical Proficiency

	Pre-depart	T/O & Climb	Cruise	Des/Appr Landing	COMMENTS
26.	Sterile cockpit SOP used in an appropriate manner; e.g., keep social conversation during taxi and below 10 000 ft to a minimum, avoid distractions during these phases.		XXX		
27.	Altitude and terrain awareness; e.g., verbalize and acknowledge altitude clearances and changes, make proper callouts, demonstrate awareness of significant terrain.				
28.	Checklist compliance; e.g., use proper normal and abnormal checklists in the prescribed manner, do not read from memory, look at items being read, complete checklist and callout completion.				

Overall Crew Rating

Overall Observations

		Overall Rating
29.	Overall technical proficiency	
30.	Overall crew effectiveness	

Operational Considerations

31.	Assess the severity of abnormals and other systems events that occur during flight. This item is rated 1 = low to 4 = high.	
32.	Assess the complexity of operating environment; e.g., WX, ATC, Traffic, MELs, XCMs, rated 1 = low to 4 = high. Comment on conditions affecting flight.	

In those cases where the *actions of a particular crew member* may be particularly significant to the outcome of the observed behavior, enter the relevant item number from the LLC, the crew position involved, the rating assigned, check one or more phases of flight and include supporting comments.

LLC Item #	Crew Position	Rating	Indicate Phase(s) of Flight				Comments
			Pre-depart	T/O & Climb	Cruise	Des/Appr Landing	

Additional comments on this flight segment

Flight Crew Member ASAP Report

This form is to be filled out by **each** flight crew member involved in the incident and reported to the Event Review Committee within 24 hours/48 international. An ASRS report will be automatically filed from this submission. Note: *=Required for ASRS submission.

*Date of occurrence (Z)	*Location of event	*Time of event (Z)	*Altitude	Flight number
Origination	Scheduled destination	*Airport landed	Out/Off (Z) /	On/In (Z) /
Amount of departure delay for this flight	*Your crew position (CA, FO, SO) Other _____	Domicile	*Aircraft type	*Aircraft #
Hours commuted previous to this flight pairing	*Hours flown: 7 days prior _____ 90 days prior _____	Off-duty hours prior to duty period	Time since awakening	Hours worked before event
*Were you **Pilot Flying** or **Pilot Monitoring** at beginning of event?		*Total flight hours	*Hours in A/C type	Hours in type *and* position
*Crew member mailing address:		*Phone number and times of day you can be reached:		
*Date of report: (Z)		Time of report: (Z)		
*Crew member name:		Signature:		Employee #

Was this an ETOPS segment? (Y or N)		**Time zone change in 24 hours previous to event?** (Y or N)	
Captain/FO first day ever together? (Y or N)		How many hours change?	
Captain/FO first flight ever together? (Y or N)		Flying **East** or **West**?	

TOPOGRAPHY		***WEATHER**	
Over water			
Flat		Ceiling _____ ft/meters	
Mountainous		Visibility _____ miles/ft/meters/sm/km	
Densely populated		VMC	
Shoreline		IMC	
*LIGHTING		Mixed/marginal	
Dawn		Scattered/broken/overcast clouds	
Daylight		Fog	
Dusk		Rain	
Night		Thunderstorms	
TRAFFIC		Snow	
Light		Ice	
Medium		Turbulence	
Heavy/saturated		Windshear	

NAME OF ATC FACILITY: (Enter frequency, if known, or check)				*CONTROL STATUS*	
Clearance delivery		Departure		Cleared route	
Ramp control		Center		On vector	
Ground		Approach		On SID/STAR	
Tower (local)		CTAF		Published FMS departure/arrival	

PHASE OF FLIGHT AT TIME OF OCCURRENCE								
Parked		Takeoff		Descent		Landing		Missed approach/GA
Powerback/pushback		Climb		Arrival		Taxi-in		
Taxi-out		Cruise		Final approach		Parking		

TYPE OF APPROACH	
Precision to visual	
Non-precision to visual	
Visual to landing	
Precision to landing	
Non-precision to landing	

WHAT WAS THE URGENCY?	
How quickly was it necessary to take action to maintain/restore the safety of flight?	
Immediate action required	
Timely, but not immediate, action required	
Action could be completed anytime, at crew's discretion	
No action required	

WHAT WERE THE CONSEQUENCES?			
SPACE		**RESOURCES**	
Runway incursion		Aircraft damage	
Runway excursion			
Taxiway excursion			
Improper spatial location (lost in space)		**OPERATIONS**	
Aircraft diversion		Unstable flight	
Air return			
*Near mid-air collision			
Was evasive action taken? (**Y or N**)		**TIME**	
Was TCAS a factor?(**Y or N**)		Flight cancellation	
Crew follow TCAS RA?(**Y or N**)		Schedule delay	
Miss distance horizontal		**PEOPLE**	
		Personal injury	
Miss distance vertical		Passenger dissatisfaction	
		Interpersonal conflict	
(E)GPWS caution activate? (**Y or N**)		**RULES**	
(E)GPWS caution followed? (**Y or N**)		SOP violation	
(E)GPWS warning activate? (**Y or N**)		Clearance deviation	
(E)GPWS warning followed? (**Y or N**)		Exercise of emergency authority	

NOTE: If a second aircraft was involved, please describe the additional aircraft in the "What Happened?" description section.

ASAP CHECKLIST

- Please complete this checklist for the event you have reported to the ASAP system. Not all items will be pertinent to this event. **Check only those that are clearly relevant to this incident.**

- **Check the + (plus) column** if the item contributed to a successful outcome or reduced the severity of the event. **Check the – (minus) column** if the action had a negative effect on the outcome or contributed to the occurrence of the event. Some examples are provided for clarification, but this is not intended to be an exhaustive list.

- If the factor involved something you should have done that you did not do (an omission), clarify and explain in the comments section beside the factor.

- Please read through the entire form and consider all factors. Items may sound similar but they are not. Read them carefully. Items refer to technological, physiological and technical **inputs** to the incident, to mental, procedural, cockpit crew interaction **processes**, and to the extended flight team **support and interactions** (ATC, F/A's, etc.).

Check positive (+) ....or negative (–) column, IF APPLICABLE.

	Factor	Positive Contribution Examples	+	Negative Contribution Examples	–	Comments
			RESOURCES			
1.	Airport facilities/ design	Expedited prompt and efficient resolution		Hindered/ delayed resolution of event		
2.	Company policy	Clear, appropriate, adequate		Confusing, conflicting, overly restrictive or demanding		
3.	Procedural guidance	Clear, appropriate, adequate		Confusing, conflicting, overly restrictive or demanding		
4.	Publications	Adequate and accurate		Complex, disorganized, conflicting		
5.	Flight paperwork	Accurate, complete		Inaccurate, incomplete		
			PHYSIOLOGY			
6.	Crew physiological state	Rested		Fatigue, hunger, illness		
7.	Perceptions (visual, auditory, tactile, olfactory, intuition, fear)	Noted and constructively utilized		Not available, misleading, ambiguous, or not acted upon, misheard calls.		
			TECHNOLOGY			
8.	Aircraft systems and equipment	Functional, easy to use, adequate, reliable		Broken, unreliable, unreasonably complex		
9.	Aircraft capabilities	Required performance available		A/C cannot perform to request, ex: climb capabilities		
10.	Aircraft displays	Informative and unambiguous		Confusing or poorly placed		
11.	Communications and navigation equipment (ground or space-based)	Functioning properly		Poorly tuned, maintained, operated, inoperable		

	Factor	Positive Contribution Examples	+	Negative Contribution Examples	-	Comments
		THOUGHT				
1.	Crew's knowledge	Extensive		Inadequate		
2.	Crewmember memory	Accurate, complete		Inaccurate, critical lapse		
3.	Calculation/computation	Complete, accurate		Incomplete, inaccurate		
4.	Situational awareness	Crewmembers agree on status - even in retrospect situation interpreted the same		Crew "misread" situational cues		
		INFORMATION GATHERING				
5.	Inquiry and reducing ambiguity	Results in discovery of appropriate and sufficient information, resolves ambiguity and uncertainty		Insufficient, results in use of inappropriate information, fails to reduce ambiguity or uncertainty		
6.	Monitoring and cross-checking (vigilance)	Adequate awareness maintained of configuration, flight parameters, environmental circumstances		Inattention to available cues/information, missed calls, etc.		
7.	Risk assessment	Appropriate, probable hazards anticipated, reasonable action taken		Inappropriate, underestimates hazards or aborts reasonably safe course of action		
8.	Crew self-critique	Progress monitored through task completion		Failure to note incomplete tasks, failure to assess progress toward goal		
		INFORMATION DISTRIBUTION				
9.	Briefings	Pertinent and thorough, contingencies covered, continuing as required		Poor, or none, failed to consider contingencies, too short, or overly detailed		
10.	Flying pilot's plan	Articulated, clear, appropriate		Unstated, ambiguous, conflicting, inappropriate		
11.	Communications regarding FMC programming	Verified, verbalized		Not verified, not verbalized		
12.	Crewmember suggestions/challenges	Timely, constructive, explicit		Insulting, indirect, confrontational, withheld		
13.	Crewmember acknowledgement of communications, instructions, settings	Verbalized, explicit, complete, timely		Not verbalized, inexplicit, incomplete		
14.	Verbal observations	Clear, informative, articulate implications		Withheld, ambiguous, neglect implications		

	Factor	Positive Contribution Examples	+	Negative Contribution Examples	-	Comments
				TASK MANAGEMENT		
1.	**Contingency planning**	Likely events foreseen and discussed		Insufficient, or try to cover more than needed		
2.	**Level of automation used**	Appropriate, helpful		Inappropriate, over- or under-used		
3.	**Distribution of duties of the Pilot Flying & Pilot Monitoring**	Discussed, followed, prevented overload, confusion, or redundancy		Not discussed or followed, led to omissions or complacency		
4.	**Workload distribution**	Realistic, workable, prevented overload, confusion, or redundancy		Poorly managed, overload, led to omissions or complacency		
5.	**Task prioritization**	Secondary tasks managed appropriately, clear priorities		Inappropriate, unclear, or conflicting priorities		
6.	**Crewmember initiative**	Appropriate tasks initiated in a timely manner		crewmembers fail to take appropriate action, require excessive direction		
7.	**Time management**	Pace appropriate to needs		Rushed, overloaded, rushing to comply		
8.	**Timing of FMC programming**	Timely, time allocated for programming		Done at inappropriate times, high workload		
				PROCEDURES		
9.	**Aircraft configuration**	Safe, economical, expeditious, appropriate, timely		Unsafe, inefficient, inappropriate		
10.	**FMC operation**	Reduced workload, monitored and cross-checked, appropriate to circumstances		Under utilization, over-reliance, failure to monitor or crosscheck		
11.	**Fuel management**	Efficient, safe, legal, sufficient amount		Inefficient, unsafe, illegal, insufficient amount		
12.	**Preflight inspection**	Thorough		Incomplete		
13.	**Adherence to SOP's and FAR's**	Consistent		Selective compliance		
14.	**Procedure selection**	Correct procedures chosen		Incorrect procedure chosen, unclear which procedure to choose, procedure too complex/ confusing, none available		
15.	**Procedural implementation**	Standard, complete		Procedure omitted, items omitted, or out of order		
16.	**Systems operation**	Standard, appropriate		Non-standard, inappropriate		
17.	**Checklist use**	Timely, complete		Non-standard, omitted, from memory		

	Factor	Positive Contribution Examples	+	Negative Contribution Examples	-	Comments
		MOTOR ACTIVITY				
1.	Aircraft handling	Skilful, precise, smooth		Overly aggressive, timid, inept		
2.	MCP/CDU entries	Accurate		Inaccurate		
3.	Instrument, radio and control switch settings/positioning	Accurate, appropriate		Inaccurate, inappropriate		
4.	Copying ATIS, clearance	Accurate, complete		Inaccurate, incomplete		
		COCKPIT CREW INTERACTION				
5.	Captain's leadership	Competent, communicative, supportive		Autocratic, incompetent, unassertive, hostile, non-supportive		
6.	Crew conflict resolution	Successful, consensus attained		Unresolved		
7.	Social conversation	Stimulating during low workload, contributed to team cohesion		Sterile cockpit violation, distracting, inappropriate		
		ADAPTATION				
8.	Precautionary action	Increased v-speeds, de-icing, etc. when necessary		Continued operation in conditions at or near limits		
9.	Operational limitations/ setting boundaries	Followed as briefed		Not adhered to, "slipping bottom lines"		
10.	Choice of error management countermeasures	Good plan, helpful in resolving the situation		Ineffective, nonexistent, or made things worse		
11.	Crew flexibility	Task abandoned when appropriate, plan adapted as necessary		Failure to abort or amend planned course of action as necessary		

	Factor	Positive Contribution Examples	+	Negative Contribution Examples	-	Comments
				SUPPORT		
1.	Check airman/ air carrier inspector/ ACM	Contributed information, expertise, or experience		Negative training effect caused by training role or lack of proficiency		
2.	ATC clearance or instructions	Unambiguous, expeditious, safe		Confusing, incomplete, unrealistic, hazardous, incorrect		
3.	ATC timing	Helpful, no delay of clearance when expedited handling needed		Late descent or slam dunk, complicated, non-critical instructions given at points of high cockpit workload		
4.	Coordination between flight crew and cabin crew	Adequate, appropriate information exchanged between cockpit and cabin about circumstances and activities		Flight crew condescending toward cabin crew, no briefing, or cabin crew aloof/resist information exchange		
5.	Communication/ coordination with support team (gate agents, ramp, maintenance, dispatch)	Sufficient, cooperative, collaborative, informative, explicit, clear		Ambiguous, confrontational, inadequate		
6.	Support personnel's knowledge	Superior		Inadequate		
7.	Passenger relations	Passengers note and communicate hazards or comply fully with crewmember instructions		Uncooperative, drunk		

*WHAT happened? (continue on back of form, if necessary)

_____

_____

_____

_____

_____

_____

_____

_____

_____

_____

_____

_____

*WHY do you think it happened?

_____

_____

_____

_____

_____

*ONE SENTENCE SUMMARY

_____

_____

*In your opinion, what could the WORST END RESULT of this situation have been?

_____

_____

_____

CORRECTIVE ACTION:

In your opinion, *who* (columns) could make *improvements in what area* (rows) to help prevent a recurrence of this event?

	Flight ops	Cockpit crew	FA	ATC	Maintenance	FAA	Dispatch	Ground ops	Ramp ops	Safety	Manufacturer	Airport authority	Emergency services	Passenger services
Hiring/staffing														
Cooperation														
Facilities														
Resource utilization														
Priorities														
Leadership														
Planning														
Training content														
Training delivery														
Signs/alerts														
Publications														
Supervision														
Standardization														
Equipment/tools														
Scheduling														
Communications														
Procedures														
Policy														
Techniques														
Design														

How long did it take you to fill out this form? _____ minutes

Comments:

References

Aronson, E. & Mills, J. (1959), 'The effect of severity of initiation on liking for a group', *Journal of Abnormal and Social Psychology*, **59**, 177–81.

Bakeman, R. & Helmreich, R. (1975), 'Cohesiveness and performance: Covariation and causality in an undersea environment', *Journal of Experimental Social Psychology*, **11**, 478–89.

Bales, R.F. (1950), *Interaction Process Analysis: Theory, research and application*, Reading, MA: Addison-Wesley.

Barnlund, D.C. & Yoshioka, M. (1990), 'Apologies: Japanese and American styles', *International Journal of Intercultural Relations*, **14**, 193–206.

Beckmann, U., Baldwin, I., Hart, G.K. & Runciman, W.B. (1996), 'The Australian incident monitoring study in intensive care: AIMS-ICU. An analysis of the first year of reporting', *Anaesthesia and Intensive Care*, **24**, (3), 320–29.

Beckmann, U., West, L.F., Groombridge, G.J., Baldwin, I., Hart, G.K., Clayton, D.G. & Runciman, W.B. (1996), 'The Australian incident monitoring study in intensive care: AIMS-ICU. The development and evaluation of an incident reporting system in intensive care', *Anaesthesia and Intensive Care*, **24**, (3), 314–19.

Belkin, L. (1997), 'How can we save the next victim?', *New York Times Magazine*, June, pp. 28–70.

Bennett, M.J. (1993), 'Toward ethnorelativism: A developmental model of intercultural sensitivity', in R.M. Paige (ed.), *Education for the Intercultural Experience*, Yarmouth, ME: Intercultural Press.

Berry, J.W. (1980), 'Introduction to methodology', in H.C. Triandis & J.W. Berry (eds), *Handbook of Cross-Cultural Psychology*, **2**, Boston, MA: Allyn & Bacon, Inc.

Berwick, D.M. (1989), 'Continuous improvement as an ideal in health care', *New England Journal of Medicine*, **320**, 53–6.

Bochner, S. (1981), *The Mediating Person: Bridges between cultures*, Boston, MA: G.K. Hall.

Boeing Center for Leadership and Learning (1996), *Applying CRM methods and best practices in developing high performance management teams*, Renton, WA.

Bogner, M.S. (1994), *Human Error in Medicine*, Hillside, NJ: Lawrence Erlbaum.

Bond, M.H. (1988), 'Finding universal dimensions of individual variation in multicultural studies of values: the Rokeach and Chinese value surveys', *Journal of Personality and Social Psychology*, **55**, (6), 1009–15.

Bond, M.H. (1991), *Beyond the Chinese Face: Insights from Psychology*, Hong Kong: Oxford University Press.

Bond, M.H. (1994), 'Into the heart of collectivism: A personal and scientific journey', in U. Kim, H. Triandis, C. Kağitçibasi, A. Choi & G. Yoon (eds), *Individualism and Collectivism: Theory, methods and applications*, vol. 18, Cross-Cultural Research and Methodology Series. Newbury Park, CA: Sage.

Bond, M.H. & Hwang, K.K. (1986), 'The social psychology of Chinese people', in M.H. Bond (ed.), *The Psychology of the Chinese People*, Hong Kong: Oxford University Press.

Bond, M.H. & King, A.Y.C. (1985), 'Coping with the threat of westernization in Hong Kong', *International Journal of Intercultural Relations*, **9**, 351–64.

Bond, M.H. & Smith, P.B. (1996), 'Cross-cultural social and organizational psychology', *Annual Review of Psychology*, **47**, 205–35.

Brennan, T.A., Leape, L.L., Laird, N. et al. (1991), 'Incidence of adverse events and negligence in hospitalized patients: Results of the Harvard Medical Practice Study I', *New England Journal of Medicine*, **324**, 370–76.

Britt, H., Miller, G.C., Steven, I.D., Howarth, G.C. & Nicholson, P.A. (1997), 'Collecting data on potentially harmful events: A method for monitoring incidents in general practice', *Family Practice*, **14**, 101–6.

Byrnes, R.E. & Black, R. (1993), 'Developing and implementing CRM programs: The Delta experience', in E. Weiner, B. Kanki & R. Helmreich (eds), *Cockpit Resource Management*, San Diego, CA: Academic Press.

Chidester, T.R., Kanki, B.G., Foushee, H.C., Dickinson, C.L. & Bowles, S.V. (1990), *Personality factors in flight operations: Vol. 1. Leader characteristics and crew performance in full-mission air transport simulation* (NASA Technical Memorandum 102259), Moffett Field, CA: NASA–Ames Research Center.

Chinese Culture Connection (1987), 'Chinese values and the search for culture-free dimensions of culture', *Journal of Cross-Cultural Psychology*, **18**, 143–64.

Chopra, V., Bovill, J.G., Spierdijk, J. & Koornneef, F. (1992), 'Reported significant observations during anaesthesia: A prospective analysis over an 18–month period', *British Journal of Anaesthesia*, **68**, 13–17.

Chopra, V., Engbers, F.H.M., Geerts, M.J., Filet, W.R., Bovill, J.G. & Spierdijk, J. (1994), 'The Leiden anaesthesia simulator', *British Journal of Anaesthesia*, **73**, 287–92.

Christensen, U.J., Laub, M. & the Sophus Group (1995), 'The Sophus anaesthesia simulator', *British Journal of Anaesthesia*, **74**, 22–3, Abstract 72.

Chun, K.T., Campbell, J.B. & Yoo, J.H. (1974), 'Extreme response style in cross-cultural research', *Journal of Cross-Cultural Psychology*, **5**, 465–79.

Chute, R.D. & Wiener, E.L. (1996), 'Cockpit–Cabin Communications: Shall we tell the pilots?', *International Journal of Aviation Psychology*, **6**, 211–32.

Connelly, E.P. (1997), 'A resource package for CRM developers: Behavioral markers of CRM skill from real world case studies – and accidents', University of Texas Crew Research Project Technical Report 97–03.

Cooke, R.A. & Rousseau, D.M. (1988), 'Behavioral norms and expectations: A quantitative approach to the assessment of organizational culture', *Group and Organizational Studies*, **13**, 245–73.

Cooper, G.E., White, M.D. & Lauber, J.K. (eds) (1979), *Resource management on the flightdeck* (NASA Conference Publication 2120), Moffett Field, CA: NASA–Ames Research Center.

Copeland, L. & Griggs, L. (1985), *Going International*, New York: Random House.

Cramér, H. (1946), *Mathematical Methods of Statistics*, Princeton, NJ: Princeton University Press.

Davies, J.M. (1994), 'Mortality/morbidity and audit', in W.S. Nimmo, D.J. Rowbotham & G. Smith (eds), *Anaesthesia*, 2nd edn, Oxford: Blackwell Scientific.

Davies, J.M. (1995), 'Critical incidents during anaesthesia', in T.E. Healy & P.J. Cohen (eds), *Wylie and Churchill Davidson's A Practice of Anaesthesia*, London: Edward Arnold.

Davies, J.M. & Helmreich, R.L. (1996), 'Simulation: It's a start' (editorial), *Canadian Journal of Anaesthesia*, **43**, (5), 425–9.

Dawson, J.L. (1967), 'Traditional versus Western attitudes in West Africa: the construction, validation and application of a measuring device', *British Journal of Social and Clinical Psychology*, **6**, 81–96.

De Vellis, R.F. (1991), *Scale Development: Theory and Applications*, Newbury Park, CA: Sage.

Deal, T. & Kennedy, A. (1982), *Corporate Cultures: The rites and rituals of corporate life*, Reading, MA: Addison-Wesley.

Denison, D.R. (1990), *Corporate Culture and Organizational Effectiveness*, New York: Wiley.

Denison, D. & Mishra, A. (1995), 'Toward a theory of organizational culture and effectiveness', *Organization Science*, **6**, 204–23.

DiTomaso, N. (1987), 'Symbolic media and social solidarity: The foundations of corporate cultures', *Research in the Sociology of Organizations*, **5**, 105–34.

Donabedian, A. (1968), 'Promoting quality through evaluating the process of patient care', *Medical Care*, **11**, 166–206.

Ekman, P. (1973), 'Cross-cultural studies of facial expressions', in P. Ekman (ed.), *Darwin and Facial Expression*, New York: Academic Press.

Federal Aviation Administration (1997), 'Aviation safety action programs', Advisory Circular 120–66.

Festinger, L. (1957), 'A theory of social comparison processes', *Human Relations*, **7**, 117–40.

Foushee, H.C. (1984), 'Dyads and triads at 35,000 feet: Factors affecting group process and aircrew performance', *American Psychologist*, **39**, 886–93.

Freiberg, K. & Freiberg, J. (1996), *Nuts!*, Austin, TX: Bard Press.

Frost, P., Moore, L., Louis, M., Lundberg, C. & Martin, J. (1991), *Reframing Organizational Culture*, Beverly Hills, CA: Sage.

Gaba, D.M. & DeAnda, A. (1988), 'A comprehensive anesthesia simulating environment recreating the operating room for research and training', *Anesthesiology*, **69**, 387–94.

Gandt, R. (1995), *Skygods: The Fall of Pan Am*, New York: William Morrow & Co.

Gann, E.K. (1961), *Fate is the Hunter*, New York: Simon & Schuster.

Gertsen, M. (1990), 'Intercultural competence and expatriates', *Journal of Human Resource Management*, **4**, 341–61.

Gibson, R.H. (1990), 'Managerial leadership assessment: Personality correlates of and sex differences in ratings by leaders, peers and followers', unpublished doctoral dissertation, The University of Texas at Austin, Austin, Texas.

Ginnette, R. (1987), 'First encounters of the close kind: The first meetings of airline flight crews', unpublished doctoral dissertation, Yale University, New Haven, CT.

Good, M.L., Gravenstein, J.S., Mahla, M.E., White, S.E., Banner, J.J., Carovano, R.G. & Lampotang, S. (1992), 'Anaesthesia simulator for learning basic skills', *Journal of Clinical Monitoring*, **8**, 187–8.

Goode, W.J. (1957), 'Community within a community: The professions', *American Sociological Review*, 194–200.

Gordon, G. & DiTomaso, N. (1992), 'Predicting corporate performance from organizational culture', *Journal of Management Studies*, **29**, 783–98.

Greenwood, E. (1957), 'Attributes of a profession', *Social Work*, 45–55.

Gudykunst, W., Guzley, R. & Hammer, M. (1996), 'Designing intercultural training', in D. Landis & R. Bhagat (eds), *Handbook of Intercultural Training*, 2nd edn, London: Sage.

Hansman, R.J., Midkiff, A., Vakil, S., Vaneck, T., Corwin, W., Irving, S., Irving, J. & Polson, P. (1995), 'Mode awareness in advanced autoflight systems', paper presented to the FAA Human Factors Advisory Committee, Langley, VA, January.

Helmreich, R.L. (1975), 'Applied social psychology: The unfulfilled promise', *Personality and Social Psychology Bulletin*, **1**, 548–61.

Helmreich, R.L. (1980), 'Social psychology on the flight deck', *Proceedings of the NASA Workshop on Resource Management Training for Airline Flight Crews*, NASA CP-2120a, Moffett Field, CA: NASA–Ames Research Center.

Helmreich, R.L. (1983), 'Applying social psychology in outer space: Unfulfilled promises revisited', *American Psychologist*, **38**, 445–50.

Helmreich, R.L. (1984), 'Cockpit management attitudes', *Human Factors*, **26**, 63–72.

Helmreich, R.L. (1987), 'Exploring flight crew behaviour', *Social Behaviour*, **2**, 63–72.

Helmreich, R.L. (1992), 'Human factors aspects of the Air Ontario crash at Dryden, Ontario: Analysis and recommendations', in V.P. Moshansky (Commissioner), *Commission of Inquiry into the Air Ontario Accident at Dryden, Ontario: Final report. Technical appendices*, Ottawa, Ontario: Minister of Supply and Services.

Helmreich, R.L. (1994), 'Anatomy of a system accident: The crash of Avianca Flight 052', *International Journal of Aviation Psychology*, **4**, (3), 265–84.

Helmreich, R. (1997d), 'Managing human error in aviation', *Scientific American*, pp.62–7.

Helmreich, R.L. (in press), 'The Evolution of Crew Resource Management in Commercial Aviation', *International Journal of Aviation Psychology*.

Helmreich, R.L. & Davies, J. (1996), 'Human factors in the operating room: Interpersonal determinants of safety, efficiency and morale', in A.A. Aitkenhead (ed.), *Balliere's Clinical Anaesthesiology: Safety and Risk Management in Anaesthesia*, London: Balliere Tindall.

Helmreich, R.L. & Davies, J.M. (1997), 'Anaesthetic simulation and lessons to be learned from aviation' (editorial), *Canadian Journal of Anaesthesia*, **44**, (9), 907–12.

Helmreich, R.L. & Foushee, H.C. (1993), 'Why Crew Resource Management? Empirical and theoretical bases of human factors training in aviation', in E. Wiener, B. Kanki & R. Helmreich (eds), *Cockpit Resource Management*, San Diego, CA: Academic Press.

Helmreich, R.L. & Hines, W.E. (1997), 'Crew performance in the approach/landing phase: Observations in 2600 flights', talk presented at the Approach/Landing Advisory Report: Bogota, Colombia. University of Texas Aerospace Crew Research Project Technical Report 97–1.

Helmreich, R.L. & Schaefer, H.-G. (1994), 'Team performance in the operating room', in M.S. Bogner (ed.), *Human Error in Medicine*, Hillside, NJ: Lawrence Erlbaum.

Helmreich, R.L., Schaefer, H.-G. & Sexton, J.B. (1995), Operating Room Checklist (ORC), NASA/UT/FAA Technical Report 95–4, Austin, TX: The University of Texas.

Helmreich, R.L. & Schaefer, H.-G. (1997), 'Turning silk purses into sows' ears: Human factors in medicine', in L. Henson, A. Lee & A. Basford (eds), *Simulators in Anesthesiology Education*, New York: Plenum.

Helmreich, R.L., Sexton, J.B. & Merritt, A.C. (1997), The Operating Room Management Attitudes Questionnaire (ORMAQ), University of Texas Aerospace Crew Research Project Technical Report 97–6, Austin, TX: The University of Texas.

Helmreich, R.L. & Spence, J.T. (1978), 'The Work and Family Orientation Questionnaire: An objective instrument to assess components of achievement motivation and attitudes toward family and career', JSAS *Catalog of Selected Documents in Psychology*, **8**, 35, MS 1677.

Helmreich, R.L. & Stapp, J. (1974), 'Short forms of the Texas Social Behavior Inventory (TSBI), an objective measure of self-esteem', *Bulletin of the Psychonomic Society*, **4**, 473–5.

Helmreich, R.L., Hines, W.E. & Wilhelm, J.A. (1996), 'Common issues in human factors and automation use: Data from line audits at three airlines', NASA/UT/FAA Technical Report 96–1, Austin, TX: The University of Texas.

Helmreich, R.L., Hines, W.E. & Wilhelm, J.A. (1997), 'The University of Texas Aerospace Crew Research Project Line/LOS/Error Checklist', experimental version 5.0.

Helmreich, R.L., Merritt, A.C. & Wilhelm, J.A. (in press), 'The evolution of Crew Resource Management training in commercial aviation', *International Journal of Aviation Psychology*.

Helmreich, R.L., Butler, R.E., Taggart, W.R. & Wilhelm, J.A. (1994), 'The NASA/University of Texas/FAA Line/LOS Checklist: A behavioral marker-based checklist for CRM skills assessment', NASA/UT/FAA Technical Report 94–02, revised 12/8/95, Austin, TX: The University of Texas.

Helmreich, R.L., Butler, R.E., Taggart, W.R. & Wilhelm, J.A. (1995), 'Behavioral markers in accidents and incidents: Reference list', NASA/UT/FAA Technical Report 95–1, Austin, TX: The University of Texas.

Helmreich, R.L., Foushee, H.C., Benson, R. & Russini, R. (1986), 'Cockpit management attitudes: Exploring the attitude–performance linkage', *Aviation, Space and Environmental Medicine*, **57**, 1198–1200.

Helmreich, R.L., Chidester, T.R., Foushee, H.C., Gregorich, S.E. &

Wilhelm, J.A. (1990), 'How effective is Cockpit Resource Management training? Issues in evaluating the impact of programs to enhance crew coordination', *Flight Safety Digest*, **9**, (5), 1–17, Arlington, VA: Flight Safety Foundation.

Helmreich, R.L., Merritt, A.C., Sherman, P.J., Gregorich, S.E. & Wiener, E.L. (1993), 'The Flight Management Attitudes Questionnaire (FMAQ)', NASA/UT/FAA Technical Report 93–4, Austin, TX: The University of Texas.

Helmreich, R.L., Spence, J.T., Beane, W.E., Lucker, G.W. & Matthews, K.A. (1980), 'Making it in academic psychology: Demographic and personality correlates of attainment', *Journal of Personality and Social Psychology*, **39**, 896–908.

Hilburn, B., Molloy, R., Wong, D. & Parasuraman, R. (1993), 'Operator versus computer control of adaptive automation', in R.S. Jensen & D. Neumeister (eds), *Proceedings of the Seventh International Symposium on Aviation Psychology*, Columbus, OH: Ohio State University.

Hines, W.E. (1996), 'Dimensions of personality across professions: Comparisons of aviators, astronauts and medical teams', unpublished master's thesis, The University of Texas at Austin.

Hines, W.E. (1998), 'Teams and technology: Flightcrew performance in standard and automated aircraft', unpublished doctoral dissertation at The University of Texas at Austin.

Hofstede, G. (1980), *Culture's Consequences: International differences in work-related values*, Beverly Hills, CA: Sage.

Hofstede, G. (1982), *Values Survey Module*, Maastricht, the Netherlands: Institute for Research on Intercultural Cooperation.

Hofstede, G. (1991), *Cultures and Organizations: Software of the mind*, Maidenhead, UK: McGraw-Hill.

Hofstede, G., Neuijen, B., Ohayv, D. & Sanders, G. (1990), 'Measuring organizational cultures: A qualitative and quantitative study across 20 cases', *Administrative Science Quarterly*, **35**, 286–317.

Howard, S.K., Gaba, D.M., Fish, K.J., Yang, G. & Sarnquist, F.H. (1992), 'Anesthesia crisis resource management training: Teaching anesthesiologists to handle critical incidents', *Aviation Space and Environmental Medicine*, **63**, 763–70.

Hughes, D. (1995), 'Studies highlight automation "surprises"', *Aviation Week and Space Technology*, **142**, (6), 6 February, pp. 48–9.

Hughes, E.C. (1958), *Men and Their Work*, New York: Free Press.

Hui, C.H. & Triandis, H.C. (1986), 'Individualism–collectivism: A study of cross-cultural researchers', *Journal of Cross-Cultural Psychology*, **17**, 222–48.

Hui, C.H. & Triandis, H.C. (1989), 'Effects of culture and response format on extreme response style', *Journal of Cross-Cultural Psychology*, **20**, 296–309.

Inkeles, A. & Smith, D. (1974), *Becoming Modern*, Cambridge, MA: Harvard University Press.

Jahoda, G. (1992), 'J'Accuse', in M.H. Bond (ed.), *The Cross-Cultural Challenge to Social Psychology*, Vol. 11, Cross-Cultural Research and Methodology Series, Newbury Park, CA: Sage.

Janis, I.L. (1972), *Victims of Groupthink*, Boston, MA: Houghton Mifflin.

Johnston, N. (1996), 'Blame, punishment and risk management', in C. Hood, D. Jones, N. Pidgeon & B. Turner (eds), *Accident and Design – Contemporary debates in risk management*, Dublin: University College Press.

Jones, E.E. (1985), 'Major developments in social psychology during the past five decades', in G. Lindzey & E. Aronson (eds), *Handbook of Social Psychology*, 3rd edn, Vol. 1, New York: Random House.

Jones, S.G. (in press), 'Air traffic control: A starting point', in R.S. Jensen (ed.), *Proceedings of the Ninth International Symposium on Aviation Psychology*, Columbus, OH: The Ohio State University.

Josephs, R.A., Larrick, R.P., Steele, C.M. & Nisbett, R.E. (1992), 'Protecting the self from the negative consequences of risky decision', *Journal of Personality and Social Psychology*, **62**, 26–37.

Kağitçibasi, C. (1994), 'A Critical Appraisal of Individualism and Collectivism: Toward a new formulation', in U. Kim, H. Triandis, C. Kağitçibasi, A. Choi & G. Yoon (eds), *Individualism and Collectivism: Theory, methods and applications*, Vol. 18, Cross-Cultural Research and Methodology Series, Newbury Park, CA: Sage.

Kağitçibasi, C. & Berry, J.W. (1989), 'Cross-cultural psychology: Current research and trends', *Annual Review of Psychology*, **40**, 493–531.

Kealey, D. (1990), *Cross-cultural effectiveness*, Hull, Quebec: CIDA.

Kealey, D. (1996), 'The challenge of international personnel selection', in D. Landis & R. Bhagat (eds), *Handbook of Intercultural Training*, (2nd edn), London: Sage.

Kim, U., Triandis, H., Kağitçibasi, C., Choi, A. & Yoon, G. (eds) (1994), *Individualism and Collectivism: Theory, methods and applications*, Vol. 18, Cross-Cultural Research and Methodology Series, Newbury Park, CA: Sage.

Kumar, V., Barcellos, W.A., Mehta, M.P. & Carter, J.G. (1988), 'An analysis of critical incidents in a teaching department for quality assurance: A survey of mishaps during anaesthesia', *Anaesthesia*, **43**, 879–83.

Kurrek, M.M. & Fish, K.J. (1996), 'Anaesthesia crisis resource management training: An intimidating concept, a rewarding experience', *Canadian Journal of Anaesthesia*, **43**, 430–34.

Leape, L.L. (1994), 'Error in medicine', *Journal of the American Medical Association*, **272**, 1851–7.

Leape, L.L., Brennan, T.A., Laird, N., Lawthers, A.G., Localio, A.R., Barnes, B.A., Herbert, L., Newhouse, J.P., Weiler, P.C. & Hiatt, H.

(1991), 'The nature of adverse events in hospitalized patients', *New England Journal of Medicine*, **324**, (6), 377–84.

Lesar, T.S., Briceland, L. & Stein, D.S. (1997), 'Factors in medication prescribing', *Journal of the American Medical Association*, **277**, 341–2.

Leung, K. (1989), 'Cross-cultural differences: Individual-level vs. culture-level analysis', *International Journal of Psychology*, **24**, 703–19.

Leung, K. & Bond, M. (1989), 'On the empirical identification of dimensions for cross-cultural comparisons', *Journal of Cross-Cultural Psychology*, **20**, 133–51.

Levy, M., Jr. (1966), *Modernization and the Structure of Societies*, Princeton, NJ: Princeton University Press.

Lewin, K. (1946), 'Action research and minority problems', *Journal of Social Issues*, **2**, 34–46.

Lloyd, B.B. (1972), *Perception and Cognition: A cross-cultural perspective*, Harmondsworth: Penguin.

Markus, H. & Kitayama, S. (1991), 'Culture and the self: Implications for cognition, emotion and motivation', *Psychological Review*, **98**, 224–53.

Maurino, D.E., Reason, J.T., Johnston, A.N. & Lee, R.B. (1995), *Beyond Aviation Human Factors*, Aldershot: Avebury Aviation.

McCrae, R.R. & Costa, P.T., Jr. (1987), 'Validation of the five-factor model of personality across instruments and observers', *Journal of Personality and Social Psychology*, **52**, 81–90.

McDonald, J.S. & Peterson, S. (1985), 'Lethal errors in anesthesiology', *Anesthesiology*, **63**, A497.

McGuire, (1967), 'Personality and susceptibility to social influence', in E.F. Borgatta & W.W. Lambert (eds), *Handbook of Personality Theory and Research*, Chicago: Rand McNally.

Merritt, A. (1995), 'Commercial pilot selection and training in the next ten years: Some global cultural considerations', *Proceedings of the Royal Aeronautical Society Conference, 'Commercial Pilot Selection and Training – The Next Ten Years'*, 4.1–4.8, London, 10 October.

Merritt, A.C. & Helmreich, R.L. (1996), 'Human factors on the flightdeck: The influences of national culture', *Journal of Cross-Cultural Psychology*, **27**, (1), 5–24.

Merritt, A. & Ratwatte, S. (in press), 'Who are you calling a threat? A debate on safety in mono- versus multi-cultural cockpits', in R.S. Jensen (ed.), *Proceedings of the Ninth International Symposium on Aviation Psychology*, Columbus, OH: The Ohio State University.

Meshkati, N. (1994), 'Cross-cultural issues in the transfer of technology: Implications for aviation safety', *Proceedings of the International Civil Aviation Organization (ICAO): Report of the flight safety and human factors seminar and workshop*, Amsterdam, 16–19 May, 116–37.

Mischel, W. (1968), *Personality and Assessment*, New York: Wiley.

Misumi, J. (1985), *The Behavioral Science of Leadership*, Ann Arbor: University of Michigan Press.

Moshansky, V.P. (1992), *Commission of Inquiry into the Air Ontario Accident at Dryden, Ontario: Final report* (Vols 1–4), Ottawa, Ontario: Minister of Supply and Services.

National Insurance Law Service (1996), *Rupp's Insurance Glossary*, Chatsworth, CA: NILS Publishing Co.

National Research Council (1993), Team leadership and crew coordination', in B.M. Huey & C.D. Wickens (eds), *Workload Transition*, Washington, DC.

National Transportation Safety Board (1980), *Aircraft Accident Report: Air New England, Inc., DeHavilland DHC-6–300, N383X, Hyannis, Massachusetts, June 17, 1979* (Report No. NTSB-AAR-80–1), Washington, DC.

National Transportation Safety Board (1991), *Aviation Accident Report: Avianca, The Airline of Columbia, Boeing 707-321B, HK 2016, Fuel Exhaustion, Cove Neck, New York, January 25, 1990* (Report No. AAR-91-04), Washington, DC.

National Transportation Safety Board (1994), *Safety study: A review of flightcrew involved, major accidents of U.S. air carriers, 1978 through 1990* (NTSB/SS-94/01), Washington, DC.

National Transportation Safety Board (1997), *Marine Accident Report: Grounding of the Panamanian Passenger Ship Royal Majesty on Rose and Crown Shoal near Nantucket, Massachusetts, June 10, 1995* (Report No. NTSB-MAR-97.01), Washington, DC.

Nauman, E. (1992), 'A conceptual model of expatriate turnover', *Journal of International Business Studies*, **23**, (3), 499–532.

Nel, E., Helmreich, R. & Aronson, E. (1969), 'Opinion change in the advocate as a function of the persuasibility of his audience: A clarification of the meaning of dissonance', *Journal of Personality and Social Psychology*, **12**, 117–24.

Nyquist, L. & Spence, J. (1986), 'Effects of dispositional dominance and sex-role expectations on leadership behaviors', *Journal of Personality and Social Psychology*, **50**, 87–93.

Orasanu, J., Davison, J. & Fischer, U. (in press), 'What did he say? Culture and language barriers to efficient communication in global aviation', in R.S. Jensen (ed.), *Proceedings of the Ninth International Symposium on Aviation Psychology*, Columbus, OH: The Ohio State University.

Ouchi, W. & Price, R. (1978), 'Hierarchies, clans and theory Z: A new perspective on organizational development', *Organizational Dynamics*, **7**, 25–44.

Parasuraman, R., Molloy, R. & Singh, I. (1993), 'Performance consequences of automation-induced "complacency"', *International Journal of Aviation Psychology*, **3**, 1–23.

Paries, J. (1996), 'Evolution of the aviation safety paradigm: Towards systemic causality and proactive actions', in B. Hayward & A. Lowe (eds), *Applied Aviation Psychology: Achievement, Change and Challenge*, Aldershot: Avebury-Ashgate Publishing Limited.

Perrow, C. (1984), *Normal Accidents*, New York: Basic Books.

Peters, T. & Waterman, R. (1982), *In Search of Excellence: Lessons from America's best run companies*, New York: Harper & Row.

Pettigrew, A. (1979), 'On studying organizational cultures', *Administrative Science Quarterly*, **24**, 570–81.

Poortinga, Y.H. & Berry, J.W. (1989), 'Introduction to special issue', *International Journal of Psychology*, **24**, 661–3.

Predmore, S.C. (1991), 'Microcoding of communications in accident investigation: Crew coordination in United 811 and United 232', in R.S. Jensen (ed.), *Proceedings of the Sixth International Symposium on Aviation Psychology*, Columbus, OH: The Ohio State University.

Radloff, R. & Helmreich, R., (1968), *Groups under stress: Psychological research in SEALAB II*, New York: Appleton-Century-Crofts.

Radloff, R. & Helmreich, R. (1969b), 'Stress under the sea', *Psychology Today*, **3**, 28–9, 59–60.

Reason, J. (1990), *Human Error*, New York: Cambridge University Press.

Reason, J. (1997), *Managing the Risks of Organizational Accidents*, Aldershot: Ashgate.

Redding, S.G. & Ogilvie, J.G. (1984), 'Cultural effects on cockpit communications in civilian aircraft', *Proceedings of the Flight Safety Foundation Conference, Zurich*, Washington: Flight Safety Foundation.

Ring, K. (1967), 'Experimental social psychology: Some sober questions about frivolous values', *Journal of Experimental Social Psychology*, **3**, 113–23.

Robins, N. (1996).*The Girl Who Died Twice: The Libby Zion case and the hidden hazards of hospitals*, New York: Delacorte Press.

Robinson, W.S. (1950), 'Ecological correlations and the behavior of individuals', *American Sociological Review*, **15**, 351–7.

Rochlin, G.I. (1997), *Trapped in the Net: The unintended consequences of computerization*, Princeton, NJ: Princeton University Press.

Rose, R.M., Fogg, L.F., Helmreich, R.L. & McFadden, T.J. (1994), 'Psychological predictors of astronaut effectiveness', *Aviation, Space and Environmental Medicine*, **65**, 910–15.

Runciman, W.B., Sellen, A., Webb, R.K. et al. (1993), 'Errors, incidents and accidents in anaesthetic practice', *Anaesthesia and Intensive Care*, **21**, 506–9.

Saint Exupéry, Antoine de (1942), *Night Flight*, New York: Harcourt, Brace and Co.

Sampson, E.E. (1977), 'Psychology and the American ideal', *Journal of Personality and Social Psychology*, **35**, 767–82.

Sarter, N.B. & Woods, D.D. (1992), 'Pilot interaction with cockpit automation I: Operational experiences with the flight management system', *The International Journal of Aviation Psychology*, **2** (4), 303–321.

Sarter, N.B. & Woods, D.D. (1994), 'Pilot interaction with cockpit automation II: An experimental study of pilots' model and awareness of the flight management system', *The International Journal of Aviation Psychology*, **4** (1), 1–28.

Schaefer, H.G., Helmreich, R.L. & Scheidegger, D. (1995), 'Safety in the operating theatre – Part 1: Interpersonal relationships and team performance', *Current Anaesthesia and Critical Care*, **6**, 48–53.

Schall, M. (1983), 'A communication-rules approach to organizational culture', *Administrative Science Quarterly*, **28**, 557–81.

Schein, E. (1992), Organizational Culture and Leadership, 2nd edn, San Francisco: Jossey-Bass.

Schein, E. (1996), 'Culture: The missing concept in organization studies', *Administrative Science Quarterly*, **41**, 229–40.

Schwartz, S.H. (1992), 'Universals in the content and structure of values: Theoretical advances and empirical tests in 20 countries', in M. Zanna (ed.), *Advances in Experimental Social Psychology*, Vol. 25, Orlando, FL: Academic Press.

Schwartz, S.H. (1995), 'Identifying culture-specifics in the content and structure of values', *Journal of Cross-Cultural Psychology*, **26**, 92–116.

Schwartz, S.H. & Bilsky, W. (1987), 'Toward a psychological structure of human values', *Journal of Personality and Social Psychology*, **53**, 550–62.

Schwartz, S.H. & Bilsky, W. (1990), 'Toward a theory of the universal content and structure of values: Extensions and cross-cultural replications', *Journal of Personality and Social Psychology*, **58**, 878–91.

Segall, M., Dasen, P., Berry, J. & Poortinga, Y. (1990), *Human Behavior in Global Perspective: An introduction to cross-cultural psychology*, New York: Pergamon Press.

Seglin, J.L. (1996), 'The happiest workers in the world', *State of Small Business*, 62.

Sexton, B. (1997), personal communication.

Sexton, B., Marsch, S., Helmreich, R.L., Betzendoerfer, D., Kocher, T. & Scheidegger, D. (1997a), 'Jumpseating in the Operating Room', *Proceedings of the Second Conference on Simulators in Anesthesiology Education*, New York: Plenum.

Sexton, B., Marsch, S., Helmreich, R.L., Betzendoerfer, D., Kocher, T. & Scheidegger, D. (1997b), 'Participant Evaluation of Team

Oriented Medical Simulation', *Proceedings of the Second Conference on Simulators in Anesthesiology Education*, New York: Plenum.

Sherman, P.J., Helmreich, R.L. & Merritt, A.C. (1997), 'National culture and flightdeck automation: Results of a multi-nation survey', *International Journal of Aviation Psychology*, **7**, (4), 311–29.

Siehl, C. & Martin, J. (1990), 'Measuring the organizational culture: Mixing qualitative and quantitative methods', in M.O. Jones, M.D. Moore & R.C. Synder (eds), *Inside Organizations: Understanding the human dimension*, London: Sage.

Sinha, J.B.P. (1981), *The Nurturant Task Manager: A model of the effective executive*, Atlantic Highlands, NJ: Humanities Press.

Smircich, L. (1982), 'Organizations as shared meanings', in L.R. Pondy, P. Frost, G. Morgan & T. Dandridge (eds), *Organizational Symbolism*, Greenwich, CT: JAI Press.

Smith, P.B. & Bond, M.H. (1993), *Social Psychology Cross Cultures: Analysis and Perspectives*, Boston, MA: Allyn & Bacon.

Smith, P.B. & Peterson, M.S. (1988), *Leadership, Organization and Culture*, London: Sage.

Smith, P.B., Dugan, S. & Trompenaars, F. (1996), 'National culture and the values of organizational employees', *Journal of Cross-Cultural Psychology*, **27**, 231–64.

Smith, P.B., Trompenaars, F. & Dugan, S. (1995), 'The Rotter locus of control scale in 43 countries: A test of cultural relativity', *International Journal of Psychology*, **30**, 377–400.

Spence, J.T. (1985), 'Achievement American style: The rewards and costs of individualism', *American Psychologist*, **40**, 1285–95.

Spence, J.T. & Helmreich, R.L. (1978), 'Masculinity and femininity as personality dimensions', *Society for the Advancement of Social Psychology Newsletter*, **4**, 2–3.

Spence, J.T., Deaux, K. & Helmreich, R.L. (1985), 'Sex roles in contemporary American society', in G. Lindzey & E. Aronson (eds), *Handbook of Social Psychology*, 3rd edn, Reading, MA: Addison-Wesley.

Spence, J.T., Helmreich, R.L. & Holahan, C.K. (1979), 'Negative and positive components of psychological masculinity and femininity and their relationships to self-reports of neurotic and acting out behaviors', *Journal of Personality and Social Psychology*, **37**, 1673–82.

Staender, S. (1997), Critical Incident Reporting System Website, *www.medana.unibas.ch*.

Staender, S., Davies, J., Helmreich, B., Sexton, B. & Kaufmann, M. (1997), 'The Anesthesia Critical Incident Reporting System: An experience-based database', *Journal of Medical Informatics*, **47**, 87–90.

Stening, B.W. & Everett, J.E. (1984), 'Response styles in a cross-cultural managerial study' *The Journal of Social Psychology*, **122**, 151–6.

Stephens, G. & Black, J. (1991), 'The impact of spouses' career orientation on managers during international transitions', *Journal of Management Studies*, **28**, (4), 417–29.

Stogdill, R.M. & Coons, A.E. (1957), *Leader Behavior* (Monograph 88), Columbus: Ohio State University, Bureau of Business Research.

Swann, W.B., Jr. (1996), *Self-traps: The elusive quest for higher self-esteem*, Freeman: New York.

Swann, W.B., Jr. & Read, S.J. (1981a), 'Self-verification processes: How we sustain our self-conceptions', *Journal of Experimental Social Psychology*, **17**, 351–72.

Swann, W.B., Jr. & Read, S.J. (1981b), 'Acquiring self-knowledge: The search for feedback that fits', *Journal of Personality and Social Psychology*, **41**, 1119–28.

Tang, S. & Kirkbride, P. (1986), 'Developing conflict management skills in Hong Kong: An analysis of some cross-cultural implications', *Management Education and Development*, **17**, 287–301.

Thibaut, J. & Kelley, H. (1959), *The Social Psychology of Groups*, New York: John Wiley & Sons.

Ting-Toomey, S. (1988), 'A face-negotiation theory', in Y. Kim & W. Gudykunst (eds), *Theory in Intercultural Communication*, Newbury Park, CA: Sage.

Ting-Toomey, S. (1994), *The Challenge of Facework: Cross-cultural and interpersonal issues*, Albany: SUNY Press.

Triandis, H.C. (1972), *The Analysis of Subjective Culture*, New York: John Wiley & Sons.

Triandis, H.C. (gen. ed.) (1980), *Handbook of Cross-Cultural Psychology*, Vols 1–6, Boston, MA: Allyn & Bacon, Inc.

Triandis, H.C. (1994), 'Theoretical and methodological approaches to the study of Collectivism and Individualism', in U. Kim, H. Triandis, C. Kağitçibasi, S. Choi & G. Yoon (eds), *Individualism and Collectivism: Theory, Methods and Applications*, Newbury Park, CA: Sage.

Triandis, H.C., McCusker, C. & Hui, C.H. (1990), 'Multimethod probes of individualism and collectivism', *Journal of Personality and Social Psychology*, **59**, 1006–20.

Triandis, H.C., Bontempo, R., Leung, K. & Hui, C.H. (1990), 'A method for determining cultural, demographic and personal constructs', *Journal of Cross-Cultural Psychology*, **21**, 302–18.

Triandis, H.C., Bontempo, R., Villareal, M.J., Asai, M. & Lucca, N. (1988), 'Individualism and collectivism: Cross-cultural perspectives on self–ingroup relationships, *Journal of Personality and Social Psychology*, **54**, 323–38.

Triandis, H.C., Betancourt, H., Bond, M.H., Leung, K., Brenes, A., Georgas, J., Hui, C.H., Marin, G., Setiadi, B., Sinaha, J., Verma, J., Spangenerg, J., Touzard, H. & Montmollin, G. (1986), 'The measurement of etic aspects of individualism and collectivism across cultures', *Australian Journal of Psychology*, **38**, 257–67.

Trice, H.M. & Beyer, J.M. (1993), *The Cultures of Work Organizations*, Englewood Cliffs, NJ: Prentice-Hall.

Trompenaars, F. (1994), *Riding the Waves of Culture: Understanding diversity in global business*, New York: Irwin.

Tullo, F. (in press), 'Instructor/evaluator training in error management', in R.S. Jensen (ed.), *Proceedings of the Ninth International Symposium on Aviation Psychology*, Columbus, OH: The Ohio State University.

Van de Vijver, F. & Leung, K. (1997), *Methods and Data Analysis for Cross-cultural Research*, Thousand Oaks, CA: Sage.

Van de Vijver, F. & Poortinga, Y.H. (1997), 'Towards an integrated analysis of bias in cross-cultural assessment', *European Journal of Psychological Assessment*, **13**, 21–9.

Waller, M.J. (1997), 'Keeping the pins in the air: How work groups juggle multiple tasks', in M. Beyerlein, D. Johnson & S. Beyerlein (eds), *Advances in Interdisciplinary Studies of Work Teams*, **4**, 217–247, Greenwich, CT: JAI Press.

Waller, M.J. (in press), 'Multiple-task performance in groups', *Academy of Management Journal*.

Wickens, C.D. (1992), *Engineering Psychology and Human Performance*, 2nd edn, New York: Harper Collins.

Wiener, E. (1993), 'Crew coordination and training in the advanced-technology cockpit', in E. Wiener, B. Kanki & R. Helmreich (eds), *Cockpit Resource Management*, San Diego, CA: Academic Press.

Wiener, E., Kanki, B. & Helmreich, R. (eds) (1993), *Cockpit Resource Management*, San Diego, CA: Academic Press.

Williamson, J.A., Webb, R.K., Sellen, A., Runciman, W.B. & van der Walt, J.H. (1993), 'Human failure: An analysis of 2000 incident reports', *Anaesthesia Intensive Care*, **21**, 678–83.

Wolfe, T. (1979), *The Right Stuff*, New York: Farrar, Straus & Giroux.

Xenikou, A. & Furnham, A. (1996), 'A correlational and factor analytic study of four questionnaire measures of organizational culture', *Human Relations*, **49**, 349–72.

Yamamori, H. & Mito, T. (1993), 'Keeping CRM is keeping the flight safe', in E. Wiener, B. Kanki & R. Helmreich (eds), *Cockpit Resource Management*, San Diego, CA: Academic Press.

Yang, K. (1988), 'Will societal modernization eventually eliminate cross-cultural psychological differences?', in M.H. Bond (ed.), *The Psychology of the Chinese People*, Hong Kong: Oxford University Press.

Zax, M. & Takahashi, S. (1967), 'Cultural influences on response style: Comparisons of Japanese and American college students', *The Journal of Social Psychology*, **71**, 3–10.

Index